IMPORTANT PLACES OF ISTANBUL AT FIRST SIGHT

⓳ *Zeyrek Mosque* (p. 98),
⓴ *Fatih Mosque* (p. 98),
㉑ *Fethiye Mosque and Museum* (p. 101),
㉒ *Kariye (Chora) Museum* (p. 105),
㉓ *Tekfur Palace* (p. 110),
㉔ *Gül Mosque* (p. 110),
㉕ *Fener Greek Orthodox Patriarchate* (p. 111),
㉖ *Eyüp Sultan Mosque* (p. 113),
㉗ *Pierre Loti,*
㉘ *Taksim Square* (p. 124),
㉙ *İstiklal Avenue,*
㉚ *Saint Antonio Church* (p.130),
㉛ *Tunnel* (p. 131),
㉜ *Galata Tower* (p. 133),
㉝ *Dolmabahçe Palace* (p. 136),
㉞ *Yıldız Palace* (p. 141),
㉟ *Çırağan Palace* (p. 155),
㊱ *Yıldız Park* (p. 155),
㊲ *Ortaköy* (p. 156),
㊳ *Üsküdar* (p. 178),
㊴ *Leander's Tower* (p. 181),
㊵ *Haydarpaşa Train Station*
㊶ *Kadıköy* (p. 182).
㊷ *The City Walls* (p. 19)

ISTANBUL
CITY GUIDE

Door of Blue Mosque.

Küçüksu Summer Palace.

Archaeology Museum.

Dolmabahçe Palace.

Mosaic of Gabriel, Hagia Sophia.

Tile detail, Sokullu Mehmet Pasha Mosque.

Blue Mosque.

Mihrab of the Çinili Mosque.

Binbirdirek Cistern.

Detail of Alexander Sarcophagus, Archaeology Museum

Mosaic of Hagia Sophia.

Last Judgement scene, Chora Museum.

AS BOOK

ISTANBUL
CITY GUIDE

Published and Distributed by
AS & 64 Ltd. Co.

Çatalçeşme Sk. No: 15/1
34110 Cağaloğlu
Istanbul / Türkiye
Tel : +90 (212) 513 39 90
Fax : +90 (212) 513 65 20
Web : www.asbook.org
e-mail : info@asbook.org

Editor : Avni Alan

Writer : Hakan Alan

Cover : Fatih M. Durmuş

Photographs : Avni Alan, Güngör Özsoy and Sercan Alan

Page Layout : AS&64 Ltd. Co.

Maps used in the book have been printed with the permission of the Map Directorate of Istanbul Metropolitan Municipality

Print and Volume :
Acar Basım ve Cilt San. Tic. A.Ş.

ISBN : 978-975-01147-1-7

Cover Pictures :
Front cover ***Hagia Sophia Museum,***
Back cover ***Sultanahmet Mosque.***

TABLE OF CONTENTS

HOW TO USE THE GUIDE

Istanbul City Guide consists of four sections:

1. ***Historical Peninsula,***
2. ***Beyoğlu and Surroundings,***
3. ***European and Asian Sides of the Bosphorus,***
4. ***The Guide*.**

Separately in each section, the *Historical and Touristic buildings, Museums, Palaces, Summer Palaces (Qasr), Mosques, and Bazaars* are examined and supported with many current photographs.

At the end of each section; practical information is provided on *Hotels, Restaurants, and places to shop, where to eat and dine and how to reach the locations.*

The pages with yellow background at the beginning of the sections include historical information about the region.

Maps of Istanbul Regions and **Shortest Road Descriptions** are organized in a way that you can easily visit the locations without any need for additional sources.

Region colors stated on the cover of the book enables you to easily find the locations you want to visit and the boxes on the maps show the places of the mentioned locations with numbers.

In the ***Guide***, the last section of the book, *general transportation information, addresses and telephone numbers you may need, culture and art activities and some practical information etc*. are provided.

Introduction of the Sections: *The pages with yellow background are the introduction sections where historical information is given.*

Colors of Sections: *On the annex of the front cover, the colors that belong to each section is explained and these colors will help you easily find the section you want to check.*

Historical, Touristic Structures and their Places on the Map: *The locations of the topics are shown on the map with numbers. You may see the places you want to visit on the map, follow the road route and easily reach the places you want.*

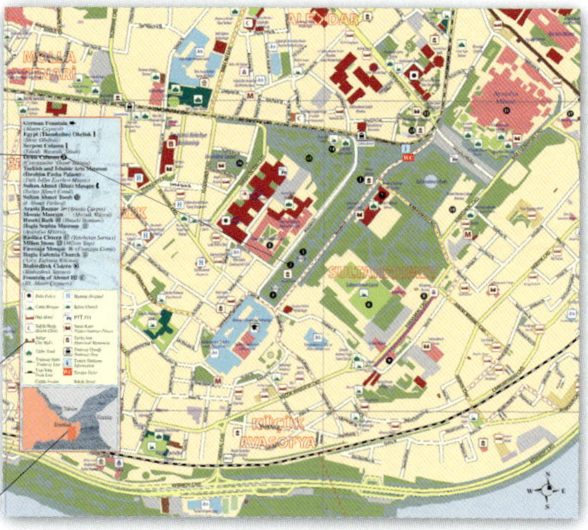

Symbols and their explanations: *You may find the meanings of the symbols and where they are on the map.*

Where you are: *You can see which region and where you are in Istanbul with the drawing.*

Travel map: *The maps will help you reach where you want to go.*

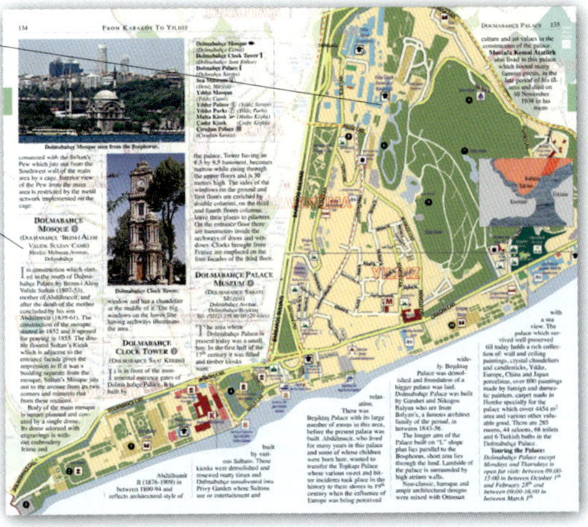

Main text: *You may find the necessary information about the place you want to visit in these topics.*

Short road descriptions: *The texts on the gray background include some practical information on some places you can see on foot.*

Shopping, where to dine and wine, Transportation: *These useful pages at the end of each section gives practical information on What you can eat, Where you can shop, How you will reach a location and Where you can entertain in the region that you are located.*

Hotels-Restaurants: *At the end of each section; the addresses, telephones and price range is given on the Hotels and Restaurants of the region.*

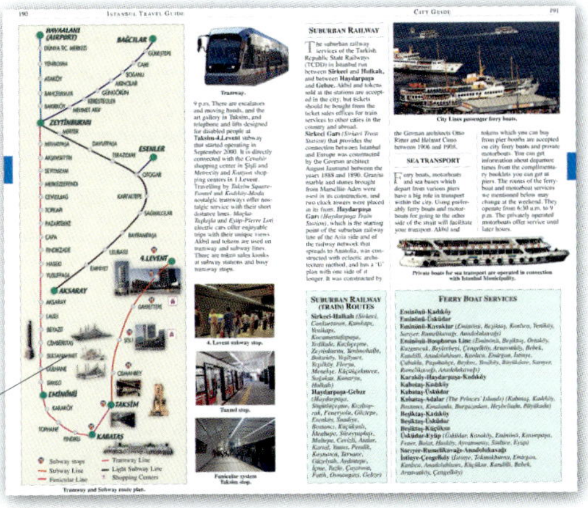

The Guide: *Transportation, Communication, Culture-Art activities and necessary telephone and addresses can be found at this section.*

ΜΡ
Η ΧΩΡΑ

ISTANBUL

Welcome to Istanbul. Istanbul, one of the important cities in the world, is on a very special center with its geopolitical situation. It is located on the two sides of the Bosphorus bordering Asian and European continents and has the reputation of being a city with lands on two continents.

Istanbul is the most crowded city of Turkey with its population that exceeds twelve million. It has been the capital of Roman, Byzantine and Ottoman Empires and has been constructed for ages with magnificent religious and civil structures that suit its fame.

The first foundation of the city is told through legends. A sea horde leaded by Byzas around 650 B.C. started to search for a new location out of their city Megara. In the tradition of the age, prophets were always consulted and the prophets of Apollo Temple at Delphi, the famous prophecy center of the age advised Byzas to settle "across the land of the blind". After long research, when the nomads looking for such a place reached Istanbul peninsula and admired the wealth of the surroundings and opportunities of the "Golden Horn", they met people who settled on the other side of the Bosphorus. The nomads who believed that one has to be "blind" to settle on the other shore when there is an ideal place with such opportunities believed that they reached the place stated in the prophecy.

Since the day of its foundation, Byzantion sometimes lived as subjects of the superior powers in the region and sometimes within its own free will. The region of today's Topkapı Palace was the Acropolis of the city. It had a calm harbor at the entrance of Golden Horn which is still used today. Powerful city walls starting from here surrounded the city and reached Marmara Sea. While Byzantion continued to live during the times of the Roman Empire as a city of harbor and commerce, it defended the wrong side during a conflict for a throne that started on 191 B.C. and afterwards following a siege for more than 2 years, it was conquered by Roman Empire Septimus Severus and burned down to pieces. The city was later reconstructed by the same Emperor and ornamented with new city walls and structures.

Base of the Egypt Obelisk at Hippodrome.

On 4th century A.D., the Roman Empire was largely extended and the capital Rome was left in a corner of the Empire. Emperor Constantine the Great (306-337) chose here when he was looking for a capital because he understood the importance of the great strategical position, ideal climate of the city and its position of intersecting land and sea routes. With the city walls that were reconstructed in more than 6 years; the city was extended, many temples, official buildings, palaces, hammams and hippodrome were built and on 330, it became the official capital of Roman Empire with a great ceremony. A golden age started at the city that was named as **Second Rome** and **New Rome** and

Mosaic of Saint Ioannes Khrysostomos, the Patriarch of Istanbul
(Museum of Hagia Sophia).

Remains of Bukoleon Palace, Çatladıkapı.

⬅

The Virgin Mary and Child Jesus Christ
(Museum of Kariye).

Ottoman Emblem.

after these names that were quickly forgotten, it was named as **Byzantion** and in later ages as **Constantinople.**

The efforts to make the city more beautiful continued with the emperors after Constantine the Great and they had new constructions, streets, aqueducts and monuments built. The first churches in the city were constructed after Constantine. Even though Roman Empire was divided into two in 395 and Western Roman Empire collapsed in 5th century, Eastern Roman Empire continued its existence under capital Istanbul for more than 1000 years. Contemporary historians named this empire "**Byzantine Empire**".

Byzantine Empire that developed under the influence of early civilizations in Anatolia and the grandeur, rules and laws taken from the East and Rome and most importantly under the influence and principles of Christian religion has a very interesting history. Istanbul city was extended once again in the first half of the 5th century with the reconstructed city walls. These city walls of the land site that can still be seen today were built by Empire Theodosius II (408-450) and its length was 6492 meters. The city with a population exceeding half a million in 6th century lived another golden age under the administration of Emperor Justinian I (527-565). The well-known Hagia Sophia that has come to today is the work of this empire.

The later history of Byzantine Empire and capital Istanbul is full of palace and church contrivances, attacks from Iran and Arabians and bloody conflicts between the fast-changing descendants of empires. All kinds of icons were banned during *Iconoclastic* move that took place between 726 and 843.

The Latin rule which is a black era of its history started with the siege of the city in 1204 during the Crusades and the city was exposed to a robbery for years against its churches, monasteries and even towards its monuments. Even though the administration of the city was left to the Byzantions again in 1261, Istanbul could not reach its wealth again. The threat of growing Turkish Ottoman Empire increased and eventually after 53 days of siege, the city was taken over by the Turks in 1453. One of the reasons for overcoming Istanbul city walls was the large balls used for the first time in war history by Fatih Sultan Mehmet. Another reason that enabled the conquest was the fact that the natural end of Byzantine Empire had come.

Fatih carried the capital of Ottoman Empire here and increased the population of the city with the nomads he brought from various parts of the country and started constructing the empty and ruined city. He gave freedom of religion and social rights to the previous folk of the city and enabled them to continue living there. Due to the rights that he bestowed, the Patriarchate which is the head of Christian Orthodox Church has stayed in its place until today. Among with some other churches in the city, the Hagia Sophia was also turned into a mosque and saved from its ruined condition.

After Istanbul was conquered by the Turks, it was improved and reconstructed again in a short time. A century after the conquest, Turkish Art was dominant and domes and minarets were seen in the silhouette

Sultan Mehmet the Conqueror entering the city through Topkapı.

of the city. After 16th century, because the Ottoman Sultans were the caliphates, Istanbul became the center of the whole Islamic world.

Under the rule of the sultans, the city was completely constructed and gained an enchanting atmosphere. In the colorful pages of Istanbul history at this age, there are no wars; however, the frequent fires burned large sections of the city. After the contacts that became more frequent after 19th century, the mosques and palaces were built on the side of the Bosphorus in European architectural style. Many palaces built in short time were also symbols of the decline period. Istanbul witnessed the end of another world empire at the end of the 1st World War.

While the empire was divided and the inner and outer enemies struggled for their shares, a noble commander of the Turkish army started struggling for Turkish Nation. This national hero named Mustafa Kemal founded Turkish Republic in 1923 after the War of Independence that lasted 4 years.

Mustafa Kemal Atatürk who became the head of this first Republic of Asia directed his country towards the basis of Western Civilization and modernity. Sultan and his family were sent abroad, caliphacy was banned, Latin alphabet was accepted, fez and garment that covered women were banned, and the right to vote was extended to women as well.

When Atatürk died in 1938, the young Turkish Republic had taken its place by the western world. The capital of the country became Ankara but it did not decrease the importance of Istanbul and this unique city continued its enchanting view and life.

M. Kemal Atatürk, the founder of the Republic of Turkey.

"The group that Ottoman State was a member of, was defeated in the 1 World War, Ottoman army was damaged in many places, and a ceasefire with heavy burdens had been signed... Those who took the country and its people to the war started to worry about their own lives and escaped from the country... As soon as ceasefire was signed, the warrior soldiers of the units were demobilised, their weapons and ammunition were taken away and they were turned into some groups lacking the ability for war... The enemy states started to attack Ottoman nation and state in financial and moral ways. They had decided to destroy and share it. The person who is the sultan and the caliphate does not think any other solution than the one that will save his life and comfort... Commanders and officials are devastated to see that with all the suffering and difficulties of the 1 World War, their nation is being torn to pieces... Sirs, there was only one decision upon this condition. And that was to form a new Turkish Nation that is independent and based on national domination without any conditions!... No matter how rich or abundant it is, a nation without independency is never treated more than a servant before civilized humanity... Although, the honor, pride and capabilities of the Turks are very high and great. Such a nation shall be destroyed rather than live as a captive. Thus, either independence or death!"

Nutuk,
Mustafa Kemal Atatürk

EASTERN ROMAN AND BYZANTINE EMPIRES

Constantine I *(306-337)*
Constantine II *(337-340)*
Constans I *(337-350)*
Constantie II *(337-361)*
Magnentius *(350-353)*
Iulianus *(361-363)*
Iovianus *(363-364)*
Valens *(364-378)*
Procopius *(365-366)*
Theodosius I *(378-395)*
Arcadius *(395-408)*
Theodosius II *(408-450)*
Markianos *(450-457)*
Leon I *(457-474)*
Leon II *(474)*

Emperor Alexandros *(912-913).*

Zenon *(474-491)*
Anastasios I *(491-518)*
İustinos I *(518-527)*
Justinian *(527-565)*
İustinos II *(565-578)*
Tiberios Constantine II *(578-582)*
Flavios Maurikios Tiberios *(582-602)*
Phokas *(602-610)*
Herakleios *(610-641)*
Herakleios - Constantine III *(641)*
Herakleios (Heraklonas) *(641)*
Konstans II *(641-668)*
Constantine IV *(668-685)*
Justinian II Rhinotmetos *(685-695)*
Leontios *(695-698)*
Tiberios II *(698-705)*
Justinian II Rhinotmetos *(705-711)*
Philippikos *(711-713)*
Anastasios II *(713-715)*

Theodosios III *(715-717)*
Leon III *(717-741)*
Constantine V Kopronymos *(741-775)*
Leon IV *(775-780)*
Constantine VI Porphyrogenetos *(780-797)*
Eirene *(797-802)*
Nikephoros I *(802-811)*
Stavrakios *(811)*
Mikhail I Rhangabe *(811-813)*
Leon V *(813-820)*
Mikhail II Balbus *(820-829)*
Theophilos *(829-842)*
Mikhail III *(842-867)*
Basileios I *(867-886)*
Leon VI *(886-912)*
Aleksandros *(912-913)*
Constantine VII Porphyrogenetos *(913-919)*
Romanos I Lekapenos *(920-944)*
Romanos II *(959-963)*
Nikephoros II Phokas *(963-969)*
İoannes I Tzimiskes *(969-976)*
Basileios II Bulgaroktonos *(976-1025)*
Constantine VIII *(1025-28)*
Romanos III Argyros *(1028-34)*
Mikhail IV *(1034-41)*
Mikhail V Kalaphates *(1041-42)*
Zoe *(1042-56)*
Constantine IX Monomakhos *(1042-55)*
Theodora *(1055-56)*
Mikhail VI Stratiotikos *(1056-57)*

Empress Zoe *(1042-56).*

Emperor Constantine IX Monomakhos *(1042-55).*

Emperor Ioannes I Komnenos *(1118-43).*

İsaakios I Komnenos *(1057-59)*
Constantine X Dukas (1059-67)
Romanos IV Diogenes (1068-71)
Mikhail VII Dukas (1071-78)
Nikephoros III Botaniates (1078-81)
Aleksios I Komnenos *(1081-1118)*
İoannes I Komnenos *(1118-43)*
Manuel I Komnenos *(1143-80)*
Aleksios II Komnenos *(1180-83)*
Andronikos I Komnenos *(1183-85)*

You can see the mosaics of the Byzantine Empire in the Hagia Sophia Museum.

İsaakios II Angelos *(1185-95)*
Aleksios III Angelos *(1195-1203)*
İsaakios II Angelos *(1203-04)*
Aleksios V Dukas Murtzuphios *(1204)*
NIKAIA
Theodoros I Laskaris *(1204-22)*
İoannes III Dukas Vatatzes *(1222-54)*
Theodoros II Laskaris *(1254-58)*
İoannes IV Laskaris *(1258-61)*

CONSTANTINOPLE
Mikhail VIII Palaiologos *(1261-82)*
Andronikos II Palaiologos *(1282-1328)*
Andronikos III Palaiologos *(1328-41)*
İoannes V Palaiologos *(1341-76)*
İoannes VI Kantakuzenos *(1347-54)*
Andronikos IV Palaiologos *(1376-79)*
İoannes V Palaiologos *(1379-90)*
İoannes VII Palaiologos *(1390)*
İoannes V Palaiologos *(1390-91)*
Manuel II Palaiologos *(1391-1425)*
İoannes VIII Palaiologos *(1425-48)*
Constantine XI Palaiologos *(1448-53)*

Osman I *(1299-1324).*

Süleyman I (The Magnificant) *(1520-66).*

OTTOMAN SULTANS

Osman I *(1299-1324)*
Orhan *(1324-62)*
Murat I (Hüdavendigar) (1362-89)
Bayezid I (Yıldırım) *(1389-1402)*
Mehmet I (Çelebi) *(1403-21)*
Murat II *(1421-44/1445-51)*
Mehmet II (Fatih) *(1444-45/1451-81)*

Mehmet II (Conqueror) *(1444-45/1451-81).*

Bayezid II *(1481-1512)*
Selim I (Yavuz) *(1512-20)*
Süleyman I (Kanuni) *(1520-66)*
Selim II (Sarı) *(1566-74)*
Murat III *(1574-95)*
Mehmet III *(1595-1603)*
Ahmet I *(1603-17)*
Mustafa I *(1617-18/1622-23)*
Osman II (Genç) *(1618-22)*
Murat IV *(1623-40)*
İbrahim *(1640-48)*
Mehmet IV (Avcı) *(1648-87)*
Süleyman II *(1687-91)*
Ahmet II *(1691-95)*
Mustafa II *(1695-1703)*
Ahmet III *(1703-30)*
Mahmut I *(1730-54)*
Osman III *(1754-57)*
Mustafa III *(1757-74)*
Abdülhamit I *(1774-89)*
Selim III *(1789-1807)*
Mustafa IV *(1807-08)*
Mahmut II *(1808-39)*
Abdülmecit *(1839-61)*
Abdülaziz *(1861-76)*
Murat V *(1876)*
Abdülhamit II *(1876-1909)*
Mehmet V *(1909-18)*
Mehmet VI *(1918-22)*

Mahmut II *(1808-39).*

You can see the portraits of Ottoman Sultans in the Imperial Portraits Collection of Topkapı Palace.

OTTOMAN COMPLEX *(KÜLLİYE)*

The name *külliye* is used for a complex set of structures that cover a part or whole of a school, hospital, hammam, bazaar, soup kitchen, caravanserai adjacent to a mosque. From this perspective, *külliye* was the center with important functions in city life where public social, cultural and

Sultanahmet (Blue) Mosque with all six minarets visible.

health necessities were met. *Külliye* brought vivacity to the place it was built at and increased the pace of urban development.

Mosque: Mosques that stand alone or are built within a *külliye*, are religious constructions where the Muslims carried out their salah *(namaz)*. Salah is one of the Five Pillars of Islam that has to

People pray generally together in mosques.

be carried out five times a day (morning, noon, midafternoon, evening, dusk).

Before performing salah; a ritual ablution *(abdest)* is performed requiring the cleaning of the head, hands until the elbows and the feet. *Adhan* (*Ezan* – Islamic call to prayer) is a call for salah made before each salah period by *muezzins*. Among the traditional music maqams of Islamic world, Adhan spreads around the city from *minarets* that rises like a tower near to the mosques.

The largest of the mosques were *Selatin Mosques* that were generally built by the sultans and where they had their Friday salah. These mosques had two or four minarets and uniquely of the age, *Sultanahmet Mosque* had six minarets. Classical period mosques generally had outer courtyards and inner courtyards. Vaulted arcades *(revak)* that are covered with domes consisting of columns attached to each other surround the inner courtyard.

A *şadırvan* (fountain) is located in the middle of the inner courtyard and it has the fauucets for the ritual ablution. The arcade of the courtyard that extends throughout the entrance side of the mosque is called the last location for the congregation. *The last place for congregation* with two *mihrab* niches on each

The *Mihrab* and *Minber* of Rüstem Pasha Mosque, which are decorated with İznik ceramic tiles.

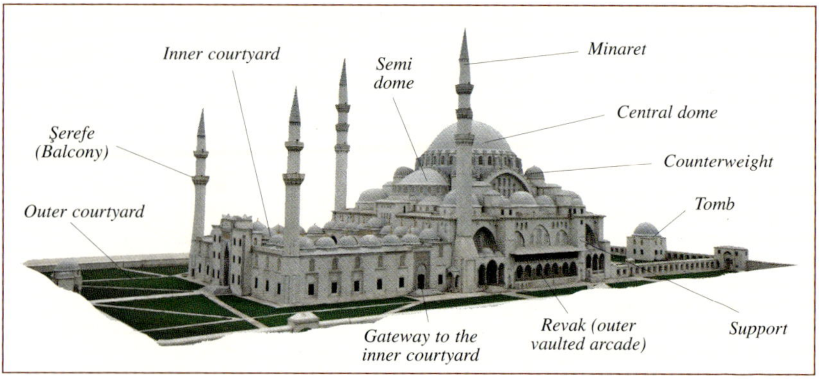

Classical period Ottoman Mosque (Süleymaniye Mosque).

People performing *abdest* (ritual ablution) before prayer.

side is considered for those who arrive late for the salah or who can not enter due to the crowd.

The niches of the mosques are directed towards Kaaba at Mecca. Since the direction of the Kaaba is on southeast of Istanbul, the mosques are built on southeast-northwest axis. When you enter the location of religious services, in the middle of *kıble* (Kıblah) wall right across the entrance, there is a *niche* where the *imam* (prayer leader) stands

***Müezzin Mahfili* (the platform of the assistant of the *imam*, the *müezzin*, stands during prayer).**

enabling the entire congregation to move together. On the right of the niche, *pulpit* is placed for sermons or addressing the crowd. The *sermon pulpit* is on the left of the niche.

The royal loge (hünkar mahfili) is the private place for the sultan who performs the salah at the mosque and it has detailed ornaments. The gallery floors higher than prayer areas are called *Kadınlar* (Women's) *Mahfili* for the performance

View of the inner courtyard of Sultanahmed Mosque.

***Hünkar Mahfili* (Royal loge) in the Museum of Hagia Sophia.**

of salah by women. Ottomans who started state process after sultanade period in 1299 had their first mosques covered with single dome with a caliber of 8-10 meters. Afterwards, mosques with "T" shape were built that had rectangular plan under two domes and where *tabhane*s (book

The pulpit.

printing rooms) bulged on the line of the back dome. These examples are mostly seen in Bursa and Edirne. Again, there are different implementations with the roofing system covered with a number of domes. The plan of *Üç Şerefeli Mosque* in Edirne built by Murat II between 1438 and 1447, constitutes an important phase for transition from mosques with multiple feet to large mosques with a central dome. The dome of this mosque is set on the hexagonal arch system and carries different innovations from the features of the period with its arcaded courtyard and four minarets.

Fatih Mosque (1463-70) built after the conquest of Istanbul had a large dome covering the middle section and under the influence of Hagia Sophia, a half dome supporting it on the side of *mihrab*. An improved version of first Fatih Mosque that was collapsed was successfully implemented at Beyazıt Mosque, supported with two half domes on its axis.

When the Ottomans were turning into an empire, Classical Period started in architecture in 16th century when the most beautiful works were created. The greatest architect of this period is Mimar Sinan who further improved the level of architecture. Later on,

Davut Ağa and Sedefkar Mehmet Ağa also continued his style. *Mihrimah Sultan Mosque* at Üsküdar completed by Mimar Sinan in 1548 achieved its perfection level with the three semidomes developed from the plan scheme of Beyazıt Mosque. Also, *Şehzade Mosque* he built between 1543 and 1548 did so with the four semidomes supporting the central dome. Again, the hexagon plan line of Üç Şerefeli Mosque was implemented with the support of corner trompe l'oeil at *Sokullu Mehmet Pasha Mosque* in Kadırga and *Atik Valide Mosque* in Üsküdar, both built by Mimar Sinan. These structures were further improved at *Rüstem Pasha Mosque* at Istanbul and *Sokullu Mehmet Pasha Mosque* at Azapkapı with octagonal schema with eight ranks. This plan shape reached its peak with *Selimiye Mosque* at Edirne which is among the most important structures of world architecture history and one of the most perfect works of central plan. Beginning with the middle of 18th century, art trends of European origin were increasingly felt. The trends used for ornamentation at the beginning were reflected on architecture in 19th century. The mosques that were reduced in size at the period manifested themselves while addressing the eye. At the beginning of 20th century, 1th National Architecture trend, which was the new classical, started to be influential.

RULES AT THE MOSQUES

Since the mosques are open everyday, you can visit them except for salah hours. In large mosques when the time is near or during the call of adhan, the visits are delayed by the attendants until the end of salah. Since salah time changes every day with slight differences, the calling of adhan would be your guide. The salah lasts for approximately thirty minutes after adhan is called. If there are any specific mosques you would like to see apart from the large ones, please do not forget that they may be closed until the noon salah. Some mosques in small neighborhoods can even be closed between the times of two salah. Some rules that need to be obeyed while visiting the mosques are as follows:

Hünkar Hammam *(Turkish Bath)* in the Harem of Topkapı Palace.

- Because the inside of the mosques are covered with carpet, no shoes are allowed due to hygiene and showing respect. You will notice small bags at the entrance of the mosques for placing your shoes. In smaller mosques, there are cabinets with numbers and keys or shoe cupboards for placing the shoes. Place your shoes on these cabinets, lock it and keep the key in your pocket until you exit. Do not forget to replace the key when you leave. While visiting tombs, shoes are removed and placed in the shoe cupboard.
- Women should cover their heads and wear long skirts.
- Since you may always meet someone performing salah, you shall not speak loudly and proceed further than the sections reserved for visits.

Madrasah: They are the education institutions for middle and higher education after *Sıbyan Mektebi* is completed that constitutes primary education. They generally had one floor and consisted of student rooms called cells and a class surrounding the courtyard. The students had their allowances from the charitable fund of the madrasah, sheltered in their rooms and had their meals at alms house.

Hammam: The fame of "*Turkish Hammam*" spread due to the importance that Islam gave to hammam as a result Islam's care for hygiene and the admiration Europeans towards the structures here. Hammams of Ottoman period were generally in double hammam shape with sections for women and men. These sections with symmetrical plan features were preferably on different roads or streets. The hammams were divided in three sections and the first section was called *soyunmalık*, that is called hotbed *(camekan)*. In this location that is made for the rest of the people entering hammams, there are sections for dressing and undressing. The second section called *Soğukluk* (the cold room) is the place where the warm air prepared the body for the heat. From this section on, comes the third section of the hammam named *sıcaklık* (or caldarium). The person is placed on a *heated marble platform* for sweating and *massage* is made by rubbers. On the corners, there is halvet, that is the cells used for washing. The caldarium with marble walls receive the light from the holes on the dome above.

Tabhane (Guesthouse): The rooms *(zaviye)* that were first used to shelter the mobile dervishes within the mosque were taken as separate places afterwards with complex and they were turned into tabhane with multiple rooms.

Tomb of Ahmet I, who had Sultanahmet Mosque constructed.

Ground plan of the Grand Bazar (Kapalıçarşı).

İmaret (soup kitchen): They were the institutions that provided free meals for the attendants serving at various parts of complex, the teachers and students of the schools, the visitors accommodating at the guest house and the poor and homeless around.

Dar al-shifa (Hospital): It served as a hospital and for some period, it also was a medical school.

Tomb (Türbe): They were grave structures consisting of single structure with square, polygon or circle plan covered with a dome. In general, they were structures where sultan, women members of the dynasty, sultan's son, and members of dynasty or high level officials were buried.

Fountain: They were made to meet the need for hygiene and drinking water. After 18th century, building fountains was more widespread and they had richer designs. Particularly, the fountains at squares are noteworthy with their monumental look.

Water dispenser: They mostly had circle or polygon plans and they were made to deliver drinking water. On special occasions such as *Bayram* (national festival), they also delivered sherbet.

Caravanserai / Inn: Caravanserai was the place where travelers and merchants stayed with their animals. They were founded in the cities and on the road where caravans passed. Later on, the buildings with commercial structures in the towns were called inns.

Arasta: They are generally the bazaars with a line of shops.

Fountain of Ahmet III.

Levent, where some shopping centers are located.

TODAY'S ISTANBUL

İstanbul, a metropolis with a population exceeding twelve million is a city that meets all kinds of needs and tastes. You are in a wealthy city that has been structured throughout its history dating back to Roman period. The **Historical Peninsula** surrounded by city walls, in a more narrow description, Sultanahmet Square and its surroundings is almost like an open air museum with its monuments. Wandering around the mystical atmosphere of *Hagia Sophia* with admiration, going about under the domes of the elegant *Sultanahmet (Blue) Mosque*, living this spirit under a monument of Hippodrome where car races were held is a peaceful experience. Witness the rich collections of *Topkapı Palace* and *Archaeological Museum*. *Basilica Cistern* which is still under the water, the priceless mosaics of *Kariye* and *Fethiye Museums* will leave you in awe. You will enjoy the view of the Historical Peninsula from *Galata Tower* and want to reflect on paper the silhouette of *Süleymaniye Mosque* on the **Golden Horn** that will not be possible for any other structure. While wandering around the wealthy history of Istanbul, it will be a different joy to shop at historical *Grand Bazaar* and smell the various spices of *Spice Bazaar*. In addition to historical bazaars, modern shopping malls with a large capacity such as İstinye Park (İstinye-Maslak), Kanyon (1. Levent), Metrocity (1. Levent), Akmerkez (Etiler), Profilo (Mecidiyeköy), Cevahir (Şişli) are also ready to serve you with its many shops, restaurants, cafes and movie theaters. Apart from these, the boutiques of Nişantaşı, shops of Bağdat Avenue at **Kadıköy** are also ready to serve you any time. In addition to modern shopping malls, Istanbul has many four and five star hotels for accommodation. Among all these, do not forget to view Istanbul with 360° from *Leander's Tower* located on a small island at the entrance of the Bosphorus. After visiting *Dolmabahçe Palace* on **Bosphorus**, you will feel a higher admiration. One should not leave the city

Metrocity and Kanyon, two of the shopping centers in 1. Levent.

Modern subway which offers service between Taksim and 4.Levent.

Bosphorus Bridge 29th October Lazer shows.

View of Eminönü, Galata and Bosphorus region from New Mosque.

without walking on *İstiklal Avenue* at **Beyoğlu** which is the most famous avenue of the city and without smelling the air of Bosphorus. The transportation network includes the street railway between Kabataş-Zeytinburnu-Airport, the tunnel that

General gravur of Istanbul *(Rouargue).*

goes up to **Taksim**, the funicular system and the ships that work with short intervals between the two continents.

THE CITY WALLS OF ISTANBUL

Istanbul city walls contributed greatly to the existence of Byzantium Empire for more than a thousand years. It was the most efficient defense system of the city with its length of approximately 22 km. The city was surrounded by the walls for four times after its first foundation. The first one was built by *Megarians* who settled here on 7th century B.C.. These walls were torn down by the Roman Emperor Septimus Severus (193-211) who entered the city on 196 A.D. and a second line of city walls was constructed. The first two city walls surrounded the acropolis and settlement area around Sarayburnu. The third line of city walls was built by *Constantine the Great* (306-337) who moved the capital of Roman Empire to Istanbul. These walls started from Marmara Sea and went towards the Golden Horn from Aksaray and followed the side of the sea.

The fourth city wall that reached today was built at the time of *Theodosius II* (408-450) and it extended the border of the city to double its size. At Marmara Sea and the Golden Horn, the city walls were laid parallel to the shore. Marmara city walls were 8.5 km long and the walls of the Golden Horn were 5 km long. The land city walls that unite Yedikule on the shore of Marmara and Ayvansaray at the shore of the Golden Horn were 6 km long. Because of the construction of railroads that passed from the shores of Marmara between 1870 and 1873, some of Marmara city walls were brought down. Even though very little are left from the city walls of the Golden Horn, the land city walls are in better shape. The city walls were taken under protection after the declaration of the Republic and they were partly restorated.

Walls of Marmara, and Topkapı Palace.

SULTAN AHMET SQUARE AND HIPPODROME

Sultanahmet and its surrounding which is the center of the Historical Peninsula is also the most lively tourism center of Istanbul. During Byzantine and Ottoman period, this area also experienced a lively past that suits its identity today. It is the most important area one has to see in Istanbul with **Hagia Sophia Museum** and **Sultanahmet Mosque** rising at both ends of the square, museums with rich collections, artists and monuments of hippodrome.

Museum of Hagia Sophia.

The square at the south of Hagia Sophia was called Augusteion on Byzantine period. The reason was because it was presented in the memory of Augusta Helena, the mother of Constantine the Great who moved the capital of Rome to Istanbul. On the large column in the middle of the square, there was the statue of Helena. With the Constantine Forum *(Çemberlitaş)* nearby, this was the most important square of the town. On its southeast, there was Khalke Gate, the entrance of **Grand Palace** and hammams and palaces of important people were lined around the square.

Hippodrome on the west of Sultanahmet Mosque was the most glorious and lively square of Byzantine and Ottoman period. Hippodrome had rectangular plan with a circle on south side and it was the race area for horse cars that could be

Detail from the Egypt Obelisk and Constantine (Bonded) Column.

of wild animals and rope dancers were held apart from the races. The walls of the Hippodrome were ornamented with many statues and paintings and were used until the end of 12th century and the car races ended after 1261 at the end of Latin invasion Byzantine Palace moved to Blahernai.

The Head of the Serpent Column *(Archaeology Museum).*

The name of the Hippodrome was changed as **Atmeydanı** during Ottoman period. The palace weddings, big ceremonies, javelin games and riots were carried out at this square. The Hippodrome area today is reduced in size compared to its original. On the east side, at the area where there used to be the viewers' stands, there is Sultanahmet Mosque; on the west there is İbrahim Pasha Palace *(Turkish-Islamic Arts Museum)* and on the south at the section with a square plan, there is Marmara University building.

watched by approximately a hundred thousand people. The racing cars used to travel around the wall called Spina. Only three of the monuments on Spina have reached today; these are: **Egypt Obelisk**, **Serpent Column** and **Constantine (Bonded) Column.** The emperor watched the races from his box named Kathisma which was linked to the Great Palace. Hippodrome was also an area where dances and shows

Window Facade, *(Tiled Pavilion).*

Sultan Ahmet Square and Hippodrome.

German Fountain 1
(Alman Çeşmesi)
Egypt (Theodosius) Obelisk 2
(Mısır Obeliski)
Serpent Column 3
(Yılanlı 'Burmalı' Sütun)
Constantine (Bonded) Column 4
(Örme Sütun)
Turkish and Islamic Arts Museum
(İbrahim Pasha Palace) 5
(Türk İslâm Eserleri Müzesi)
Sultanahmet (Blue) Mosque 6
(Sultanahmet 'Mavi' Cami)
Sultan Ahmet Tomb 7
(I. Ahmet Türbesi)
Arasta Bazaar 8 (Arasta Çarşısı)
Mosaic Museum 9 (Mozaik Müzesi)
Haseki Hammam 10 (Haseki Hamamı)
Hagia Sophia Museum 11
(Ayasofya Müzesi)
Basilica Cistern 12 (Yerebatan Sarnıcı)
Milion Stone 13 (Milion Taşı)
Firuzağa Mosque 14 (Firuzağa Camii)
Hagia Eufemia Church 15
(Azize Eufemia Kilisesi)
Binbirdirek Cistern 16
(Binbirdirek Sarnıcı)
Fountain of Ahmet III 17
(III. Ahmet Çeşmesi)
Sokullu Mehmet Pasha Mosque 18
Small Hagia Sophia Mosque 19
Polis Police
Hastane Hospital
Cami Mosque
Kilise Church
Otel Hotel
PTT PTT
Sağlık Ocağı Health Clinic
Saray-Kasır Palace-Summer Palace
Surlar City Walls
Tarihi Anıt Historical Monument
Türbe Tomb
Tramvay Durağı Tramway Stop
Tramvay Hattı Tramway Line
Turizm Danışma Information
Tren Yolu Train Line
Tuvalet Toilet
CAD. Avenue
Sk. Street
Taksim
Üsküdar
Eminönü
MOLLA FENARİ
BİNBİRDİREK
KÜÇÜK AYASOFYA
YENİÇERİLER CAD.
DİVANYOLU CAD.
VEZİRHAN CAD.
BAB-I ALİ CAD.
PİYER LOTİ CAD.
PEYKHANE CAD.
KLODFARER CAD.
İMRAN ÖKTEM CAD.
KADIRGA LİMANI CAD.
AKSAKAL CAD.
KENNEDY CAD.
Eminönü Belediye Başkanlığı
Cağaloğlu Anadolu Lisesi
Türk Ocağı Kültür Sanat Merkezi
Marmara Üniversitesi Rektörlüğü
İstanbul Cumhuriyet Eğitim Müzesi
Sultanahmet A.T.L A.M.L Teknik Lisesi ve E.M.L
Küçük Ayasofya Camii
Küçük Ayasofya Spor Kulübü
Necip Fazıl Kısakürek Kültür Merkezi
İSMEK
Turizm Meslek Lisesi
Kadırga Parkı
Çemberlitaş
Kaleci Sk.
Kasap Osman Sk.
Şehit Mehmet Paşa Sk.
Şehit Çeşmesi Sk.
Terzihane Sk.
Üçler Sk.
Nakilbent Sk.
Aksakal Sk.
Mustafa Paşa Sk.

SULTANAHMET
Ayasofya Müzesi
Aya İrini Müzesi
Sultanahmet Camii
Sultanahmet Parkı
Yerebatan Sarnıcı
Million Taşı
Alman Çeşmesi
İstanbul Türbeler Müdürlüğü
Sultan I. Ahmet Türbesi
Sultanahmet Camii Sarnıcı
Haseki Hürrem Sultan Hamamı
Hz. Abdurrahman Eş Şami Türbesi
Yeşil Ev
Four Seasons Hotel
Sırca El Sanatları Merkezi
Gül Sultan
Akropol Hotel
Magnuara Sarayı
Aşkın Hotel
Arhtamara Bazaar
Halı Müzesi
Mozaik Müzesi
Sultanahmet Sarayı
Sarı Konak Hotel
Angel's Home
Hotel Avicenna
Yusufpaşa Hoteli
Sokullu Mehmet Paşa Camii Türbesi
Sokullu Mehmet Paşa Camii
Tarım Orman ve Köyişleri
Mescit
Tashi Konak Hotel
Kapıağası Mahmutağa Camii
Almima Hotel
Akbıyık Camii
Kalyon Hotel
Firuz Ağa Camii
Firuz Ağa Camii Türbesi
Sultanahmet
Dikilitaş
Şehzadeler Türbesi
III. Sultan Murat Türbesi
II. Sultan Selim Türbesi
III. Sultan Mehmet Türbesi
III. Ahmet Çeşmesi
Üçyüzlü Çeşmesi
Cafer Ağa Türbesi
Ömerağa Çeşmesi
Yücel Kültür Vakfı
Zeynep Sultan Camii
Yerebatan Camii Türbesi
Yerebatan Camii
İstanbul İli Özel İdare Müdürlüğü
Turizm Şube Müdürlüğü
Türk Edebiyat Kurumları
Sultanahmet Sağlık Merkezi
Namede Otel
Otel Pamphylia
Kubele Hotel
T.C. Başbakanlık Devlet Arşivleri Genel Müdürlüğü
Kültür Bakanlığı Anıtlar Müdürlüğü
Sultanahmet A.T.M.L. ve Ticaret Meslek Lisesi
Çevrikalfa İ.Ö.O
İshak Paşa
Erol Taş Kültür
YEREBATAN CAD.
ALEMDAR CAD.
DİVANYOLU
KABASAKAL CAD.
BAB-I HÜMAYUN CAD.
MİMAR MEHMET AĞA CAD.
AKBIYIK CAD.
CANKURTARAN CAD.
AHIRKAPI CAD.
KENNEDY CAD.
AYASOFYA CAD.
Sultanahmet Meydanı
Atmeydanı Sk.
Tevkifhane Sk.
Kutlugün Sk.
Akbıyık Değirmeni Sk.
Oyuncu Sk.
Kapı Ağası Hisar Sk.
Torun Sk.
Dalbastı Sk.
Utangaç Sk.
Seyit Hasan Sk.
Bayram Fırını Sk.
Çetinkaya Sk.
Amiral Tafdil Sk.
Yeni Saraçhane Çıkmazı
Terbıyık Sk.
Adliye Sk.
Soğukçeşme Sk.
Caferiye Sk.
Mustafa Dede Sk.
Salkım Söğüt Sk.
Ticarethane Sk.
İncili Çavuş Sk.
Şeftali Sk.
Tavukhane Sk.
Küçük Ayasofya Cad.
Kapıcılar Sk.
Akbıyık Camii Sk.
Şadırvan Sk.
Yeni Güvey Sk.
Fenerli Kapı Sk.
Sultan Yegah Sk.
Mustafapaşa Çıkmazı
Oyuncu Çıkmazı
WC
Ptt
N
E
S
W

GERMAN FOUNTAIN (1)
(ALMAN ÇEŞMESİ)
At Meydanı (Hippodrome)

German Fountain.

The German Emperor Wilhelm II had built the fountain on the north side of the Hippodrome in memory of his second visit to Istanbul on 1898. The fountain prepared in Germany was moved to Istanbul in 1901 and mounted to its today's place. The fountain reflecting an octagon plan is covered by a dome with mosaics carried by eight onyx column. On four of the eight medallions engraved within the dome, there is the signature of Sultan Abdülhamit on green background and on the other four medallions, there is the letter "W" on Prussian blue background which was the symbol of Emperor Wilhelm II.

EGYPT (THEODOSİUS) OBELISK (2)
(MISIR OBELİSKİ)
At Meydanı (Hippodrome)

The oldest antique art in Istanbul is the obelisk made around 1500 B.C. by Tutmosis III, one of the pharaohs of Egypt. It was placed in front of Amon-Re Temple at Karnak with a similar one. It was brought to Alexandria for a period and kept laid down there for long years. The obelisk that was brought to Istanbul by Emperor Theodosius I (379-395) in 390 A.D. was erected on the marble base that was prepared earlier. On the four sides of the obelisk, there is Egyptian hieroglyph that lists the heroic deeds of Tutmosis III. On the top, Tutmosis III and Egyptian God Amon-Re are seen hand in hand in a circle. On the four sides of the marble base, there are depictions regarding Hippodrome. Here, there are engravings on how the obelisk was erected, Emperor Box, car races, musicians and dancing girls. At the bottom of the East and West side of the base, there are writings in Greek and Latin.

Tomb of Ahmet I and general view of Hippodrome. ⬅

Egypt (Theodosius) Obelisk.

SERPENT COLUMN (3)
(YILANLI 'BURMALI' SÜTUN)
At Meydanı (Hippodrome)

Small Greek city states united and won victories at Salamis (480 B.C.) and at Platea (479 B.C.) against the Persians who invaded their country. In the memory of this, they used their war captures to make the victory monument in 479 B.C. which is called Serpent Column today. This monument was placed before Apollo Temple in Delphi. In its original, three snakes holding one another looking at different sides carried a golden cauldron on their heads. The names of the cities that participated in the war were written on their bodies. The cauldron of the monument was lost long before it was brought to Istanbul at the age of Constantine the Great. The heads of the snakes were destroyed at the beginning of 18th century. One of the heads of the snakes is exhibited at the Byzantine Room at the second floor of Archaeological Museum.

Serpent Column.

CONSTANTINE (BONDED) COLUMN (4)
(ÖRME SÜTUN)
At Meydanı (Hippodrome)

It is not known when and by whom it was made. Since Constantine Porphyrogenetus VII (913-919) had it repaired; it is named after his name. Constantine Column rising on the south of Hippodrome is 32 meters high. Since it was built by stones of different sizes, it has a massive look. It has Greek writings on the

Constantine Column.

east side of its marble base. The golden facing covering its surface was looted by the Latins who invaded Istanbul.

TURKISH AND ISLAMIC ARTS MUSEUM (İBRAHİM PASHA PALACE) 5

(TÜRK VE İSLÂM ESERLERİ MÜZESİ 'İBRAHİM PAŞA SARAYI')

Atmeydanı Street No: 44

Except Mondays 09.00-16.30

Turkish and Islamic Arts Museum that was located at Complex of Süleymaniye

Plate on which God is written *(Turkish and Islamic Arts Museum).*

Mosque until 1983 was moved to İbrahim Pasha Palace after this date on the west of Hippodrome. The palace that was given as a present to İbrahim Pasha who was the grand vizier for thirteen years is the only private palace that has reached until today. The building date of the structure is unknown and the parts of the inner courtyard of the structure are used today as a museum. The museum has rich manuscripts, miniature manuscripts and collections of various Turkish-Islamic states of 7th - 20th centuries. Its has unique carpet collections of different periods.

In ethnography section, examples are exhibited regarding carpet-rug counters, wool painting techniques and public life.

Sultanahmet Mosque view from the park pool.

SULTANAHMET (BLUE) MOSQUE 6

(SULTANAHMET 'MAVİ' CAMİİ)

Atmeydanı Street No: 21-23

Can be visited everyday apart from salah hours.

The mosque built by Architect Sedefkar Mehmet Ağa between 1609 and 1616 is among the last examples of Classical Ottoman Architecture. It is called Blue Mosque due to its wall tile in blue color.

Sultan Ahmet I (1603-1617) was careful about the location of the mosque and confiscated the land on the east of Hippodrome, tearing down Ottoman palaces and chalets and started building this on 9th November 1609. Despite its huge size, the mosque located in a large courtyard of 4600 m^2 has an enchanting architecture with its elegant look. The fact that it was the only mosque with six minarets differentiates it from other mosques.

The structure constructed on a high platform is mounted through marble stairs. Its monumental entrance door is the gate with muqarnas filling

***Mihrab* of the Sultanahmet Mosque.**

on the side of the Hippodrome. In the middle of the inner courtyard surrounded by arcades, there is a marble fountain with six corners and six columns. The domes rising one after another when seen from the courtyard exhibit the wealth of the architecture.

The location of salah is about 53x50 square meters and covered with a dome that is 43 meters higher than the ground with a diameter of 23.5 meters. The dome carried by four "elephant feet" with a 5 meters diameter extends the location with its

Carpet Collection *(Turkish and Islamic Arts Museum).*

General view of Sultanahmet Mosque and Tomb of Ahmet I.

half domes opening towards four sides. The section between the semidomes is completed by independent domes and thus achieve a square plan.

Parallel to improved Ottoman architecture, tiling, woodcrafts, stone crafts and pen crafts also enrich the architecture as ornamental features. The location of salah is ornamented with tiles and pen craft from the dome down to the ground. The walls, ornamented with more than 20.000 wall tiles and especially the tiles at the gallery floor are gorgeous. The tile patterns designed at *Nakkaşhane* (the paint house) of Topkapı Palace were prepared especially at İznik (the ancient Nicaea) workshops.

The door of Sultanahmet Mosque in the direction of Hippodrome.

The upper parts of the walls of the mosque and the inner sides of the domes are decorated with pen crafts. The wings of the doors and windows are ornamented with delicate Ottoman metal and wood crafts and the *mihrab*, pulpit and royal loge are ornamented with delicate Ottoman stone crafts.

With all these features, Sultanahmet Mosque is among the most popular mosques of Istanbul.

Ceramic tile board in the mosque.

The *mihrab* wall of the mosque and stained glasses decorating the structure.

DÜNYA
AHİRETİN
TARLASIDIR

Sultan Ahmet Park and Tomb of Ahmet I.

Interior view of the tomb.

SULTAN AHMET TOMB 7

(I. AHMET TÜRBESİ)
Kabasakal Avenue
Open to visitors.

On the north of Sultanahmet Mosque, the tomb of Ahmet I who built the mosque is open to visitors. Ahmet I who was born in 1590 and who ascended the throne when he was 14, became sick in 1617 and passed away. He changed the tradition of killing siblings for the unity of the country, a tradition that started with Bayezid and became a law during the time of Fatih and Ahmet I also brought the method of the throne being ascended by the eldest one in the dynasty.

Sultan Ahmet Tomb with a square plan is covered with a dome sitting on a polygon hoop. At its entrance, there is an arcade with three domes. The inside of the tomb has rich examples of tiles, pen and wood crafts. The tiles cover the breaks between the windows with wooden wings and the upper parts of the windows. Over the tile panels, an epigraph written with white sulus calligraphy over dark blue background surrounds the structure. At the tomb, besides *Ahmet I*, his wife *Kösem Sultan (Mahpeyker Sultan)*, their sons *Murat IV* and *Osman II*, their daughter *Ayşe Sultan* and about forty members of the dynasty are buried.

ARASTA BAZAAR 8

(ARASTA ÇARŞISI)
Kabasakal Avenue

The bazaar (arasta) built with Sultanahmet Complex is located on the southeast of the mosque. It is the only open bazaar from 17th century in Istanbul and it is used today for touristic purposes.

GRAND PALACE

(BÜYÜK SARAY)

The Grand Palace of Byzantine Empire covered a large area including today's Sultanahmet Square and Blue Mosque towards the Marmara shore. As it was at Topkapı Palace, the rooms of the palace extended with additions built in different periods were decorated with rich mosaics, valuable stones and columns. The importance of Grand Palace started to decrease by 10th century and **Blahernai Palace** at Ayvansaray started to become more important. Grand Palace was used at this period as official accommodation and meeting place.

During the Latin invasion period of Istanbul (1204-1261) Grand Palace was also looted among with many other structures. Because some architectural pieces were torn down during Byzantine period to be used elsewhere, it was ruined until the Conquest of Istanbul. During Ottoman period, the fact that new neighborhoods were founded here and the building of Sultan Ahmet Complex during the time of Ahmet I caused some ruins of the palace to disappear and because of the settlement, the research regarding the palace have always been restricted.

Arasta Bazaar

Interior view of Sultanahmet Mosque.

From the Grand Palace that included many other structures within its borders, some ruins and the ruined walls of **Bukoleon Palace** at Çatladıkapı near Small Hagia Sophia have come until today.

MOSAIC MUSEUM 9

(MOZAİK MÜZESİ)
Torun Street
Except Mondays 09.00-16.30

It is below Arasta Bazaar that was built with Sultan Ahmet Complex. With the work carried out by Dr. J.H. Baxter between 1933 and 1938, a courtyard with columns has been found that belonged to the palace. The works that were interrupted due to 2nd World War were continued by Prof. Dr. D. Talbot Rice between 1951 and 1954. Pieces of mosaic pavement have been found at southwest of the courtyard and some in good condition at the Northeast section of the courtyard. At the museum, these mosaics that were found and that did not include religious scenes as well as other mosaics in different regions are exhibited. On these mosaics, there are struggle figures of various animals, hunting scenes, horses and sheep on grass, a wolf eating his prey and a shepherd carrying a sheep.

Haseki Hammam (Turkish Bath) at the Sultanahmet Square.

Mosaic Museum.

Fight of leopards and hunters.

HASEKİ HAMMAM 10

(HASEKİ HAMAMI)
Sultan Ahmet Square

The structure with two domes bordering the east of Sultan Ahmet Square is Haseki Hammam that was built by Mimar Sinan between 1556 and 1557 with two sections spared for men and women. At the hammam which was active until 1910, both sections had the same plan and on men's side, there is an arcade with three domes.

A detail of the Museum.

Museum of Hagia Sophia, which is considered one of the masterpieces of the world.

HAGIA SOPHIA MUSEUM 11

(AYASOFYA MÜZESİ)
Ayasofya Square
Except Mondays 09.00-16.30
09.00-19.00 in Summer

Hagia Sophia built between 532 and 537 at the age of Justinian I (527-565) is among the foremost works in the world of architecture and art history. Its architects were Anthemios of Tralles (Aydın) and Isidoros of Miletos.

During Byzantine period, it served as a church and during the Ottoman period, it served as a mosque and today since 1935, it continues to function as a museum. Today's Hagia Sophia is the third one constructed at its place. The remains of the first structure could not reach today and the remains of the second structure found in 1935 are by the entrance.

The Virgin Mary and Child Jesus Christ.

Because the third Hagia Sophia is a very bold one for its age, it brought together some architectural deficiencies with itself; the eastern part of the dome was collapsed in 558 and one of the semidomes collapsed in the earthquake of 869. The structure that was also damaged in 1344 earthquake was only repaired through special taxes and donations. Hagia Sophia went through the danger of collapsing all together during Ottoman times, but managed to reach until today with the repairs and support footings made by Mimar Sinan.

At the center, the gorgeous dome covers the naos with its half domes on its axis; its main architectural features are two naves on each side, a boisterous apse, inner and outer narthex following the entrance. From the west, one may proceed to the plain, non-colored outer narthex and from here to the inner narthex where the ceiling is covered

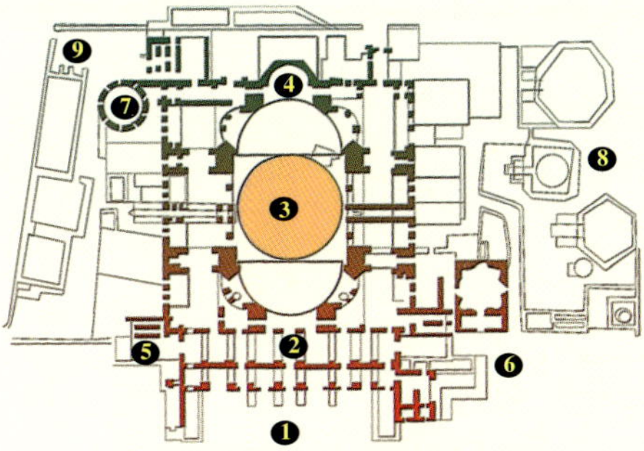

1- *Entrance to the Museum,* **2-** *Inner Narthex,* **3-** *Naos,* **4-** *Apse,* **5-** *Gallery's way-out* **6-** *Museum's way-out,* **7-** *Treasury Building,* **8-** *Tombs,* **9-** *Door of the soup kitchen.*

Plan of the Hagia Sophia.

Mosaic of Gabriel, the Angel, in the Museum of Hagia Sophia.

with non-figured mosaics. The door at the north of inner narthex opens to the platform that goes to upper gallery. The door on the south is the exit door named Horologion.

The main location of Hagia Sophia is 73,50 x 69,50 meters. The dome sitting on the pendantives carried by four big arches is 55,60 meters high and has a diameter of about 31 meters. Inner parts of Hagia Sophia are ornamented with 107 columns, 40 of which are downstairs and 67 of which are upstairs and there are monograms of Emperor Justinian I and Empress Theodora on some of the headings of the column.

Besides its architecture, Hagia Sophia is also famous for its decoration. Because the mosaics with figures were ruined during Iconoclasm period (726-843), the mosaics that can be seen are dated after the Iconoclasm period, 9th-12th centuries. The mosaic panel over Emperor's Gate which is the largest door of the inner narthex dates back to 9th century. On Horologion Gate on the south of inner narthex, there is a mosaic panel from 10th century on which Constantine the Great presents Virgin Mary and Baby Jesus presents a model of the city and Justinian I presents the model of the church.

Hagia Sophia receives daylight from 40 windows on the skirts of its dome. Inside of the dome is ornamented with a magnificent calligraphy and there is the figure of four winged angel over the four pendantives that it relies on. The cubes at the entrance of middle location were brought from Bergama (Pergamon) during the period of Murat III (1574-1595) and they are of Hellenistic age massive marble. The giant plates with a diameter of 7,5 meters hanged on the walls of the gallery were written by calligrapher Kazasker Mustafa İzzet Efendi in the middle of 19th century. It is assumed that the depictions of Baby Jesus and Mary on the semidome of the apse were the first mosaics made after Iconoclasm period. Also on the arch of the apse, the panel of Prime Angel Gabriel which is partly damaged, the royal loge made by Fossati on 1849 on the left of the apse, the pulpit on the right that dates back to 16th century are worth seeing.

Valuable mosaics can also be seen at the galleries of Hagia Sophia. One may mount this section by a spiral platform from the south of the inner narthex. On the floor of the galleries on the north, there is the mosaic of Emperor Alexandros (912-913). It is known as Empress Lodge because the empress watched religious ceremonies in the middle gallery covered with vaults over the narthex.

Deesis Mosaic in the South gallery.

One may enter the south gallery from a marble door named Gate of Heaven. After the door, just on the right, there is **Deesis Mosaic** that dates back to 12th century with a size of 6x4,7 meters and it is one of the most famous mosaics of Hagia Sophia. At the end of the gallery, there are two more mosaic panels that show two emperors and the empress with Mary and Jesus.

Seraphim Angel figure on the pendant.

Interior view of Hagia Sophia.

Emperor Constantine Monomakhos, Christ and Empress Zoe.

Emperor John II Komnenos, the Empress Eirene and Alexios, Mary with child Jesus in her lap in the middle (12th century).

Basilica Cistern.

Head of Medusa in the Basilica Cistern.

BASILICA CISTERN 12

(YEREBATAN SARNICI)
Yerebatan Avenue No: 13
Except Mondays 09.00-16.30

On the west of Hagia Sophia Square, the small structure right across the Tourism Police Station is the entrance of Basilica Cistern. It was built by Justinian I (527-565) and it is the largest Byzantine cistern with a size of 140x70 meters. 336 columns with a height of 9 meters carry the cross vaulted ceiling with bricks. During Byzantine times, the water stored here was brought from outside the city with water arcs and channels.

The structure can be visited thanks to the platforms that are constructed and there are fishes underneath due to the water level today. It is assumed that the column engraved in the shape of a tree in the middle of the cistern is brought from another structure. Nearly forty of the columns were left behind the wall that was built on the southwest of the cistern in 19th century.

On its southwest corner, the Medusa heads are interesting and they were found with the latest renovation. Two Medusa heads are used upside down linearly as the base of two columns.

Milion Stone.

MILION STONE 13

(MİLİON TAŞI)
Divanyolu Avenue

Milion Stone located nearby Basilica Cistern was the first of the stone signs in the land of the empire that showed the length of other centers to the capital.

In its original, it was a single domed structure with a square plan carried by arches over four columns. From this section, the historical Mese Avenue is directed towards Hagia Sophia Square and the Grand Palace.

FİRUZ AĞA MOSQUE 14

(FİRUZ AĞA CAMİİ)
Divanyolu Avenue

The mosque located on Divanyolu Street was built by Bayezid's senior treasury keeper Firuz Ağa between 1490 and 1491. It is a small structure covered with a single dome and a square plan. Its dome with octagon tambour rises on muqarnas

Binbirdirek Cistern.

filling pendantives. The inner walls and the *mihrab* of the mosque are ornamented with pen crafts and there is the place of last congregation on its entrance. It is assumed that the sarcophagus on the side of the minaret belongs to Firuz Ağa who died in 1512.

SAINT EUFEMIA CHURCH ⑮

(AZİZE EUFEMİA KİLİSESİ)

Eufemia was the saint of Khalkedon (Kadıköy) and he was martyred on 16th September 303 before Christianism was widespread. A section in the west of the Antiochus Palace where ruins may be seen was turned into a church in the name of the saint on 7th century. The relics of Eufemia were kept at this church between Firuz Ağa Mosque and the Court House.

Here, during the excavations of 1939 and 1942, architectural remains and frescos regarding the life of Saint Eufemia were found. The relics of Saint Eufemia are kept at *Hagios Georgios Church* which is Fener Patriarchate Church today.

BİNBİRDİREK CISTERN ⑯

(BİNBİRDİREK SARNICI)
İmran Öktem Avenue No: 4
Open to visitors

It is across the Court House on the upper street on the west of the Hippodrome. It was built in order to meet the water needs of the palace by Philoxenus, one of senators who came to the city because the capital of Roman Empire was moved to Istanbul. Binbirdirek Cistern is 64x56 meters and consists of 224 columns with plain headings. The columns attached to one another with arches carry the cross vaulted ceiling. Here, chaining two columns on one another is a different technique. Many letters engraved on the body of the column belongs to the workers who participated in the building of the cistern. It was used as a workshop by weavers.

FOUNTAIN OF AHMET III ⑰

(III. AHMET ÇEŞMESİ)
Bab-ı Hümayun Avenue

The fountain of square in front of Bab-i Hümayun Door of Topkapı Palace has rich ornaments and was built between 1728 and 1729. There is one fountain on each of the four fronts and there are niches on its two sides.

Its corners that bulge towards outside in half a circle are used as water dispensers. Its roof has wide fringes covered with lead and it is completed with five small domes, four of which are in the corners and one of which is in the middle.

Fountain of Ahmet III at the entrance of the Topkapı Palace.

Topkapı Palace Museum 1
(Topkapı Sarayı Müzesi)
Harem 2 (Harem)
Hagia Eirene Church 3
(Hagia Eirene Kilisesi)
Archaeological Museum 4
(Arkeoloji Müzesi)
Ancient Eastern Works Museum 5
(Eski Eserler Müzesi)
Tiled Pavilion 6 (Çinili Köşk)
Audience Pavilion 7 (Alay Köşkü)
Gülhane Park 8 (Gülhane Parkı)
Goths' Column 9 (Gotlar Sütunu)
Soğuk Çeşme Street 10
(Soğuk Çeşme Sokağı)
Sepetçiler Qasr 11
(Sepetçiler Kasrı)
Cağaloğlu Hammam 12
(Cağaloğlu Hamamı)
Polis Police
Hastane Hospital
Cami Mosque
Kilise Church
Otel Hotel
PTT PTT
Sağlık Ocağı Health Clinic
Saray-Kasır Palace-Summer Palace
Surlar City Walls
Tarihi Anıt Historical Monument
Türbe Tomb
Tramvay Durağı Tramway Stop
Tramvay Hattı Tramway Line
Tren Yolu Train Line
CAD. Avenue
Sk. Street
Taksim
Üsküdar
Eminönü
HOCAPAŞA
KENNEDY CAD.
SİRKECİ İSTASYON CAD.
Sirkeci Tren Garı
Sirkeci
ANKARA CAD.
İstanbul Valiliği Çevre Müdürlüğü
Başbakanlık Basın Enformasyon Müdürlüğü
Emirler Hanı Sk.
Dervişoğlu Sk.
Vezir Camii
İstasyon Arkası Sk.
Merkez Polis Karakolu
Darüssade Sk.
Nöbethane Çıkmazı Sk.
Kum Meydanı Sk.
NÖBETHANE CAD.
İBB Park ve Bahçeler Müdürlüğü
GÜLHANE PARKI YOLU
TAYA HATUN CAD.
Hüseyin Camii
Gülhane Parkı
Hasan Ünsi Hz.Tekkesi
PTT Posta İşletme Dağıtım Merkezi
Gülhane
ALEMDAR CAD.
Topkapı Müzesi Alay Köşkü
Osman Hamdi Bey Yokuşu Sk.
Darphane
Kültür Bakanlığı Anıtlar Müdürlüğü
Aya İrini Müzesi
Üçyüzlü Çeşmesi
Zeynep Sultan Camii
Zeynep Sultan Camii Sk.
Güzel Sanatlar Sk.
Otel Pamphylia
Kubele Hotel
T.C.Başbakanlık Devlet Arşivleri Genel Müdürlüğü
Yerebatan Camii Türbesi
Yerebatan Camii
İl Özel İdare Müdürlüğü
Yücel Kültür Vakfı
Cafer Ağa Türbesi
Ömerağa Çeşmesi
YEREBATAN CAD.
Muhtesem Efendi Çıkmazı
İstanbul İl Özel İdare Müdürlüğü
Mustafa Dede Sk.
Caferiye Sk.
Soğukçeşme Sk.
Turizm Şube Müdürlüğü
Ayasofya Müzesi
Ticarethane Sk.
Sultanahmet Sağlık Merkezi
Eminönü Sağlık Ocağı
Namede Otel
İncili Çavuş Sk.
Türk Edebiyat
Seftali Sk.
Yerebatan Sarnıcı
Şehzadeler
II.Sultan Selim
III.Ahmet Çeşmesi
Cağaloğlu Hamamı
Hamam Sk.
Çatalçeşme Sk.
Sallam Sk.
Hocapaşa Sk.
Hocapaşa Hamamı Sk.
Pirî Reis Sk.
Emirname Sk.

Sarayburnu Parkı
Atatürk Heykeli
DEMİRKAPI ORTA CAD.
GÜLHANE PARKI YOLU
Topkapı Saray İçi
Gotlar Sütunu
9
2
1
Topkapı Sarayı
KENNEDY CAD.
Ptt
CANKURTARAN
Topkapı Saray İçi
Topkapı Saray İçi
Tarihi Güvercinlik
Cankurtaran Futbol Sahası
Ahırkapı Feneri
CAD.

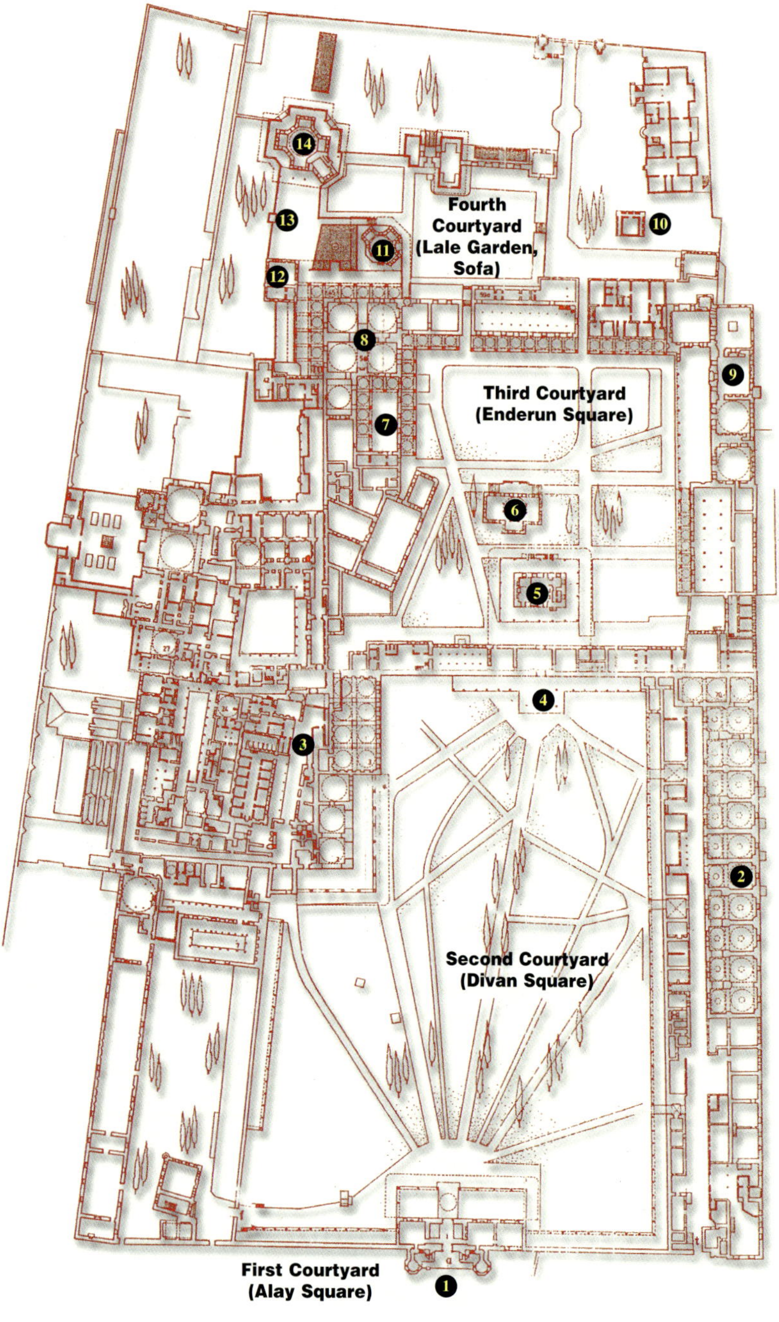

1- *Gate of Salutation (Bab-üs Selam),* **2-** *Kitchen,* **3-** *Harem Chamber,* **4-** *Gate of Felicity (Bab-üs Saade),* **5-** *Audience Chamber,* **6-** *Library of Ahmet III,* **7-** *Imperial Portraits Collection* **8-** *Chamber of the Sacred Relics (Hırka-i Saadet),* **9-** *Inner Treasury,* **10-** *Sofa Mosque,* **11-** *Yerevan Kiosk (Revan Köşkü),* **12-** *Circumcision Room,* **13-** *İftar Pavilion (İftariye Köşkü),* **14-** *Baghdad Kiosk (Bağdat Köşkü).*

Plan of the Topkapı Palace.

TOPKAPI PALACE MUSEUM ❶

(TOPKAPI SARAYI MÜZESİ)
Bab-ı Hümayun Avenue, Sultanahmet
Except Tuesdays 09.00-16.30

On the edge of the Historical Peninsula, it has a location overlooking the view of Bosphorus, Golden Horn and Marmara Sea. The main door of the palace is *Bab-i Humayun* (Imperial Gate) overlooking Fountain of Ahmet III behind Hagia Sophia. It is a wide complex which was both an administrative center of Ottoman Empire and the place where the sultans lived with their family and staff. It is among the most important museums of both Istanbul and the world due to its collections.

Topkapı Palace was built between 1461 and 1468 by Fatih Sultan Mehmet who conquered Istanbul. Since the construction of Bab-i Hümayun Gate that opens to the first courtyard was finished in 1478, it is accepted that the walls of the palace were finished at this date. It is a Classical Turkish Palace with courtyards opening to one another with large doors, lying one after another and improved with many additional parts as well as the surrounding structures.

The palace that continued to be the administration center until 19th century was deserted and became the accommodation for retired staff after Dolmabahçe Palace was built in 1856. The complex reflects what we dream about for sultans' palaces and after the declaration of the Republic, it was turned into a museum upon the orders of Atatürk on 3rd April 1924.

Entrance to the Topkapı Palace Museum *(Bab-üs Selam).*

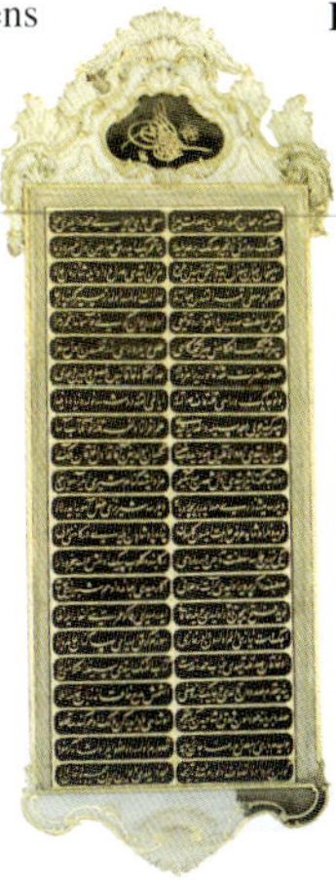

First Courtyard (Alay Square)

Topkapı Palace is entered from Bab-i Hümayun Gate. The upper floor of the door that is organized as a chalet did not reach until today. The first structure that strikes attention on First Courtyard is **Hagia Eirene Church** on the left which was used for a period as a weapon storage place. Behind it, there is the historical Imperial Mint *(Darphane-i Amire)*. Istanbul Archaeological Museums are placed lower at the Western side of the courtyard. The first courtyard was a lively square that included workshops for hospital and palace works where both the attendants and the public used.

At the end of the First Courtyard, one may see the ticket counters of the museum on the right. While purchasing tickets for visiting the palace, additional ticket shall be bought to visit Harem (Seraglio).

➡ **Gate of Felicity *(Bab-üs Saade).***

Topkapı Palace.

Second Courtyard (Divan Square)

The Second Courtyard that can be reached by passing from Bab-us Selam Gate (Gate of Salutation) is a

The *helvahane* in the kitchen of Topkapı Palace.

courtyard covered by arcades on four sides with a size of 110 m x 170 m. The official parts of the palace start from here. At the right side of thc cntrancc, behind windows, sultan cars are exhibited. The three doors that open from the arcades on the right wing of the courtyard open to the kitchen of the palace.

Pink Family Plate, Dynasty of China (1745-1765).

Palace Kitchen and Porcelain Collection: The palace kitchen, rebuilt by Mimar Sinan on 1574 after the fire in 16th century, constitutes the silhouette of the palace on Marmara direction with the domes and chimney systems. The kitchen had two sections, one of which was large and the other small. In the large kitchen, meals were cooked for the palace folk and in the small one, meals were cooked specially for the sultan. There were more than a thousand employees in the kitchen. In these sections that today host porcelain collection of 13th-19th centuries, there are various examples of Chinese and Japanese ceramic art. After leaving the kitchen on the left section, which was the accommodation for the cooks at the time, one may proceed to the room where European silvery is exhibited. On the other room at the end of the corridor named *Helvahane*, Turkish kitchen utensils are exhibited. After the visit is completed, one may again proceed to the Second Courtyard. Here, with its wide fringes and gild, the high *Adalet Kulesi (Tower of Justice)* and Kubbealtı strikes attention.

Tower of Justice.

Kubbealtı (Imperial Council) and Outer Treasury (Weapon Section): *Kubbealtı* was among the important sections of the palace. *Kubbealtı*, the meeting place of Divan-i Hümayun (Imperial Council) which was the highest decision organ of Ottoman State consisted of three sections.

The first section is the meeting area of the highest officials. On the wall behind the grand vizier seat, there is a section with a cage where the sultan could secretly watch the meetings. The section on the sides was *Defterhane* where records and files were kept by the clerks. The outside of this place, each covered with a dome is surrounded by a large fringe "L" shape.

Taxes constituting the income of the state were kept at **Outer Treasury Building** covered with double line domes adjacent to *Kubbealtı*. Today at the building, about 400 weapons are exhibited that dates back to 7th-20th centuries. Mainly Turkish-Ottoman weapons, Armenian-Abbasid swords, Egypt-Mamluk and Iran swords, shield, helmet and axes are among the important works of the collection. Weapons that belong to various Asian and European states are also exhibited here.

At the end of the Second Courtyard, one may pass to the Third Courtyard from

Imperial Council *(Kubbealtı)*.

Interior view of Imperial Council.

Bab-üs Saade Gate (Gate of Felicity) that captures attention with its wide fringes and the elegant columns carrying it. Visitors who would like to see *Harem* can enter from the counters adjacent to *Kubbealtı* and go out to the Third Courtyard from *Kuşhane Gate* when they are done.

HAREM (SERAGLIO) ❷

Starting from behind *Kubbealtı* at Second Courtyard, it extends towards the West wing until *Hırka-i Saadet Office* at the Third Courtyard. It is a complex structure that consists of hundreds of rooms with one or two floors that line around small courtyards. *Harem* was a section where Ottoman dynasty and their servers resided and a place where only the attendants could enter. Inside, it consists of about 400 rooms, 9 hammams, 2 mosques, 1 hospital, 1 laundry, pools and dormitory.

The first section that is entered from Gate of Carts *(Arabalar Kapısı)* belongs to *Kara Ağalar* of African origin who are on guard of the Harem doors. At this section, there are many locations for living and religious exercise. After this section, one may reach *Cümle Kapısı* (main gate of the *Harem*) that connects to the three main sections of the *Harem*. On the location that *Cümle Kapısı* opens to, the one on the left opens to *Cariyeler* courtyard, the middle one opens to Valide courtyard, the one on the right opens to Golden Road *(Altınyol)* and Mabeyn Courtyard (the room of Sultan and his sons).

At *Cariyeler* section, **Concubines** of many different races were seated who provided inner services at the *Harem*. Their numbers changed between 250-1000 according to age and they were generally taken by the palace at ages 10-16, provided with education and taught Turkish, writing-reading, religion rules, literature, music and handcrafts. Most of them were given to laundry, cellar, table works for service. Among the concubines, there are examples who became the wife of sultan such as Hürrem Sultan *(Russian origin)*, Safiye Sultan *(Venetian origin)*, Kösem Sultan *(Roman or Boşnak origin)* and Hatice Turhan Sultan *(Russian origin)*.

At Valide Courtyard, Chambers of the Queen Mother (Valide) is the largest and most important location after sultan's locations. Valide Sultan (Queen

Entrance to Harem.

A concubine in Harem.

Concubines in the bath-house.

A fountain in Imperial Sofa.

Mother), the mother of the sultan, had a respectful position at *Harem*. The most senior staff at *Harem* took her orders. If the sultan died or descended the throne, his mother left her position to the new Valide Sultan and moved to Old Palace. If sultan's mother died, it was upon his will to bring his wet-nurse or a faithful concubine to the condition of Valide Sultan.

Life in Harem.

Mabeyn Section which is reached through *Altınyol* opens on one side which is different from other courtyards. At *Harem*, there are structures that reflect classical Ottoman taste with their architectural features and ornamentation style.

At *Hünkar Sofrası* (the Imperial Hall) which is the largest location of the *Harem;* meetings, greeting ceremonies in *Bayram*, various entertainments and ceremonies were held. Accommodations that constitute the pieces of *Harem* life shall be visited such as *Murat III Has Room, Double Hammam, Chamber of Ahmet I, Chamber of Ahmet III* also known as Dried Fruit Room because of the plates on its walls full of flowers and fruits and *Çifte Kasırlar* (The Twin Kiosk).

Fireplace.

Imperial Sofa.

Courtyards and apartments of Sultan's favorite concubines.

The dining room of Ahmed III with wall painted with bowls of fruit.

Entrance to Audience Chamber (Chamber of Petitions).

Third Courtyard (Enderun Square)

When you pass to the Third Courtyard that has the size about 90x90 meters, *Kuşhane Gate* is seen which is the exit of *Harem*. From here towards the right wing of the courtyard, lines *Akağalar Koğuşu* and *Enderun*. *Enderun* was like a Palace University that trained civilian and military adminis-tratives. Right across the door that opens to Third Courtyard, there is *Arz Odası* (Audience Chamber) where the sultan welcomed foreign ambassadors and senior officials. The roof of the structure opens to four sides with a wide fringe that is carried by marble columns. The tiles on both sides of the door belonged to 16th century and there is a fountain on the right side of the entrance. Behind Audience Chamber, in the middle of the courtyard, there is *Library of Ahmet III* that belongs to 18th century. At this library built form marble, there were 3.500 works in writing which were Turkish, Arabic and Persian. At *Seferli Koğuşu* (Dormitory of the Expeditionary Force) on the right wing of Third Courtyard, many valuable clothes and fabric that were used by Ottoman sultans and their sons are exhib-ited. Adjacent to *Seferli Koğuşu*, one of the most impor-tant structures of the palace is Imperial Treasury which is also known as *Fatih Chalet (Conqueror's Kiosk)*.

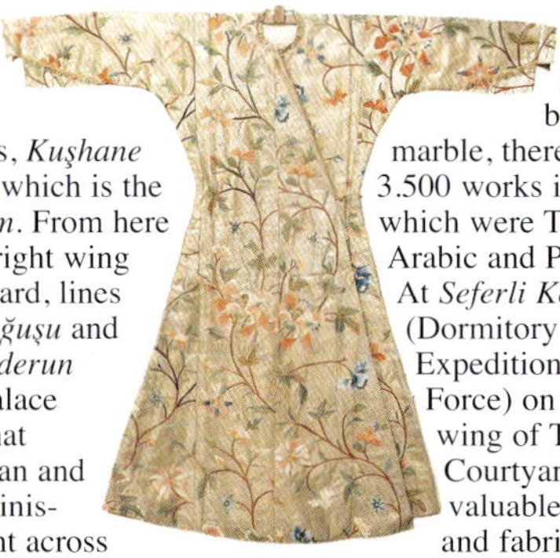

Sultan's Kaftan.

Spoonmaker's *(Kaşıkçı)* Diamond.

Treasury: It consists of three rooms lined on the right of Enderun courtyards and a fourth one that turns towards the left. On the section where the third and fourth rooms con-nect, there is a ter-race where Marmara and Bosphorus can be viewed. Many of the works displayed at Inner Treasure are the works of jewellery masters who worked at the palace.

At the first room; the throne of Murat IV and Ahmet I, throne of Nader Shah made in India in 18th century, ebony and wooden horses, sword of Kanuni, emerald crest, flasks orna-mented with valuable stones, arrow and arc are exhibited.

At the second room; Iran, Ottoman and British badges, and some works of India, Russia and China are exhibit-ed. A door that opens from second room is connected to a third room.

At the third room; Ottoman jade, rock crystal and zinc works, golden chan-deliers, golden oil lamp hanger, helmet and mace ornamented with ruby and turquoise are exhibited. After the third room, one may go out to the balcony over-looking Marmara and Bosphorus. From here, comes the fourth room.

At the fourth room; Very valuable works of Topkapı Palace are exhib-ited. **Kaşıkçı Elması** (Spoonmaker's Diamond) enrichened with 49 diamonds of 86 carat is very famous. Another valuable work of the room is **Topkapı Hançeri** (Topkapı Dagger) with emerald ornamentation. It was sent from Ottoman Sultan Mahmut I (1730-54) to Iran Shah Nader as a present; however, upon hearing on the road that he was dead, it was brought back to the palace. Apart from these, shields ornamented with valu-able stones, emerald box, crest, crystal ink holder and valuable stones and dia-monds are exhib-ited. After seeing these valuable goods of Imperial Treasury, our journey at inner treasury

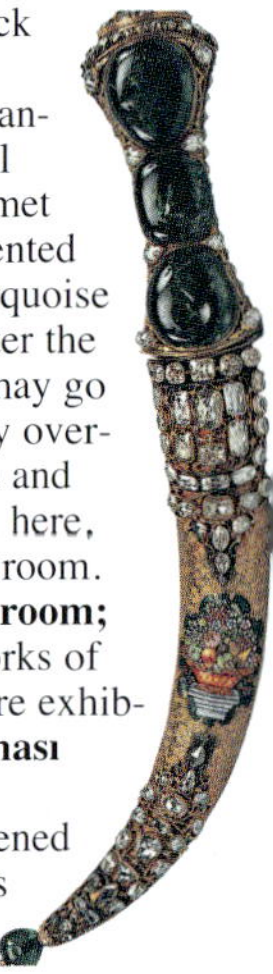

Topkapı Dagger.

Ceremonial canteen.

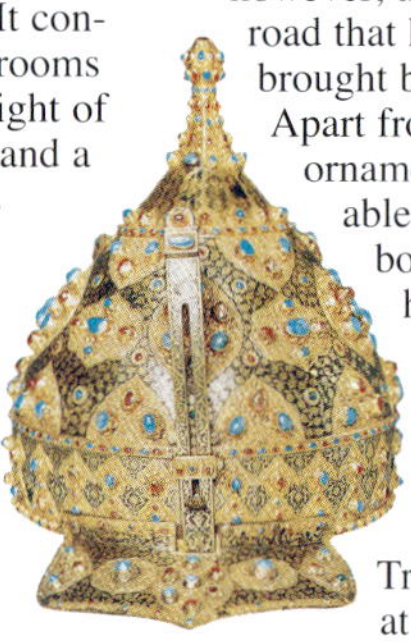

Ceremonial Helmet.

Library of Sultan Ahmed III.

ends and we proceed back to the Third Courtyard.

The marble road that goes west to the left wing of the courtyard from the Library of Ahmet III opens to **Imperial Portraits Collection**. At the end of the room; the portraits of the sultans and Sultan Selim III (1789-1807) during the accession and *Bayram* ceremonies, made by the palace artist Konstantin Kapıdağlı are worth seeing.

At the south of Imperial Portraits Collection, there is *Ağalar Mosque* (Mosque of the Agas) that is used as a library and on its north, there is the *Chamber of Sacred Relics*.

Chamber of Sacred Relics (Hırka-i Saadet): It covers the northwest corner of Third Courtyard. The two sides of the entrance are covered with century tiles. This section is made to keep the relics that Yavuz Sultan Selim brought from his Egypt Expedition on 1517. At the rooms the following are exhibited; key locks and keys brought from Kaaba, swords of the first caliphates after Prophet Mohammed, the cloak of Mohammed, his sword, his flag, his arc as well as his

footprint, his teeth broken during Uhud War, a hair from his beard and his letters inviting many people from Iran, Egypt and Byzantine to Islam.

Fourth Courtyard
(Lale Garden, Sofa)

At the right of the Fourth Courtyard, there is *Sofa Mosque*. Across the mosque, *Mecidiye Köşkü (Grand Pavilion)* that is built in 19th century baroque and empiric style serves today as a restaurant.

At the west of Fourth Courtyard, there is *Tulip Garden* that is ascended by stairs. On the north side of the garden, there is *Hekimbaşı Odası* (Tower of the Head Physician) and *Sofa Kiosk*. At the west of Tulip Garden, on the terrace ascended by stairs, there are viewing mansions of the sultan that display Istanbul's panoramic view.

At the corner of the terrace overlooking the Golden Horn, there is **Baghdad Kiosk** among the most glorious structures of the palace

Accession ceremony of Selim III or *Bayram* Ceremony (Imperial Portraits Collection).

Baghdad Kiosk in the Fourth Courtyard.

Steps to the courtyard.

Magnifican tiles of Yerevan Kiosk.

that Murat IV (1623-40) had built in memory of Baghdad conquest. Four sides of this structure with octagon plan bulges towards outside. It is covered with a dome and the skirts bulge in fringes carried by elegant columns. Inside the dome is filled with gild needlework and window wings, cupboards and wooden work are ornamented with nacre and tortoise shell and the walls are covered with tiles of the period. At the south of the same terrace,

İftar Kiosk

Door to the Circumcision Room.

there is **Yerevan Kiosk** *(Revan Köşkü)*. Murat IV had it built when he returned from his Revan (Erivan) Expedition in 1629. Yerevan Kiosk that has the same plan with Baghdad Kiosk and on the front, it has a marble pool with fountain. Across Yerevan Kiosk, the walls of **Circumcision Room** *(Sünnet Odası)* on the west side are covered with unique examples of Ottoman tile art.

Between Circumcision Room and Baghdad Kiosk, *Iftar Kiosk (Mehtaplık)* bulges like a balcony over the garden below.

Circumcision Room decorated with tiles.

The Church of Hagia Eirene.

HAGIA EIRENE CHURCH ③

(HAGİA EİRENE KİLİSESİ)
It is the 1th Courtyard of Topkapı Palace
It is closed to visitors

Hagia Eirene that is located at the First Courtyard of Topkapı Palace is the only Byzantine Church that retained its atrium (courtyard). Justinian I had the church built at the same time with Hagia Sophia within a large monastery group.

The structure that was damaged in the earthquake of 738 was repaired and attained today's look. Since it was not turned into a mosque in Ottoman period, it came to today without any changes.

The walls of Topkapı Palace separated Hagia Sophia and Hagia Eirene from each other.

The church was used as weapon warehouse from the first years of the conquest until 1846.

In Ottoman period, the main location of the structure is entered from a door with arcades that opened towards the north and covered with a dome.

Over the side naves of the structure with rectangle plan, there are gallery floors. The gilded cross motif at the apse of the church, the original mosaics from Iconoclasm period (726-843) is the only ornament that has remained from the original structure. The church left to the administration of Hagia Sophia Museum Management was repaired and since 1973, started to be used for classical music concerts due to its acoustic characteristics.

Main building of the Archaeology Museum.

ISTANBUL ARCHAEOLOGY MUSEUM ④

(ISTANBUL ARKEOLOJİ MÜZELERİ)
Osman Hamdi Bey Yokuşu
Except Mondays 09:00-16:30

At the entrance of Gülhane Park, the road that goes up from the right takes you to Archaeology Museums. Since this road opens to the First Court of Topkapı Palace, you may also reach the museum from the courtyard. Istanbul Archaeology Museums are in three separate buildings. These are the **Main Building of Archaeology Museum**, **Ancient Eastern Works Museum** and **Enameled Kiosk Museum**.

The first museum was Hagia Eirene Church where works from various parts of the country were collected and which was also used as a weapon warehouse. Many archaeological works and new foundlings from excavations were moved to Enameled Kiosk Museum in 1874 because Hagia Eirene was insufficient. When artist Osman Hamdi Bey was appointed as Museum Manager in 1881, many excavations were carried out in order to enrich the museum. The most important ones among them were excavations made in 1887 at Sayda King Necropolis (Lebanon) which was then an Ottoman land. About 20 sarcophagi found here constitutes an important collection of the museum. Since the current building was small for these sarcophagi, a new museum building was made by Alexandre Vallaury of French origin and opened on 13th June 1891. The front side of the building carries Ionic architectural effects. In later periods, the museum building was

Alexander Sarcophagus.

Sarcophagus of the Mourning Women.

extended with additions. At the entrance floor of the main building, on the south direction *(at the right section of the entrance)*, there are rooms rich in Antique Age, Hellenistic and Roman period statues. At the rooms on the north *(at the left section of the entrance)*, the collections that are rare for their sarcophagus are worth seeing. The most important of these are *Alexander Sarcophagus* (4th century B.C.), *Sarcophagus of the Mourning Women* (4th century B.C.) and *Sarcophagus of Sayda King Tabnit* (about 500 B.C.). As it is not known to whom **Alexander Sarcophagus** belongs to, the name is given due to the depiction at its long side showing Alexander on a horse. On its back, it has a lion fur which is Heracleitos' symbol. It is assumed that **Sarcophagus of the Mourning Women** that takes its name from the engravings with mourning women was made for Sayda King Straton I who died in 360 B.C. Between the columns on its long sides, there are six mourning women figures and on its narrow side there are three mourning women figures. At this room, the Mummy of Sayda King Tabnit is exhibited.

Sidamara Sarcophagus located in Konya (3rd century) exhibited in other rooms enchants its viewers with its giant size and engravings. At the end of the first floor, one may proceed to the room where friezes and architectural pieces of Ancient period temples are exhibited. Among with temple architectural examples, the floor and wall mosaics can be seen that belong to Roman period of 2nd century A.D.

The rooms at the upper floor have a very rich coin collection. At the side wall of the new annex building, the front face of Assos Athena

Sidamara Sarcophagus.

Details of sarcophagus bas-relief.

An example of bas-relief sarcophagus.

Ancient Works Museum.

Bas-reliefs of lions on the Babylon ceremonial path.

enshrine has been adopted with its original size. "Istanbul Surrounding Cultures" section is the first room where magnificent works of different ages that were found in surrounding foundlings and tumulus excavations are exhibited in a modern way. The rooms of Byzantine period works are also here.

In sections "Istanbul for Ages", "Anatolia and Troy for Ages" and "Anatolian and Neighboring Countries Civilizations" the works are exhibited in chronological order.

Facade of Tiled Pavilion.

ANCIENT EASTERN WORKS MUSEUM 5

(ESKİ ESERLER MÜZESİ)
Osman Hamdi Bey Yokuşu
Except Mondays 09:00-16:30

The first building of Archaeological Museums is Ancient Eastern Works Museum. Here sarcophagus and mummy examples of Egypt Civilization, wall plates of various periods and many foundlings are exhibited. The most interesting ones are *Lion Reliefs* (604-562 B.C.) with gloss and bricks of ceremony road at Babel and two copies of *Treaty of Kadesh* which is the first known written agreement in the world. The Treaty of Kadesh was signed in 1269 B.C. between Indian King Hattusili III and Egypt Pharaoh Ramses II. The agreement had three copies written in Akkadian which was the diplomatic language of the period. The two of the three copies found in Bogazkoy-Buyukkale in 1906 are at Ancient Eastern Works Museum.

TILED PAVILION MUSEUM 6

(ÇİNİLİ KÖŞK)
Osman Hamdi Bey Yokuşu
Except Mondays 09:00-16:30

A little further from the Ancient Eastern Works Museum, there is Enameled Kiosk Museum that was completed in 1472 during the time of Fatih Sultan Mehmet. At the Enameled Kiosk Museum which is the first structure that belongs to Topkapı Palace, tile examples of Turkish tile art from 13th-19th centuries are exhibited.

Gravure (*N.H.Bartlett, S. Bradshaw*).

Audience Pavilion.

AUDIENCE PAVILION 7

(ALAY KÖŞKÜ)
Alemdar Avenue

It is located on the left of Gülhane park over the walls. It was built by Mahmut II (1808-39) in 1819 instead of an old building for the sultan to watch the great parades. The mansion with polygon body has one room in addition to servant rooms with various sizes.

The roof is covered by a wide fringed, onion headed lead cone.

Soğukçeşme Street with historical houses.

GÜLHANE PARK 8

Soğukçeşme Street that lies between Topkapı Palace and Hagia Sophia with its historical houses or *Osman Hamdi Bey Yokuşu* that goes down to Archaeology Museums from the first court-yard of the Palace takes you to Gülhane Park. Gülhane Park that has the look of a private grove was the outer garden within the borders of Topkapı Palace.

This place was the location for various entertainment and shows including javelin and wrestling. During the construction of Archaeology Museum, the garden was laid out and opened to public with the museum.

The road that passes from the middle of the park is connected to Sarayburnu. On the right of the road, the cistern from 5th century, found in the arrangements in 1913 has a rectangular plan with a size of 18x12 meters. At the section of the park that is close to Sarayburnu, there is **Goths' Column** which is the oldest Roman work of Istanbul. The column erected on a high base is 15 meters long and it has a Corinth heading on its top.

Remains of Gülhane Park.

Column of the Goths'.

Sepetçiler Qasr ⑪

(Sepetçiler Kasri)
Kennedy Avenue

Located between Eminönü and Sarayburnu, it is the only structure that has come today from the shore mansions that belong to Topkapı Palace. Sultan İbrahim (1640-48) had it built in 1643 and it was renewed to its shape today during the period of Mahmut I. It takes its name from basket weavers who were there during Ottoman times. This was the place where the palace boats stayed, the palace folk watched navy festivals and ceremonies and sultan entered the sea. After its restoration was carried out, it was allocated to International Press Center.

Sepetçiler Qasr (literally: Basket Weavers' Palace) and Topkapı Palace behind.

Cağaloğlu Hammam ⑫ (Turkish Bath)

(Cağaloğlu Hamami)
Prof. İsmail Kazım Gürkan Avenue No: 34 Cağaloğlu
Open everyday

Hammam gravure.

It is on Ismail Kazım Gürkan Street, the extension of Yerebatan Street on Cağaloğlu that is connected to Sultanahmet. Mahmut I had it built in order to provide income to Hagia Sophia between 1741 and 1742. There is no certain information on its architect. It is a double hammam that consists of women and men sections. Innovations were tried in its inner design and baroque elements were used.

The hammam serves men between 08.00-22.00 and women between 08.00-20.00.

Düyun-u Umumiye Building

(Düyun-u Umumiye Binasi)
Türk Ocağı Avenue, Cağaloğlu

Since Ottoman State was in a condition that it could not pay its outside debts in 19th century, an institution named *Düyun-u Umumiye* was founded. Some income of Turkish Treasury was to be collected by this institution and paid to the creditors. The architect of this neo-classical building made for this institution in 1897 was Alexandre Vallaury. Today it is **Istanbul High School**.

Istanbul High School, (Düyun-u Umumiye Building).

If you finished your tour in Sultanahmet, don't neglect *Sokullu Mehmet Pasha Mosque* which is a building of Architect Sinan, in Kadırga, the lower district of Hippodrome and *Small Hagia Sophia Mosque* which is an old Byzantine Church *(page 82, See page 22-23 for map)*. These two buildings are just 5 minutes away from the Hippodrome by walk. After these you can visit *Mausoleum of Mahmut II, Çemberlitaş and Grand Bazaar* on Divanyolu (council road).

You can visit *Mausoleum of Mahmut II* which is on the right by following the tram way *(Divanyolu Avenue)* from Sultanahmet direction. Also the same road takes you to Çemberlitaş. Vezirhanı Avenue near Çembelitaş reaches the atrium gates of *Nuruosmaniye Mosque*. You can reach Nuruosmaniye gate of *Grand Bazaar* by passing this atrium.

THE COLUMN OF CONSTANTINE (ÇEMBERLİTAŞ) 1

Yeniçeriler Avenue, Çemberlitaş

This square and its sur roundings that were founded by Constantine the Great who constructed and extended Istanbul as the capital of Rome was the graveyard area of the period of Septimus Severus (193-211 A.D.). It was connected to Hippodrome and Augusteion Square (Hagia Sophia Square) as it was in Divanyolu Street with the street named Mese where shops were lined. The surrounding of the oval shaped

square, the borders of which can not be determined, was ornamented with many statues. In the middle of the square, there is the monument erected for Constantine the Great that still remains today. The pieces of porphyry stone that constitutes the body of the monument were brought from Rome and mounted to its place in 328. The gilded statue of Constantine the Great rising on its top that reminds of Sun God Helios held a globe on its left hand and a spear on its right hand. The statue that was damaged in the earthquakes fell down in the strong storm in 1106. It was restored in the period of Manuel Komnenos I (1143-1180) and a marble heading and a bronze cross was placed over it. The body was supported with iron ring to protect from fires and natural diseases. The height of the monument that used to be 37 meters is now 35 meters.

The Column of Constantine (Çemberlitaş).

TOMB OF MAHMUT II 2

(II. MAHMUT TÜRBESİ)
Divanyolu Avenue No: 82
Çemberlitaş

Mahmut II is the sultan who made important innovations in modernization of Ottoman State from the military, educational, administrative and social perspectives. After his reign of 30 years (1808-39) he died as a result of his illness on 1st, July 1839. The opening of the tomb that started after his death was made on 11th November 1840. The octagon planned tomb is covered with rich floral reliefs with a diameter of 17 meters and it constitutes a direct bulge towards Divanyolu Street. Towards Sultanahmet side, there is the water fountain built with the tomb.

In the tomb, there are sarcophagi of *Mahmut II* (1808-1839), *Abdülaziz* (1861-1876) and *Abdülhamit II* (1876-1909). The courtyard next to the tomb was turned into graveyard after 1861 and it mostly consists of graves of important officials, authors and poets.

There are graves of famous people in the courtyard of the tomb.

Interior view of the Tomb of Mahmut II.

ÇEMBERLİTAŞ HAMMAM 3 (TURKİSH BATH)

(ÇEMBERLİTAŞ HAMAMI)
Vezirhanı Avenue No: 8
Çemberlitaş
It serves between 06.00 and 24.00

It is right across Çemberlitaş. Nurbanu Sultan, wife of Selim II had it built by Mimar Sinan in 1584 and it is a double hammam with women and men sections.

NURUOSMANİYE MOSQUE 4

(NURUOSMANİYE CAMİİ)
Vezirhanı Avenue, Nuruosmaniye

The mosque that started to be built during the time of Mahmut I (1730-1754) was completed in 1755 during the time of Osman III (1754-57) and is a unique baroque work. Its two doors of the outside courtyard open to Nuruosmaniye and Grand Bazaar. Its architect is either

Interior of Nuruosmaniye Mosque.

Simeon Kalfa of Greek origin or Mustafa Ağa. The mosque is constructed on a high platform. The place of worship is covered with a single dome carried by four large arches with a diameter of nearly 26 meters. These arches are emphasized with layered molding from the outside and form the basis of its outside appearance. In the mosque that is illuminated with many windows, the medallions on the lowest line of windows are ornamented with the writings of the famous calligraphists of the age. The half dome of the *mihrab* is ornamented with rich motifs and it forms a pentagon planned bulge from the outside. Apart from the wall of the *mihrab*, roomy galleries surround the structure in three directions. One can reach the *hünkar mahfili* (the location where the sultans had their salah) of the mosque from an elevated platform rising in "L" shape from the direction of Nord-East. Some innovations were tried in the structure and its inner courtside without a fountain is organized in a circular way different from cornered courtyard application seen in other mosques.

The minarets at the two edges of the last congregation area end with stone cones instead of lead cones.

Nuruosmaniye Mosque.

GRAND BAZAAR 5

(KAPALIÇARŞI)

(For a plan, see page 64-65).

It is founded on a wide area between Nuruosmaniye and Beyazıt mosque. The seed of the bazaar stretches towards *Cevahir (inner) Bedesten* (vaulted part of a bazaar where valuable goods are kept) made during the period of Fatih Sultan Mehmet (1444-45/1451-81) and *Sandal Bedesten* made shortly afterwards. Bazaars developed around the bedesten were covered with vaults and formed the great bazaar within time.

Nuruosmaniye Gate to the Grand Bazaar.

Kalpakçılar Avenue lined with jewellery shops in Grand Bazaar.

Alaaddin's lamb.

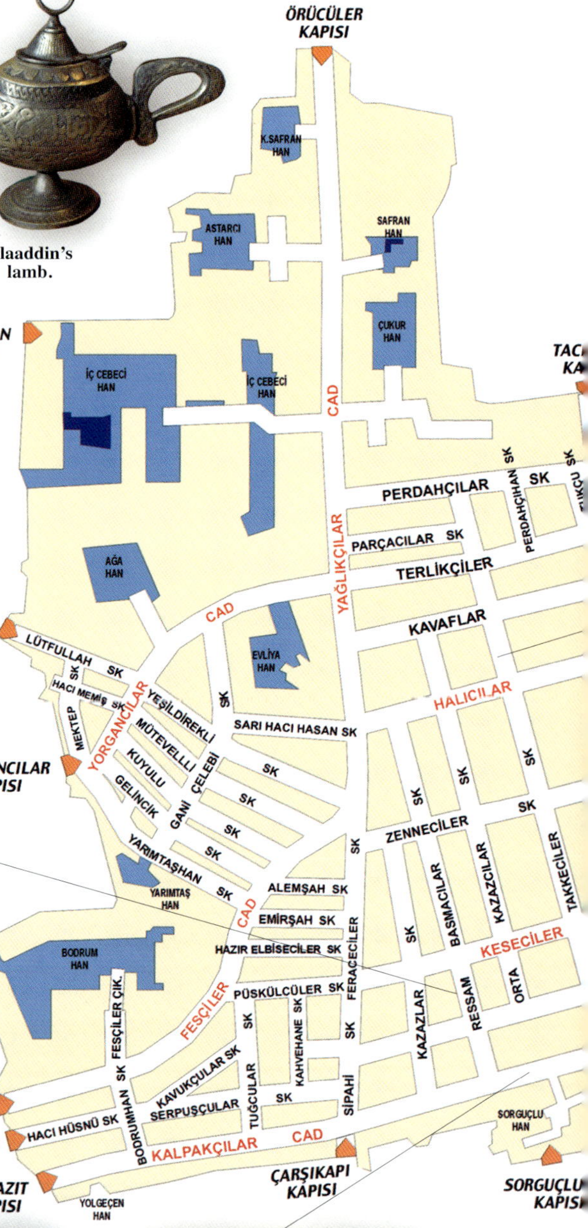

Ceramic Ewer.

Window of a souvenier shop in Grand Bazaar.

Kalpakçılar Avenue.

Ground plan of the Grand Bazar.

Ottoman Emblem.

Cevahir Bedesten.

Window of a souvenier shop in Grand Bazaar.

Cevahir Bedesten, accepted as the first structure of the bazaar, has a rectangular plan with the size of 53x68 meters. Eight large feet lined in two rows are connected to each other as well as the walls with arches, and separates the inner location to 16 units with square shapes. Each of them is covered with a dome sitting on arches.

Sandal Bedesten has the size of 35x42 meters and has the same building technique with Cevahir Bedesten. The bedesten is divided into 20 units and each one is covered

Grand Bazaar gravure.

with a dome. 61 roads of the bazaar have a complicated order resembling a labyrinth. The reasons for this are the fires and earthquakes that the bazaar was exposed to. Many repairs and annexes brought forth the complicated tissue of Grand Bazaar. A section of **Kalpakçılar Street** forming the main street opens to Nuruosmaniye and another opens to Beyazıt. Nuruosmaniye Door is ornamented with Ottoman signature and Beyazıt Door is

Grand Bazaar (Kapalıçarşı).

ornamented with the signature of Abdülhamit II (1876-1909). Under the signature, there is a writing that says "*God likes those who are merchants*".

Today, inside the bazaar, there are jewelry shops that produce and sell famous handcrafts objects and souvenirs and some shops that belong to each profession.

You reach Çadırcılar Avenue where textile products are being sold if you exit form Beyazıt and Fesçiler Gate of **Grand Bazaar**. We recommend visiting **Sahaflar** (second-hand booksellers) and **Beyazıt Mosque** if you have time. If you have limited time and want to visit **Süleymaniye Mosque**, by following the bazaar you reach Fuat Paşa Avenue which runs along the walls Istanbul University. If you follow the University walls you can easily find Süleymaniye (*See page 68-69 for map*).

SAHAFLAR BAZAAR 6

Beyazıt Square

Across the Fesciler Door of Grand Bazaar, you may see the entrance of bouquinistes *(shops that buy and sell old and new books and certificates)*. Sahaflar that used to be active at Inner Bedesten of Grand Bazaar changed places for many times as a result of earthquakes and fires and was eventually founded at Sahaflar Bazaar at this area parallel to Beyazıt Mosque. From the other door of Sahaflar, you can exit to Beyazıt Square.

Sahaflar Bazaar (The market of second hand book shop).

BEYAZIT (BAYEZID) SQUARE

Beyazit Square was named **Forum Tauri** or **Theodosius Forum** during Byzantine times. Theodosius I (379-395) made the opening of the square in 393. There used to be basilicas, churches, hammam and various buildings lined up around and among other statues, the statue of Theodosius on a horse also ornamented the square. Metal statues were ripped off from their places during the period of Latin invasion.

The first palace of Ottomans who conquered the city in 1453 was made at the area of the university in 1454 and then moved to Topkapı Palace. Beyazıt Complex *(külliye)* made during the period of Bayezid II (1481-1512) was also built by the palace.

The front side of Simkeshane Building on the side of Ordu Street was collapsed due to construction of the road and some remains were brought to light. Among these remains was a giant arch triumphal and constituted the monumental entrance at this section of the square.

Prayer time in Süleymaniye Mosque.

Some of the remains were placed at Archaeology Museum and other parts can be seen at their place.

During Ottoman times, various entertainment and shows were carried out at Beyazıt Square which was a center due to its close location to Grand Bazaar. In today's Istanbul, the fact that Grand Bazaar is lively and has many visitors as well as Istanbul University that has the most crowded number of students enables it to continue its liveliness.

Main entrance gate of the main building of Istanbul University.

Remains of the triumphal arch.

Bozdoğan Su Kemeri
KALENDERHANE
Saraçhane Parkı
ATATÜRK BULVARI
HAŞIM İŞCAN GEÇİDİ
ŞEHZADEBAŞI CAD.
İstanbul Büyükşehir Belediye Başkanlığı
Şehzadebaşı Camii
Burmalı Mescid Camii
Burmalı Mescid Sk.
Su Kemeri Sk.
İslam Sk.
CEMAL YENER TOSYALI CAD.
Revani Çelebi Sk.
İBB Reşat Nuri Sahnesi
Atatürk İ.Ö.O
Cibali Lisesi
Abdi İpekçi İlaç Sarayi
Himmet Sk.
Akif Paşa Sk.
VEFA CAD.
MOLLA HÜSRE
Mimar Mehmetağa Camii
KATİP ÇELEBİ CAD.
Ekmekçizade Ahmet Paşa Türbesi
Molla Hüsrev Camii
Vefa Anadolu Lisesi
Şehzade Camii Sk.
Çocuk Esirg Kurumu
DEDE EFENDİ CAD.
Destari Mustafa Paşa Türbesi
Şehzade Mehmet Türbesi
Fatma Sultan Türbesi
İ.Ü. Siyasal Bilgiler Fakültesi Vakfı
Damat İbrahim Paşa Camii
Delikanlı Sk.
İBB Şehzadebaşı Tıp Merkezi
İBB Gençlik Ve Spor Müd.
Onsekiz Sekbanlar Camii
Onsekiz Sekbanlar Mezarlığı
İBB Kontrol Daire Başkanlığı
Türk Dünyası Araştırmaları Vakfı
Burhan Dede Sk.
Bukali Dede Sk.
İBB Kontrol Daire Başkanlığı-Başkanlık Savunma Sekreterliği
Haşkadem Camii
Numune Çocuk Parkı
Ahmet Selahattin Sk.
History Hotel
Üryanizade Baba Türbesi
Saffet Paşa Sk.
GENÇTÜRK CAD.
Onsekiz Sekbanlar Sk.
Ömer Yılmaz Sk.
Şirvanizade Sk.
Kemal Paşa Camii
Yeşil Tulumba Sk.
Laleli Baba Türbesi
Mektep Sk.
Selim Paşa Sk.
İBB Projeler Daire Başkanlığı
MEHMET AĞA YOKUŞU CA
Defter Emini Sk.
KEMALPAŞA
Çukur Çeşme Sk.
Gümrük Emini Sk.
Mahvil Sk.
Reyhani Sk.
Mimarbaşı Sk.
Laleli Cami
Aynül Hayat Türbesi
III. Sultan Selim Türbesi
Laleli
Aksaray
ORDU CAD.
Cihan Saray Merkezi Mes
Ceylan Sk.
AKSARAY CAD.
Şair Efendi Sk.
Sait Efendi Sk.
MUSTAFA KEMAL CAD.
İhtisap Ağası Sk.
MESİHPAŞA
Bodrum Mesihpaşa Camii
MESİHPAŞA CAD.
BÜYÜK REŞİT PAŞA CAD.
KOCA RAGIP PAŞA CAD.
Bayezid Mosque 1 (Bayezid Camii)
Beyazıt Fire-Watch Tower 2 (Beyazıt Yangın Kulesi)
Laleli Mosque 3 (Laleli Camii)
Bodrum Mosque 4 (Bodrum Camii)
Valide Sultan Mosque 5 (Valide Sultan Camii)
Kalenderhane Mosque 6 (Kalenderhane Camii)
Şehzade Mosque 7 (Şehzade Camii)
Valens Aqueduct 8 (Su Kemeri)
Süleymaniye Mosque 9 (Süleymaniye Camii)
Tomb of Sultan Süleyman 10 (Kanuni Sultan Süleyman Türbesi)
Tomb of Hürrem Sultan 11 (Hürrem Sultan Türbesi)
Polis Police
Hastane Hospital
Cami Mosque
Kilise Church
Otel Hotel
PTT PTT
Sağlık Ocağı Health Clinic
Saray-Kasır Palace-Summer Palace
Surlar City Walls
Tarihi Anıt Historical Monument
Türbe Tomb
Tramvay Durağı Tramway Stop
Tramvay Hattı Tramway Line
Tren Yolu Train Line
CAD. Avenue
Sk. Street
Taksim
Eminönü
Üsküdar

SÜLEYMANİYE
Süleymaniye Camii ve Külliyesi
9
MİMAR SİNAN CAD.
Darül Kubra Türbedat Sokullu Mehmet Paşa Türbesi
Kanuni Sultan Süleyman Türbesi
10
11
Dökmeciler Sk.
Dökmeciler Hamamı Sk.
Samdancı Sk.
Süleymaniye Kadın Doğum Ve Çocuk Hastalıkları Hastanesi
Süleymaniye Kütüphanesi
PROF. SIDDIK SAMİ ONAR CAD.
Kanuni Medresesi Sk.
Molla Şemsettin Camii Sk.
Molla Şemsettin Gürani Camii
Divan Efendi Sk.
Yoğurtçuoğlu Sk.
Şifahane Sk.
Mimar Sinan Sk.
İ.Ü. Yabancı Diller Bölümü
Cenderecizade Muhittin Çelebi Türbesi
Avni Paşa Sk.
Ayla Kadın Hamamı Sk.
Elmaruf Sk.
İ.Ü. Yapı İşleri Teknik Daire Başkanlığı
Kültür Bakanlığı Tabiat Varlıklarını Koruma Müdürlüğü
Kayserili Ahmet Paşa Sk.
Emin Hoca Sk.
Kirazlı Mescit Sk.
Kirazlı Mescid Camii
İ.Ü. Spor Salonu
İ.Ü. Spor Daire Başkanlığı
SÜLEYMANİYE CAD.
İstanbul Esnaf Hastanesi
Kalender Mektebi Sk.
İ.Ü. Siyasal Bilimler Fakültesi
İ.Ü. Hukuk Fakültesi
İ.Ü. İktisat Fakültesi
İ.Ü Rektörlüğü
Medrese Çıkmazı Sk.
Çüce Çeşmesi Sk.
6
Kalenderhane Camii
ONALTI MART ŞEHİTLERİ CAD.
Helva Baba Türbesi
İ.Ü. Sosyal Bilimler Meslek Yüksek Okulu
Baharlı Sk.
Kaptan-ı Derya Sk.
Kaptan-ı Derya İbrahim Paşa Camii
BESİM ÖMERPAŞA CAD.
FUAT PAŞA CAD.
İ.Ü. Basın Yayın Meslek Yüksek Okulu
Prof. Ümit Yaşar Doğanay Sk.
İ.Ü. Fen Bilimleri
Hallaçi Mansur Sk.
İ.Ü. Öğrenci Kültür Merkezi
İ.Ü. Biyoloji Bölümü
BOZDOĞAN KEMERİ CAD.
İşitme Engelliler İ.Ö.O
Beyazıt İ.Ö.O
İ.Ü. H.Yüksel Eğitim Fakültesi
İstanbul Üniversitesi
İ.Ü. Fen Fakültesi Astronomi Bölümü
Üniversite Polis Karakolu
Prof. Cavit Orhan Sk.
İ.Ü. Sosyal Bilimler M.Y.O
Vezneciler Külhanı Sk.
VEZNECİLER CAD.
MSB Yurt Yolu
2
Ptt
İ.Ü. Eczacılık Fakültesi
İ.Ü. Atatürk İlkeleri ve İnkılap Tarihi Enstitüsü
BAKIRCILAR CAD.
Beyazıt Devlet Kütüphanesi
ÇADIRCILAR CAD.
DARÜLFUNUN CAD.
İ.Ü. Fen- Edebiyat Fakültesi
Boğaziçi Elektrik Beyazıt İşletme Müdürlüğü
Beyazıt Polis Karakolu
Türk Hat Sanatları Müzesi
1
Beyazıt Camii
Beyazıd II.Sultan Türbesi
Selçuk Sultan Türbesi
Reşitpaşa Türbesi
Kimyager Derviş Paşa Sk.
Beyazıt Külhanı Sk.
Yeni Kapan Sk.
İstanbul Üniversitesi Kütüphanesi
Üniversite
Laleli Zabıta Karakolu
Orhan Kemal İl Kütüphanesi
ORDU CAD.
Haznedar Sk.
Fırın Sk.
Kalaycı Şevki Sk.
Darphane Sk.
Sekbanbaşı Yakupağa Camii
İstanbul Çarşısı Mescidi
Sekbanbaşı Sk.
Gedik Paşa İ.Ö.O
Börekçi Ali Sk.
Ağa Çeşmesi Sk.
Mücellit Çıkmazı
Büyük Haydar Efendi Sk.
Bostan Sk.
Büyük Tulumba Çıkmazı
Dibekli Sk.
Dibekli Eminbey Camii
Tiyatro Aralığı Sk.
İstanbul Trafik Vakfı Eğitim Merkezi
Sahaflar Ç.

Beyazıt Mosque.

BEYAZIT MOSQUE 1

(BEYAZIT CAMİİ)
Beyazıt Square

It is at Beyazıt Square next to Sahaflar Bazaar. It was built by Bayezid II (1481-1512) between 1501 and 1506 with scattered kulliye buildings around it. It is important because it represents an early age classical Ottoman architecture. It is accepted that its architect is Hayreddin; however also the name Yakup Shah is considered. In the entrance, it has an inner courtyard with arcade and a marble floor with an elegant fountain in the middle. The green porphyry columns carrying the dome of the fountain, red porphyry stones scattered among the marble in the courtyard and the column bodies of different color and type in the arcades are collected pieces of Byzantine period. The main location of the mosque has a square plan and arches settled on four feet carry the dome. The main dome is supported by two half domes on the axis of Kıblah. It extends on north-south direction with naves covered with independent domes. The inner location has beautiful examples of stone craftsmanship and wooden craftsmanship besides rich pen crafts.

On the *mihrab* side of the mosque, there are tombs of *Sultan Bayezid II, his daughter Selçuk Hatun* and *Grand Vizier Reşid Pasa* (19th century). People of the palace, important officials and their families were buried to the graveyard here from 18th century until the beginning of 20th century. This section also has an entrance from Sahaflar Bazaar.

Entrance gate to Istanbul University and Beyazıt Fire-Watch Tower.

View of Beyazıt Mosque from the inner courtyard.

Interior view of the Beyazıt Mosque.

Beyazıt Fire-Watch Tower.

Another structure of complex, *sıbyan mektebi* (primary school in the neighborhood) made in 1507 is important because it is the oldest school structure of the city.

The school located further from the tombs has been turned into a library. The buildings on the right wing across the exit of Beyazıt Door of Sahaflar belonged to the alms house and caravanserai of the complex. A section of alms house structure serves as Beyazıt Government Library today. This was the first general library founded by the state in Turkey and opened on 24th June, 1884 with the contributions of Abdülhamit II. On the west of Beyazıt Mosque, there is madrasah building that was built with the complex and that strikes attention with its domes. Today, it serves as **Calligraphy Art Museum**.

BEYAZIT FIRE-WATCH TOWER 2

(BEYAZIT YANGIN KULESİ)

It rises on the garden of Istanbul University. On the place of the previous tower of wooden material that burnt down, Sultan Mahmut II had it made in 1828 by Senekerim Balyan as a stone tower. On its cylinder body, there is an observation floor with a circular plan.

The roof of the 85 meters high tower was in the shape of a cone when it was first built. It was changed in 1849 and turned into octagon plan with an addition of three floors with windows.

After touring the square, structures are separated into two directions. **Laleli**, **Bodrum** and **Valide Sultan Mosques** are on Ordu Avenue direction. On the other hand **Kalenderhane** and **Şehzade Mosque** are at Vezneciler side on *Şehzadebaşı Avenue* direction. If you want to visit all the structures, first visit Kalenderhane and Şehzadebaşı and then after seeing **Bozdoğan Aqueduct** on Atatürk Boulevard you can reach *Aksaray Square* by following the boulevard. This square has connection with the *Ordu Avenue*. However don't forget that some mosques may not be open until noon prayer (*See page 68-69 for map*).

Laleli Mosque.

LALELİ MOSQUE 3

(LALELİ CAMİİ)

Ordu Avenue, Laleli

The architect of the mosque built between 1760 and 1763 during the period of Mustafa III is Mehmet Tahir Ağa. In its middle, it has an inner court with a fountain. The section of the structure constructed on basement and overlooking Ordu Street is used as shops. Its dome covering the square main location supported by trompe l'oeil with a diameter of 12,5 meters is settled on eight marble columns.

The two columns in the entrance are independent and other columns are buried in the walls of the body. On the south of the mosque, on Ordu Street, there are tombs of *Mustafa III* (1757-74) and *Selim III* (1789-1807).

BODRUM MOSQUE 4

(BODRUM CAMİİ)

Mesihpaşa Avenue, Laleli

The church of Myrelaion Monastery built during Byzantine times is used today as a mosque. Due to the cellar underneath, it is known as Bodrum (basement) Mosque. In 10th century, Romanos Lekapenos I (920-944) turned his own palace into a monastery and this place was built as a monastery church. From the monastery, no other structure apart from the church has remained until today. The church that was left to itself after the conquest was turned into a mosque by Grand Vizier Mesih Ali Pasha during the period of Bayezid II (1481-1512).

It has the typical Byzantine architectural features with a closed cross plan and bricks on the outside. The middle

Bodrum Mosque.

Valide Sultan Mosque.

section of the structure has high tambours and the domes with windows as well as the arms of the cross are covered with vaults.

The inner surface has a plain look apart from the simple motifs on arches of Turkish period.

PERTEVNİYAL VALİDE SULTAN MOSQUE ⑤

(PERTEVNİYAL VALİDE SULTAN CAMİİ)
Aksaray Square

It was built by Pertevniyal Valide Sultan, the mother of Abdülaziz and the wife of Mahmut II between 1869 and 1871. In the courtyard of the mosque constructed by Sarkis Balyan, there is Valide Sultan Tomb. There are also sources that claim the architect to be Montani. On the north of the structure, there is Hünkar Kiosk with two minarets on its two sides. After the entrance section of the mosque comes the main location with a size of 10x10 meters and a square plan. The main location covered with a single dome is ornamented from its dome to its ground with pen crafts of blue tones. The feet rising on its four corners are connected to each other with wide arches and open to the outside in the shape of a niche.

In the outside front, the traditional atmosphere is deserted and the sharp arched windows emphasized outside such as inside are finished with head piece and the three fronts looking over to the street with selective engravings and thus reliefs achieved their monumental look.

Interior view of Valide Sultan Mosque.

FENARİ İSA MOSQUE (Constantine Lips Monastery)

(FENARİ İSA CAMİİ)
Vatan Avenue, Aksaray

At the point where Vatan Street and Halıcılar Street intersect, it is ten minutes walking distance away from Aksaray Square. The structure that served as a church during Byzantine times was turned into a mosque in Ottoman period and with the fire that took place in 1918, it waited for long years in ruined condition. After the restoration that was carried out in 1960, it was opened to service as a mosque. It consists of two adjacent churches built in different times and two graveyard chapels. The first church at the north built by Navy Commander Constantine Lips was opened in June 907 with

Fenari İsa Mosque with its magnificent view.

a glorious ceremony and the participation of Leon VI. Theodora, the wife of Michael Palaiologos VIII (1261-1282) had the second church built adjacent to the south wall of the current church. The pareccleşion (a chapel leaning to the side of the church) additional chapel in "L" shape covering the West and South of the church was built in 14th century and the complex became even larger. Over the two churches rise domes with high tambours. The inner location without paint does not have any ornamental features within.

HASEKİ SULTAN MOSQUE

(HASEKİ SULTAN CAMİİ)
Haseki Avenue No: 35, Haseki

Hürrem Sultan, wife of Kanuni Sultan Süleyman had it built by Mimar Sinan between 1538

Kalenderhane Mosque.

and 1539. It is the first mosque that Sinan built after he was appointed as Hassa Mimarbaşı (architect working for the palace).

The main location ornamented with pen crafts rich in blue and red colors has a rectangular plan covered by two domes with a diameter of 11 meters. The structure that used to have one dome when it was first built was extended in 1612 renewal with the addition of a square location on its East side and has reached today's form. The last congregation place was covered with glass panes and became a closed location.

KALENDERHANE MOSQUE 6

(KALENDERHANE CAMİİ)
On Altı Mart Şehitleri Avenue, Medrese Street No: 8 Vezneciler

It is a Byzantine Church next to Bozdoğan (Valens) aqueduct that was turned into a mosque. Here, the first church that dates back to 8th century achieved its final shape in 12th century. In 18th century, it was turned into a mosque by Darüssaade Ağası Beşir Ağa.

Şehzade Mosque gravure.

At the west of Kalenderhane, it has two narthexes one of which is outside and the other inside. The main location of the structure with a closed cross plan is covered with a dome with a high tambourine and the arms of the cross are covered with vaults. Its main apse with a plain wall did not reach today and only the marble plates have come today from the inner wall ornamentations of Byzantine period.

Its dome is ornamented with pen crafts, typically of Ottoman period and the vaults and pendantives are in plain brick without paint. New windows were opened in Ottoman period and the mosque achieved an even brighter atmosphere.

ŞEHZADE MOSQUE 7

(ŞEHZADE CAMİİ)
Şehzadebaşı Avenue No: 70 Vezneciler

It is on Şehzadebaşı Street connected to Vezneciler. After the sudden death of Shehzade Mehmet in 1543 whom Kanuni Sultan Süleyman wished to be his successor, his tomb was first made at the *mihrab* side and then the mosque was built by Mimar Sinan between 1543 and 1548. Other complex buildings are at the side of the mosque's *mihrab*.

Haseki Sultan Mosque.

Interior view of Şehzade Mosque.

Şehzade Mosque, accepted as apprenticeship work of Sinan is covered with a central dome with a width of 19 meters and four supporting semidomes. This plan was also used at Sultanahmet Mosque and New Mosque. The feet carrying the central dome from four sides are like weight towers surrounding the dome from four sides outside.

Because they did not have side galleries, there is wide integrity in the main location. The structure is ornamented by pen crafts, colored glass and muquarnas filling at the passages from the corners.

Minarets with two serefes (balcony of a minaret) rising at both edges of the Last Congregation Place exhibit beautiful examples of stone crafts with its reliefs.

BOZDOĞAN (VALENS) AQUEDUCT 8

(BOZDOĞAN SU KEMERİ)
Saraçhane

At the period of Eastern Roman Emperor Valens (364-378), it was built between 368 and 373. It was built on the lower section of the water road that is brought to the city from channels outside the city wall. With the collapsed sections on the side of Fatih and Şehzadebaşı, it had a length of 971 meters. Atatürk Street connecting to Aksaray passes below the aqueduct. Since the valley deepens at this section, it rises as vaults of two lines and reaches 28 meters. Aqueduct that continued to function during Ottoman period after a repair is a historical heritage that met the water needs of the city during Late Roman, Byzantine and Ottoman periods. You may walk from here to Unkapanı and see Zeyrek Mosque, formerly Pantocrator Church at the left hill.

You can also visit ***Zeyrek Mosque*** which was an old church by walking from Atatürk Boulevard where there is an aqueduct to Unkapanı *(page 98)*.

View of Valens Aqueduct from Saraçhane Bridge.

Süleymaniye Mosque.

SÜLEYMANİYE MOSQUE 9

(SÜLEYMANİYE CAMİİ)
Süleymaniye

Following the North and East wall of Istanbul University (Fuat Pasa Street), you may reach Süleymaniye

Medicine Madrasahs, Sıbyan Mektebi, Tabhane, İmaret and Darüşşifa. All these structures show that Süleymaniye Complex was not only a place of worship but also a group of structures that also served for social and educational purposes. Süleymaniye Mosque is the center of

Views of Rüstem Pasha and Süleymaniye Mosques.

which is the largest complex of Ottoman period. Complex buildings are lined around the mosque. These are; *Rabi and Salis Madrasahs, hammam, Darülhadis Madrasah, tombs* on the direction of the *mihrab, Evvel, Sani and*

Complex that was built by Mimar Sinan upon the orders of Kanuni Sultan Süleyman (1520-66). The mosque built between 1550 and 1557 is one of the important works of Classical Ottoman Architecture. On the third hill

Süleymaniye Mosque gravure.

of Istanbul, it constitutes a piece of the ever-changing silhouette of the Golden Horn. The opening of the mosque was made by Mimar Sinan upon the order of the sultan. Thousands of workers worked in its construction and some stone and marble used in the construction were brought from various ancient cities and some Ottoman period structures. Its inner courtyard with a fountain in the middle is floored with white marble and minarets rise at its four corners. The minarets on its west side have two serefes

Interior view of Süleymaniye Mosque with its magnificent architecture.

New Mosque in front, and Süleymaniye Mosque gravure in the background.

Tomb of Sultan Süleyman the Magnificent with outer vaulted arcade.

and a height of 56 meters and the minarets at both edges of the last congregation place are 76 meters with three serefes.

The place of worship has a rectangular plan with a size of 61x70 meters. The weight of the structure is carried by giant plates named as "elephant feet" that are placed at four corners of the dome. Sharp vaults connecting the plates to each other bulge outside at north and south direction and constitute the famous Golden Horn silhouette of Süleyman. The weight towers rising over the plates have set an example for later mosques. The dome covering the place of worship with a height of 53 meters and a diameter of 26,50 meters are supported by semidomes on its axis. At North and South direction, it extends with naves covered with independent domes. With this plan, it resembles Beyazıt Mosque.

The ornamentations of Süleymaniye Mosque renewed in 19th century displays a simpler look compared to other mosques. The alternate order of the vaults in

A view from the Tomb of Sultan Süleyman the Magnificent.

red and white and muquarnas used in the corner connection points reflects the architectural ornamentation features. The stained glass ornamenting the walls of the *mihrab* is the original work of an artist named Sarhoş (Drunk) İsmail. The tiles ornamenting the walls do not take up much space. At both sides of the *mihrab*, tile medallions ornamented with calligraphy on both sides were used and on the *mihrab*, tiles with herbal motifs were used.

At the graveyard on the side of the *mihrab* at Süleymaniye Mosque, there are some tombs that belong to Kanuni Sultan Süleyman who had the complex built and his wife Hürrem Sultan as well as some leading people.

The tomb of Koca Sinan, the architect of the palace is the beautiful structure at the northwest corner of the mosque with a modest proportion on Mimar Sinan Avenue.

Kanuni Sultan Süleyman (1495-1566)

The son of Yavuz Sultan Selim, Kanuni Sultan Süleyman, known by the westerns as "Magnificent" and "Great Turk", ascended the throne on 30th September, 1520 and during his reign that lasted for 47 years, he made Ottoman Empire one of the most powerful states in the world. The sultan who remained on the Ottoman throne for the longest period conquered Belgrade (1521), Rhodes (1522) and Hungary (1526). With the land he conquered in North Africa and Middle East, he made the Mediterranean a Turkish Lake. Eventually, he went out to Szigetvar Expedition. After a long siege, Szigetvar Castle was taken, but Kanuni, whose old body could not make it through the voyage, died before he could see the castle taken. In order not to depress the armies, his death was kept a secret for a while. His tomb is at the graveyard of Süleymaniye Mosque at the side of the *mihrab*. Here, apart from Kanuni, his daughter *Mihrimah Sultan, Ahmet II* (1691-1695) and *his wife Rabia Sultan* and *Süleyman II* are buried.

Hürrem Sultan (Roxelana) Tomb.

Hürrem Sultan (1500?-1558)

Tomb of Hürrem Sultan (Roxelana).

She was a concubine of Russian origin, Kanuni Sultan Süleyman's beloved life and the first Haseki Sultan of Christian origin *(haseki: the concubine that bears the child of the sultan)*. He was among the favorites of Kanuni who ascended the throne in 1520. In 1521, she gave birth to Shehzade Mehmet and gained the right to be the wife of the sultan. Among with her only daughter Mihrimah Sultan, she gave birth to five male children among which there was Selim II who later became the sultan. After the death of Hafsa Sultan, the mother of Kanuni in 1533, Hürrem Sultan became the sole leader of the palace and was mentioned with many contrivances. In order to pave the road for her sons, she was the main player in the incident where Shehzade Mustafa was killed by drowning; he was the son of Kanuni from Mahidevran Sultan and was loved very much by everybody. She died in 1558 and buried to the graveyard of Süleymaniye Mosque and then a tomb was made here half of which is ornamented by tiles.

Here, among with *Hürrem Sultan*, *Shehzade Mehmet* - the son of Selim II and the grandson of Hürrem- and the daughter of Hatice Sultan -sister of Kanuni- are buried.

Mimar Sinan (1490?-1588)

He is from Ağırnas village of Kayseri. He was devshirme (collection of non-Muslim children to be trained and used in troops) and taken to palace during the period of Yavuz Sultan Selim and he joined many expeditions during Kanuni period as a Janissary.

In 1538, during Kara-Boğdan expedition, he built a bridge over Prut River and received a lot of attention. Again at the same date, he was appointed as Hassa architecture and served for this purpose until the end of his life. In his long life, he was the designer or the architect of more than 400 structures. He examined previous structures and added his creativity to create unique works. Şehzade Mosque is accepted as his apprenticeship work and Selimiye Mosque at Edirne (1569-75) is accepted as his masterpiece. His tomb is on the north of Süleymaniye Mosque at the point where Mimar Sinan Street and Fetva Yokuşu Road intersect.

Tomb of Mimar Sinan (Chief Ottoman architect).

MARMARA SEA SHORES

Walls of Marmara, and Topkapı Palace.

Marmara Sea continues by the shore. The region starting from Sarayburnu that forms the first seed of the Historical Peninsula continues until Yedikule. At Kumkapı and Samatya region among the shores here, Armenians were settled after being brought to Istanbul in 15th century as a result of settlement policy of Fatih Sultan Mehmet and at Yedikule where Marmara walls meet the land walls Rums (Greek) brought from Karaman were settled.

Armenian Patriarchate Church.

Remains of the Palace of Boukoleon.

Armenian Patriarchate that continued its activities at this region was founded in 1461 during the period of Fatih Sultan Mehmet. Patriarchate that served at Surp Kevork Church at Samatya until 1640 was moved to Kumkapı afterwards where it still is today. Due to minorities who made their living through fishing for centuries, *meyhane* (bar) culture was developed at Kumkapı. Today, the streets at Kumkapı Square and its surroundings are among the famous taste regions of Istanbul with its fish restaurants.

Sokullu Mehmet Pasha Mosque 1
(Sokullu Mehmet Paşa Camii)
Small Hagia Sophia Mosque 2
Küçük Ayasofya Camii (Aziz Sergius ve Aziz Bacchus Kilisesi)
Polis Police
Hastane Hospital
Cami Mosque
Kilise Church
Otel Hotel
PTT PTT
Sağlık Ocağı Health Clinic
Saray-Kasır Palace-Summer Palace
Surlar City Walls
Tarihi Anıt Historical Monument
Türbe Tomb
Tramvay Durağı Tramway Stop
Tramvay Hattı Tramway Line
Tren Yolu Train Line
CAD. Avenue
Sk. Street
Taksim
Üsküdar
Eminönü
Sultanahmet
Kapalı Çarşı
MOLLA FENARİ
EMİN SİNAN
BİNBİRDİREK
EHSUVARBEY
Nur-u Osmaniye Türbesi
Kuyumcular Çarşısı
VEZİRHAN CAD.
Gazi Sinan Paşa Sk.
Tavuk Pazarı Sk.
Mesih Mehmet Paşa Sk.
Gazi Atik Ali Paşa Türbesi
Gazi Atik Ali Paşa Camii
Tezveren Dede Türbesi
Basın Müzesi
Çemberlitaş Anıtı
Çemberlitaş
YENİÇERİLER CAD.
Köprülü Mehmet Paşa Camii
Köprülü Mehmet Ağa Türbesi
Köprülü Kütüphanesi
Karababa Türbesi
Çemberlitaş Kız Lisesi
Çemberlitaş Anadolu Lisesi
Gedik Paşa Camii Sk.
İstanbul Sağlık Müdürlüğü-Halk Sağlığı Laboratuvarı
Emin Sinan Hamamı Sk.
PİYERLOTİ CAD.
PEYKHANE CAD.
Mina Otel
Emin Sinan Camii
PERTEV PAŞA CAD.
Silahtar Mektebi
Satır Sk.
Dizdariye Camii
Viyaletler Hizmet Birliği Polikliniği
Kececizade Fuad Paşa Türbesi
Emin Sinan Camii Sk.
Cephane Sk.
Tülcü Sk.
Gedikpaşa Surp Hovhannes Ermeni Kilisesi
Yeni Bahar Sk.
NEVRİYE CAD.
Onur Çıkmazı
Grand Yavuz Hotel
Dağhan Sk.
Kadırga Hamamı Sk.
Mühre Sk.
Fevziye Mektebi Sk.
KATİP SİNAN CAMİİ CAD.
Sokullu Mehmet Paşa Mescidi
Sokullu Mehmet Paşa Camii
Özbekler Sk.
Bostan Ali Camii Şerifi
Kumkapı Karakolu
Kadırga Spor Kulübü
KADIRGA LİMANI CAD.
Eminönü Belediyesi Kültür Merkezi
Eminönü Belediyesi Sağlık Merkezi
Kadırga Parkı
Behram Çavuş Camii
Aynül Hayat Hatun Mescidi
Kadırga İ.O.O.
Kadırga A.M.L Teknik Lisesi ve E.M.L
Şehit Çeşmesi Sk.
Şehit Mehmet Paşa Sk.
Çardaklı Fırın Sk.
Çardaklı Fırın Aralığı Sk.
Hotel Sidera
Amber Hotel
Işın Sk.
Şair Sermet Sk.
Comertler Sk.
Sehsuvarbey Camii
Cinci Meydanı Sk.
Kadırga Futbol Sahası
Cuma Meydanı
Eminönü Cinci Spor Tesisleri
Hünkar Peşrevi Sk.
Mehmet Efendi Çeşmesi
Kesikbaş Hüseyinağa Türbesi
Küçük Ayasofya Camii
Hisardibi Çıkmazı Sk.
Necip Fazıl Kısakürek Kültür Merkezi
İSMEK
KENNEDY

Sokullu Mehmet Pasha Mosque.

SOKULLU MEHMET PASHA MOSQUE 1

(SOKULLU MEHMET PAŞA CAMİİ)
Şehit Mehmetpaşa Yokuşu Street, No: 15 Kadırga

The wife of Sokullu Mehmet Pasha, İsmihan Sultan who was the daughter of Selim II had it built by Mimar Sinan in 1571 in her husband's name who was among the most famous grand viziers of Ottoman Empire. Complex building that consists of a mosque, madrasah and dervish lodge is settled masterfully on a steep hill. The place of religious exercise is 15x19 meters and is ornamented with marvelous tiles of the period. Especially the middle part of the *mihrab* wall is covered with rare tiles in green starting from the surrounding of the *mihrab* until the tambour of the dome. The pendantives, pulpit cone and the windows are also ornamented with tiles. The inside of the dome is decorated with paintings named pen crafts.

SMALL HAGIA SOPHIA MOSQUE 2

(Saint Sergius and Saint Bacchus Church)
(KÜÇÜK AYASOFYA CAMİİ)
Küçük Ayasofya Avenue

The structure at the end of Small Hagia Sophia Street and used today as a mosque was a church made between 531 and 536 by Byzantine Emperor Justinian I. Small Hagia Sophia that served as a church for nearly a thousand years was turned into a mosque by *Babüs Saade Ağası* (the chief of the Aghas) Hüseyin Ağa in 1506 during the time of Bayezid II. On the west side of the structure, a last congregation arcade suitable with Ottoman architecture, madrasah rooms to the surrounding of the small courtyard and a hammam was added on the side street.

The place of worship was of 25x28 meters in a rough square shape. Except for the *mihrab* bulge, there is a gallery floor that surrounds the whole structure in octagon shape. Since pendantives are not used in the dome that covers the main location, adopting this octagon brought forth the vawed dome structure. The dome is 19 meters high and its diameter exceeds 15 meters.

On the gallery floor, on the epigraph surrounding the structure, it is said that Justinian I had the church built in the name of Saints Sergius and Bacchus. Monograms of Justinian I and his wife Theodora can be seen on the column headings on both floors.

Small Hagia Sophia Mosque.

ARMENIAN PATRIARCHATE

(ERMENİ PATRİKHANESİ)
Sevgi Street, Kumkapı

Armenian Patriarchate in Istanbul was founded in 1461 with the support of

Armenian Patriarchate.

Mehmet II (Fatih). The rights that were bestowed to Roman Orthodox Patriarchate were also given to Armenian Patriarchate as well.

The patriarchate that was in Samatya when it was first founded and which is the religion center of Turkish Armenians in Gregorian sect was moved to its building in Kumkapı in 1641.

Across the patriarchate, there is *Surp Asdvadzadzin (Mary) Church* that was used as Patriarchate Church.

Interior view of Small Hagia Sophia Mosque.

YEDİKULE FORTRESS 3

(YEDİKULE HİSARI)
Kule Square No: 4 Yedikule
Except Wednesdays 09.00-16.30

It is on the section of land city walls that are close to Marmara Sea. Golden Gate that is made in the shape of a triumphal arch during the period of Theodosius II (408-450) was spared for the entrance of the armies that return with victory. During the period of Fatih Sultan Mehmet, five more towers were added to the East side of the door and the towers were combined with city walls that are 5 meters thick with a height of 12 meters. Thus it was connected to the land city walls and turned into a

Yedikule Fortress (Seven Towers Castle).

Land Walls in Yedikule side.

Golden Gate, one of the most important entrances to Istanbul, and Yedikule Citadel.

fortress with a polygon shape. Ottoman treasure was kept for a long time at Yedikule Citadel and ambassadors of the countries at war and Ottoman statesmen were prisoned in its dungeons.

Over the land city walls, the tower on the south that belongs to Byzantine period is restored today.

Again the tower on the North belonging to Byzantine period was collapsed in the earthquake; it was renewed during the time of Ahmet III (1703-30).

Foreign prisoners stayed on the *Epigraph Tower* on the left of the entrance door and Muslim prisoners stayed in the pylons on two sides of the Golden Gate. During Byzantine times, the *South Pylon* witnessed many death penalties.

Ottoman Sultan Genç Osman (II) was prisoned at South Pylon as a result of Janissary Riot at 1622 and was executed afterwards.

The prison function of the fortress ended during the time of Mahmut II (1808-1839).

At Yedikule Citadel, the towers can be visited, the walls can be walked upon and you can see the knitted Golden Gate from the roof of the pylons.

İMRAHOR İLYAS BEY MOSQUE ④
(Studios Monastery)

(İMRAHOR İLYAS BEY CAMİİ)
İmrahor İlyas Bey Avenue, İmam Asır Street, Yedikule
Closed to visitors

The monastery and Ioannes Prodromos Church that is pretty close to Yedikule Citadel was built by Eastern Consul Patricius Studios on his own land between 454 and 463. Starting from 9th century, it became a cultural center where hundreds of monks lived and religious works were prepared. After the con-

Bas-relief of anchor made by a prisoner. Yedikule Citadel.

Eastern side of İmrahor İlyas Bey Mosque.

quest of Istanbul, it was turned into a mosque by İlyas Bey in 1486. The wooden roof of the structure that was damaged with various fire and earthquakes collapsed in 1908. After this, it was not repaired and only with small repairs, it was prevented from collapsing further. The sarcophagus and mosaic pieces belonging to Byzantine period that were found in researches in 1907 are now in Istanbul Archaeology Museum. The structure in ruined condition today is very important due to its architectural features of Early Christianism. The mosaics on the floor date back to 13th century.

Zoodohu Pege "Balıklı" Church.

ZOODOHU PEGE "BALIKLI" CHURCH

(ZOODOHU PEGE 'BALIKLI' KİLİSESİ)

Seyit Nizam Avenue Kazlıçeşme

It is further away from the city walls, at Kazlıçeşme which is within Zeytinburnu region among Balıklı Ayazma (Holy Spring) which is the most famous ayazma of Istanbul, Merkezefendi and Silivrikapı graveyards. The ayazma of the church that was first founded in the period of Emperor Leon I (457-474) was used as a health center.

This region outside of the city became important after the church and ayasma were built. The church was repaired many times during Byzantine period and was reconstructed from its base in 1834 by Patriarchate Constantinos I.

Its courtyard surrounded by high walls is covered with gravestone in Karamanlı language.

It is believed that the ayasma in northwest corner gave health to patients. It also has a graveyard on the west of the church that is entered from a door opening from the narthex of patriarchates and donators.

EMİNÖNÜ AND BAZAARS

Eminönü is founded at the entrance of the Golden Horn by the shore. It is one of the centers where commercial life gained importance and it was frequently visited by Istanbul folk. At the shops under Galata Bridge that provides the connection between Karaköy-Eminönü, there are fish restaurants and cafes. Tahtakale and Mercan districts starting from

Eminönü Square, New Mosque and Bosphorus.

Spice Bazaar and extending towards Grand Bazaar are the most crowded economical shopping districts. At the shops in and around Spice Bazaar, you may find various products such as spices, various plants and seeds, dried fruits and delicatessens.

The shops that line at two sides of Mahmutpaşa Yokuşu stretching towards Grand Bazaar mainly sell inexpensive textile products.

Galata Bridge and Galata Tower in the background.

Fisherman in Eminönü.

Mahmutpaşa.

New (Valide) Mosque.

NEW (VALİDE) MOSQUE 1

(YENİ 'VALİDE' CAMİİ)
Eminönü Square

The construction of the mosque started in 1597 upon the orders of Safiye Sultan, the mother of Mehmet

Detail from the Mosque.

III (1595-1603). It was left unfinished when the sultan died in 1603 and Valide was sent to the Old Palace. Ahmet I who ascended the throne did not care for the structure and paid attention to the construction of Sultan Ahmet Mosque. The mosque that

Interior view of the Mosque.

remained without an owner was only completed half a century later during the period of Mehmet IV (1648-87) with the own means of his mother Hatice Turhan Sultan and built by Architect Mustafa Ağa between 1660 and 63. Spice Bazaar was constructed at this period next to this structure that was considered as complex.

The place of worship was 35x41 meters with a rectangular plan. Its dome with a diameter of 17,5 meters is supported by half domes from four sides. With this plan, it shows similarity with

Minber.

◀ View of Galata Bridge and Bosphorus from Süleymaniye Mosque.

Hatice Turhan Sultan Tomb.

Şehzade Mosque and Sultan Ahmet Mosque. With its dome that was kept high and other structural elements, it creates a pyramidal effect from the outside.

The blue-green tiles and pen crafts that portray the most beautiful examples of 17th century ornament the structure from top to bottom as it was in Sultan Ahmet Mosque.

At the south of Yeni Mosque, at the tomb across the street; *Hatice Turhan Sultan* as well as six Ottoman sultans; *Mehmet IV (1648-87), Mustafa II (1695-1703), Ahmet III (1703-30), Mahmut I (1730-54), Osman III (1754-57)* and *Murat V*

View of historical Spice Bazaar and details from the interior of the bazaar.

(1876) are buried. At the graveyards here, there are graves of many shehzade and sultans.

SPICE BAZAAR ❸

(MISIR ÇARŞISI)
Eminönü Square

Spice Bazaar which is the arasta of New Mosque Complex has an "L" plan at the south of the mosque and was built between 1663 and 1664. It is named as such (Egypt) because the spices sold in the shops at the bazaar during Ottoman period are brought through Egypt road. Shops are lined at two sides of the structure that is covered with vault and a length of 270 meters. The bazaar that sells spices, seeds of flowers, various plants, dried fruits and delicatessen is among the liveliest shopping centers. At the point where "L" is united, there is **Flower Bazaar** on the side of the mosque. Here; besides plants and seeds, pets are sold.

RÜSTEM PASHA MOSQUE ❷

(RÜSTEM PAŞA CAMİİ)
Hasırcılar Avenue No: 90, Tahtakale

The only structure with a single minaret on the shore, west of New Mosque was built by Mimar Sinan between 1561 and 1562 upon the orders of Rüstem Pasha, grand vizier and son-in-law

Interior view of Rüstem Pasha.

Tiles decorated with tulip motifs in the Mosque.

of Kanuni Sultan Süleyman (1520-66). Since it was built with two floors, the courtyard is reached through the stairs on its four sides. The place of worship has a rectangular plan with a size of 20x27 meters. The main location supported by tromps and covered with dome extends towards the sides with the gathering place and gallery floors. Rüstem Pasha Mosque is especially famous for the magnificent Iznik tiles of 16th century, the time when Ottoman tile art reached its peak. The walls of the Last Congregation Place, inner walls, feet, pendantives, the inside of the *mihrab* and its surroundings are ornamented with tiles from the base until the middle.

GRAND POST OFFICE 4

(BÜYÜK POSTANE)

Büyük Postane Avenue, Eminönü

This building which is a product of National Architectural period was built by Architect Vedat Tek between 1905 and 1909. The structure with four floors carries the features of a selective architecture as of its plan and front features. It is used today for postal services function. At the Jackie Chan movie "Accidential Spy" that was partly shot in Istanbul, Grand Post Office was presented to the audience as the bank.

Grand Post Office building.

After you finish your tour in Eminönü, transportation to other directions will be easy. Kabataş-Zeytinburnu tram line passes from Eminönü. Kadıköy, Üsküdar and Bosphorus line steamboats are in service within short intervals from the piers on the quay. You can reach **Sultanahmet, Grand Bazaar** and **Süleymaniye Mosque** on foot from Eminönü. It is advised going to Sultanahmet by tram because the road is a little rough. If you prefer walking Yenicami Avenue which is on the side, Hatice Turhan Sultan Mausoleum takes you the square. Hoca Hanı Street at the highest left corner of the square is connected with Yerebatan Avenue and so with Sultanahmet. Vasıf Çınar Avenue which is at the right corner of the same square, turning left takes you to Süleymaniye. Mahmutpaşa Hill turning up from the first left of Vasıf Çınar Avenue, which starts asphalt and then turns to cobble open into Mahmutpaşa Gate of Grand Bazaar *(See page 86-87 for map)*.

THE REGION OF GOLDEN HORN AND FATİH

The Golden Horn is a narrow, deep and calm, small bay next to the meeting point of Bosphorus and Marmara Sea separating the Historical Peninsula from Beyoğlu.

It was formed as a result of sea level rise and filling the valley here at the end of Ice Age. It is about 8 km long with a width of 200-700 meters. Due to the silt carried by the rivers, its depth decreases at the north sections and forms little islands. During Ottoman times, the shores of Golden Horn that was always a place of leisure became more intense especially during *Lale Period* (Tulip Period) and it was ornamented with palaces, kiosks and groves and was famous for its entertainment and boat trips. During *Lale Period* when Sultan Ahmet III (1703-30) had *Sadabad Qasr* built in Kağıthane for his entertainment, Kağıthane River and the surroundings of the Golden Horn reached a new look. Tulip gardens around Sadabad Qasr also caused the trend of planting tulips among wealthy families. This way, the negative atmosphere brought by war years left itself to a lively and fun, elite life-style. With *Patrona Halil İsyanı (Riot)* in 1730, *Lale Period* ended and the structures were brought down. The region of Golden Horn kept its feature of being a leisure center.

Sarayburnu, the starting point of the Golden Horn and the first hill of the city is the area for the first acropolis settlement in the Historical Peninsula. During Byzantine and Ottoman times, Latin Colonies among which was Genoa continued their commercial life at the region of Sirkeci-Unkapanı. Genoa Colony later on settled at Galata and developed there. The Jewish lived at Eminönü until 17th century and than immigrated to Balat and Hasköy.

Most of the works and topics mentioned at Golden Horn are the regions in the shores and hills of Fatih. At the shore section of Haliç, there are the regions Ayakapı, Fener, Balat and Ayvansaray connected to Fatih.

View of the Golden Horn from Pierre Loti.

Following the collapse of Byzantine Empire, because Fatih Sultan Mehmet guaranteed their safety and religious freedom, the local folk continued their beliefs and social life. Greek Patriarchate still continues their activities in Fener. At the shores of **Fener**, there were the *yalıs* (residence) of well-known Greek families. Families with lower income settled in the inner sections, in houses with window seats. Fener protected its identity of being a Greek region until the middle of 20th century and lost this feature upon the Greek's immigrating to different places. **Balat**, the neighbor of Fener is the region where Jewish people brought from Macedonia after the conquest were settled at and during the time of Bayezid II (1481-1512) Jewish immigrants were settled. With the founding of Israel state, most families emigrated from here. At this place, there used to be many synagogues including Ahrida Synagogue at Kürkçü Çeşmesi Street that could not reach until today. Compared to the calm streets of Fener, it had a lively merchant class.

Ayvansaray that comes after Balat was called Blakhernai during Byzantine times. Emperor's Palace that was moved here with the desertion of the Grand Palace was a wide complex settled on the hills with the view of the Golden Horn right within the land city walls. Now only the walls of *Tekfur Palace* remain at the hills. Since there are many tombs and graves from the martyrs during the Arabs siege of Istanbul, the region is important for Muslims as

Fener Greek Orthodox High School with its interesting architecture.

Floating bridge in the Golden Horn in the 19th century *(Miss Pardoe).*

well. With this region, the Golden Horn border of the historical city ends and Golden Horn city walls connect with Land Walls and stretch towards Eğrikapı-Edirnekapı-Sulukule and Topkapı. The Golden Horn borders of the Historical Peninsula used to extend from Sarayburnu until Ayvansaray; however today no other part remains than that of a small part in Ayvansaray.

Beyond the third Golden Horn Bridge, the region **Eyüp** starts. Because Eyüp was out of the city walls, it was not an important settlement area during Byzantine period. When Fatih Sultan Mehmet made a complex and tomb at the graveyard of Eyüp Sultan, the surrounding of the complex developed as a Muslim neighborhood. The identity of Ottoman period religious center has been protected until today. **Eyüp Sultan Tomb** is among the most visited places in Istanbul by the Muslims.

At the hills of Eyüp, at a point overlooking the Golden Horn, there is **Pierre Loti Café** that still functions today where the French author Pierre Loti often visited and stayed for a long time to write. Between the panorama of the Golden Horn of Ottoman period and this period there is subtle difference also brought by time. Especially the intense and unorganized settlements at the hills are brought by today. During its period, it was a perfect place to rest with its magnificent *yalı*, the greens ornamenting its hills and boat delights. With the cable car that has been completed in recent years, one may reach from Eyüp to the hill of Pierre Loti in a short time.

***Merdivenli Yokuşu* (Climbing street with steps), Balat.**

General view of the Golden Horn from the aerial perspective.

HALİÇ
GOLDEN HORN
ABDÜLEZELPAŞA CAD.
DR. SADIK AHMET CAD.
VODİNA CAD.
SULTAN SELİM CAD.
YAVUZ SELİM CAD.
MANYASİZADE CAD.
BEYCEGİZ CAD.
DARÜŞŞAFAKA
SARAYAĞASI CAD.
NİŞANCA CAD.
FEVZİPAŞA CAD.
ALTAY CAD.
HIRKAİ ŞERİF CAD.
KÜÇÜK MUSTAFAPAŞA CAD.
AYAKAPI CAD.
KİREMİT CAD.
TAHTA MİNARE
ABDİ SUBAŞI
HATİP MUSLAHİTTİN
SALAHİTTİN
KOCA DEDE
BEYCEGİZ
Zeyrek Mosque 1 (Zeyrek Camii)
Fatih Mosque 2 (Fatih Camii)
Tomb of Sultan Mehmet 3
(Fatih Sultan Mehmet Türbesi)
Yavuz Sultan Selim Mosque 4
(Yavuz Sultan Selim Camii)
Fethiye Mosque and Museum 5
(Fethiye Camii ve Müzesi)
Kariye Museum (page 104) 6
(Kariye Müzesi)
Mihrimah Sultan Mosque (page
7 (Mihrimah Sultan Camii)
Tekfur Palace (page 104) 8
(Tekfur Sarayı)
Gül Mosque 9 (Gül Camii)
Fener Greek Orthodox Patriarch
(Fener Rum Ortodoks Patrikhanes
Hagios Georgios Patriarchal Ch
(Hagios Georgios Patrikhane Kili
Fener Greek Orthodox High Scl
(Fener Rum Lisesi)
Panagia Muhliotissa (Mother M
Church 13 (Panagia Muhliotissa
'Meryem Ana' Kilisesi)
Sveti Stefan Bulgarian Church
(Sveti Stefan Bulgar Kilisesi)
Polis Police
Hastane Hospit
Cami Mosque
Kilise Church
Otel Hotel
PTT PTT
Sağlık Ocağı Health Clinic
Saray-Kasır Palace-Summer
Surlar City Walls
Tarihi Anıt Historical Mon
Türbe Tomb
Tramvay Durağ Tramway Stop
Tramvay Hattı Tramway Line
İDO İskele Pier
CAD. Avenue
Sk. Street
Taksim
Eminönü

ABDÜLEZELPAŞA CAD.
ÜSKÜPLÜ CAD.
SALİHPAŞA CAD.
ATATÜRK BULVARI
HAYDAR CAD.
KARADENİZ CAD.
YEŞİLZADE CAD.
NEVŞEHİRLİ İBRAHİMPAŞA CAD.
ÇIRÇIR CAD.
ZEYREK CAD.
İTFAİYE CAD.
HATTAT NAFİZ CAD.
MİHCİLAR CAD.
ESKİ MUHAFIZLAR CAD.
HALİÇ CAD.
İSLAMBOL CAD.
BÜYÜK KAHRAMAN CAD.
HAYDARBEY CAD.
MACAR KARDEŞLER CAD.
FEVZİPAŞA CAD.
KIZTAŞI CAD.
HORHOR CAD.
KARAÇİ
KARA MEHMET
HAYDAR
KASAP DEMİRHUN
SİNANAĞA
HACIKADIN
YAVUZ SİNAN
KIRMASTİ
HÜSAM BEY
ÇEŞME
Fatih Camii ve Külliyesi
Fatih Sultan Mehmet Türbesi
Fatih Mezarlığı
Fatih Parkı
Teyyare Parkı
Zeyrek Parkı
Kadir Has Üniversitesi
Fatih Müftülüğü
1
2
3

Giant Zeyrek Mosque.

On the way to Zeyrek
It can be reached by following the **"Zeyrekhane"** signs on İftaiye Avenue which is on the right when going up from Unkapanı to **Bozdoğan Aqueduct**. The gizzard road, which is higher and parallel to İftaiye Avenue, a little bit further on the right, is a short-cut *(See page 96-97 for map)*.

ZEYREK MOSQUE (Pantocrator Monastery) 1

(ZEYREK CAMİİ)
İbadethane Street, Zeyrek

It is between İbadethane Street which is a back street of Atatürk Street on the direction of Fatih and İbadethane Arkası Street. The large structure formed with connecting three churches dates back to 12th century. Eirene, the daughter of Hungarian King Laszlo and the wife of Ioannes Komnenos II (1118-1143) had the first building constructed on the south. After the death of Eirene, Ioannes Komnenos II had a new church built at the north of the church which is a smaller copy of the one in South. When two churches close to each other existed, the Emperor decided to connect them and in between them, he had a graveyard chapel built in 1136 which was the smallest of the three where Emperor and the Empress were buried.

The North and South churches have a cross plan. Their middle locations are covered with a high tambour dome and they were surrounded from four sides with vaults forming the arms of the cross. The four columns in the middle location are replaced by arches today. At the west fronts of both the north and the south church, there are narthex sections. The chapel in the middle is covered with two domes lined in East and West direction.

The structure that was turned into a mosque after the conquest of Istanbul was named as Zeyrek Mosque due to its first *müderris* (tutor) Molla Zeyrek Mehmet Efendi. At the end of 18th century, it went through a major restoration and after 1966 it was restored again. The south church of the structure continues to function as a mosque.

Plan of Zeyrek.

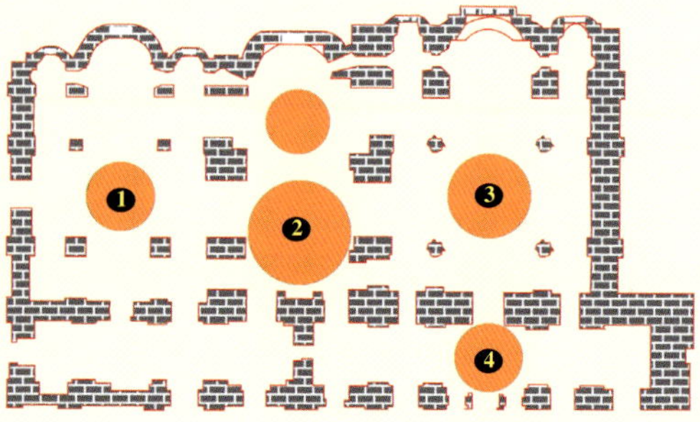

1- *Northern Church*, **2-** *Parecclesion*, **3-** *Zeyrek Mosque*, **4-** *Narthexes*.

Fatih direction follows in two ways as coast and upper parts after touring Zeyrek. You should reach Edirnekapı if you want to see **Kariye** first. It is enough to get on the Edirnekapı bus from Zeyrek side of Atatürk Boulevard. Get off at Edirnekapı, stop and walk down. Vaiz Street on the first left and Şeyh Eyüp Street which is lower intersect with Kariye Camii Street which is connected with Kariye Museum. If you choose Şeyh Eyüp Street it will be easier for you. You will see **Mihrimah Sultan Mosque** while going down on this road. After visiting **Kariye Museum** you can visit **Mihrimah Sultan Mosque, Tekfur Palace** and **Fethiye Museum** which are very close to the museum *(See page 104 for map)*.

FATİH MOSQUE 2

(FATİH CAMİİ)
Fevzi Paşa Avenue, Fatih

It was built between 1463 and 1470 during the period of Fatih Sultan Mehmet with complex structures to the place of Havariyyun Church ruins which was among the most important churches in the city after Hagia Sophia. At this church overlooking the city, there were grave-

Fatih Mosque.

Interior view of Fatih Mosque.

yards of many Byzantine Emperors among which is Constantine the Great who carried the capital of Rome to Istanbul. The monastery of Havariyyun Church was used by Orthodox Patriarchate after the conquest and was moved to Pammakaristos Church (Fethiye Mosque) in 1455. Afterwards, the complex started to be built at the place of Havariyyun Church. In the flooring of the courtyard, some of the marble used to keep the processed side underneath is among the pieces that belong to the church.

The architect of the first great complex made after the conquest of Istanbul is Atik Sinan. As it was in Süleymaniye Complex, it consists of social and educational institutions located around the mosque; however, some of the structures including the first mosque that was built could not reach until today. The mosque of this period had a square plan and covered with one large dome and a half dome on the direction of the *mihrab*. The other sections of the square plan were completed with small domes. The mosque that was damaged in different periods collapsed in 1766 earthquake in a way that it could not be repaired again. According to a different plan than the first one, Fatih Mosque was rebuilt between 1767 and 1771 during the period of Mustafa III (1757-74). The architect of the new mosque was Mehmet Tahir Ağa who was also the architect of Lale Mosque. The tile plates that ornament the headpiece of the two windows in the inner court are the ornamentations of the first mosque. Also

Minber.

cümle gate, the three walls of its inner courtyard and the bodies of the minarets until the line of lower *şerefe* are left from the previous structure.

The place of worship is covered with a central dome that sits on the arches supported by four half domes. The wide main location has a spacious look. In the ornamentation of the mosque built according to the classical architectural order, also Turkish baroque art influences of 18th century are seen. At the direction of the *mihrab* of the mosque, there is **Fatih Sultan Mehmet Tomb** which was damaged in the earthquake of 1766. In the tomb that was renewed with its baroque features in a short time, there is only the sarcophagus of Fatih. The structure with octagon plan is cov-

Cover system of Fatih Mosque.

ered with a single dome. It was repaired many times during Ottoman period and its inner ornamentations were renewed. At the east of the tomb, there is a smaller tomb where Gülbahar Hatun, Fatih's wife and his daughter Gevheri Sultan are placed.

Fatih Sultan Mehmet (1432-1481)

He is the son of Murat II and Hüma Hatun and one of the most famous sultans of Ottoman Empire. He was raised by the scholars of the period and besides his poetic spirits, he was also interested in other sciences as well. Upon the death of his father Murat II in 1451, he ascended the throne for the second time. Fatih, who decided the conquest of Istanbul during the first years of his reign, had Rumeli Fortress on Bosphorus which was the largest castle of his age and thus aimed to prevent support forces that could come from the Black Sea.

Sultan Mehmet the Conqueror.

In 1453 after a siege of 53 days, Sultan Mehmet II who conquered Istanbul at the age of 21 took the title of Fatih (Conqueror) after this date. On the first day that he entered the city he visited Hagia Sophia and ordered it to be turned into a mosque but also that none of its parts shall be damaged. He worked hard to prosper Istanbul, the new capital of Ottoman Empire and turn it into a glorious center. His good behavior towards the noble of the Byzantine and Christian folk is a result of his wide world view. After conquering Istanbul, he gathered Italian humanists and Greek scholars at his palace. He brought Gentile Bellini from Venice and had the walls of the palace ornamented with frescoes and had his portrait made which is exhibited today at *National Gallery* in London. As a sultan with a wide perspective and civilized thought, he pioneered in modernization in art and culture and he was careful to apply his orders and laws. Fatih Sultan Mehmet extended Ottoman land to large areas with the conquests he made. He ended other Turkish beyliks (sultanade) in Anatolia and Pontus Roman State in Trabzon and united Anatolia strictly to Ottomans. In the west, he reigned over Serbia, Wallachia- Moldavia, Bosnia-Herzegovina and Albania. He had a new Patriarch appointed to Fener Greek Patriarchate, activated it again and he provided the foundation of Armenian Patriarchate and Jewish Chief Rabbi in Istanbul.

Gate of the Tomb of Sultan Mehmet the Conqueror

Mehmet II became sick when he was about to go on a new expedition in Anatolia in the spring of 1481 and died 25 kilometers outside of Istanbul. His tomb is at the graveyard of Fatih Mosque.

Interior view of the Tomb of Sultan Mehmet the Conqueror.

YAVUZ SULTAN SELİM MOSQUE ④

(YAVUZ SULTAN SELİM CAMİİ)
Yavuz Selim Avenue, Yavuzselim

Yavuz Sultan Selim (1512-20), ended the Mamluk reign in Egypt and brought the Sacred Relics to Istanbul and also he brought the title of calliphacy to Ottomans. Thus, Ottoman sultans used the calliphacy title until 1924 when it was abandoned. Sultan Selim Mosque was built by his son Kanuni Sultan Süleyman (1520-66) between 1520 and 1522 upon the death of the sultan in 1520. There is no certain information about its architect. The place of worship at the mosque is covered with a single dome of 24,5 meters and the mosque is the last example of its kind with its tabhanes in two sides. The tile plates over the windows of the inner location and the boards over the windows of the last congregation place have reached today as its original.

The Tomb of Yavuz Sultan Selim at the *mihrab* side of the mosque has an octagon plan. The tomb where there is only the sarcophagus of Sultan Selim has doors and windows rich with mother-of-pearls. At *Shehzades Tomb* at the northeast of Sultan Selim Tomb, the three sons of Kanuni and his two sisters are buried. The other tomb which is in a ruined condition in the east belongs to Kanuni's mother, *Hafsa Sultan*. The remains of the tomb wall that rise about a meter from the ground as well as the iron bars of the windows still remains. Behind Shehzades Tomb, there is the **Tomb of Abdülmecit** (1839-61).

From Fatih to Fethiye

You can reach Fethiye Museum by approximately 20 minutes walk from Fatih Mosque. Don't forget that it is just a Parecclesion made museum, other parts serve as a mosque and may not be open even between prayers. Follow Fevzi Pasha Avenue where Fatih Mosque is on, and then turn right into Yavuz Sultan Selim Avenue after passing Fatih District Police Department. You see **Yavuz Sultan Selim Mosque** and its two minarets after you ascend the avenue. Before the mosque, turn left to Darüşşafaka Avenue after Çarşamba Park. Follow Fethiye Avenue which turns right after passing the Çarşamba and Fethiye bus stops. You will see Fethiye Medresesi Street sign while the road sweeps down, that sign will take you to **Fethiye Museum**. If you don't want to walk, this road is where Draman buses pass. You should get off at Fethiye stop after Çarşamba stop if you prefer going with bus (*See page 96-97 for map*).

Tomb of Shehzades (The son or male line descendant of an Ottoman Sultan).

Yavuz Sultan Selim Mosque.

FETHİYE MOSQUE AND MUSEUM ⑤

(FETHİYE CAMİİ VE MÜZESİ)
Fethiye Avenue, Fethiye Medresesi Street, No: 4
Çarşamba-Draman
Except Wednesdays 09:00-16.30

Pammakaristos Monastery Church which is a Byzantine period structure continues to function today as a mosque and museum. It is made of two churches side by side, one of which is small. It's most important section, the main church was built by Ioannes Komnenos (1118-43) and his wife Anna Dukaina at the beginning of 12th century. The nephew of Emperor Michael Palaiologos (1261-82), Mihail Glabas had the structure repaired between 1290 and 1294. After the death of Glabas, towards 1315, his wife Maria had the parecclesion built that formed the second church to the south of the structure. This additional building where there are graves of Michael Glabas and Maria is a small structure like the parecclesion of Kariye.

South-Western view of Fethiye Museum.

Parecclesion.

Greek Patriarchate that was moved to here in 1455 from Havariyyun Church served until 1586. In honor of Murat III's (1574-95) conquest of Georgia and Azerbaijan it was turned into a mosque in 1587 and named Fethiye Mosque in memory of the victory. It was repaired between 1845 and 1846. Between 1936 and 1938, it was restored and turned into a small parecclesion museum and the main building was opened for worship again as a mosque.

Parecclesion has 14th century mosaics that were rare but of high importance in art. In the middle of its dome of

Mosaic of Jesus Christ.

Babtism scene on the eastern wall.

Saint Mosaic.

Saint Mosaic.

2,30 meters, there is the mosaic of *Pantocrator Jesus* and the 12 parts are ornamented with the mosaics of Old Testament prophets. In the *Deesis* scene in its apse, there is Jesus in the middle and on the side walls of the apse, the scene is completed with Mary and John the Baptist. In its east wall, Baptism can be seen and on the arches and headpieces of arches, various saint figures can be seen.

From Fethiye to Balat

You will see Draman bus stop and Tercuman Yunus Mosque on Draman Avenue which is continuation of Fethiye Avenue. Opposite of them is Draman Çeşmesi Street descending from the hills of Golden Horn. Enter this street and continue from the right of the street which is split into two. Follow Ayan Avenue where small retailers are crowded in between historical Balat houses. You reach the coast by following Leblebiciler Street, the right of the avenue that separates in to two at the end. Şucaiddin Mosque, built by alternating white stone and red bricks will be the first to greet you on the coast.

From Balat to Fethiye

If you want to go to Fethiye from Balat, like the opposite of this description enter the street across the Şucaiddin Mosque which has traffic lights in front of it. The street takes you to Ayan Avenue by turning left. Likewise Ayan Avenue will take you to Draman Avenue where Tercuman Yunus Mosque is on. By turning left from this avenue you reach **Fethiye Museum**, and turning right you reach **Kariye Museum**. If you want to se Fethiye first continue from the left of the street, the Fethiye Merdresesi Street sign that you will see soon shows Fethiye Museum. For Kariye see the section "from Fethiye to Kariye".

From Fethiye to Kariye

Fethiye Museum is very close to Kariye. Fethiye Avenue continues as Draman Avenue from a point. Move on in direction of Tercüman Yunus Mosque and Draman bus stop. You will see the dome of Kariye in the end of the street. Turn left from the Selma Tomruk Avenue at the end of the street, if you continue from the gizzard road of Kariye Türbesi Street which departs from the left and you will reach the entrance of the museum.

Mosaics of Saints decorating the walls.

Christ Pantocrator in the middle and prophets of the Torah around him.

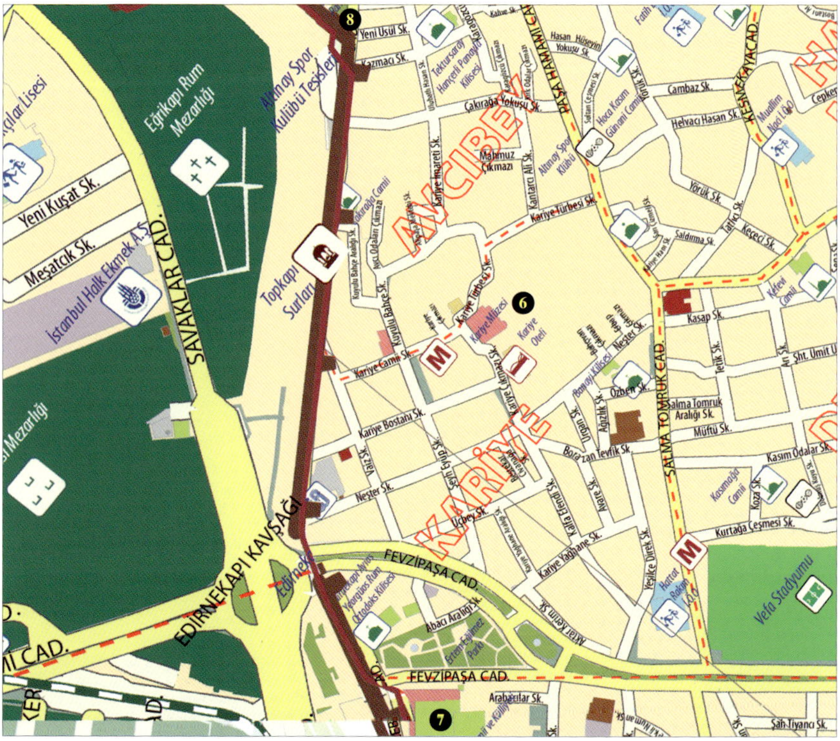

Mosaic of Pantocrator Jesus.

Kariye (Chora) Museum.

KARİYE MUSEUM (Chora Monastery) 6

(KARİYE MÜZESİ)

Kariye Camii Street, Edirnekapı

Except Wednesdays 09:00-16:30

Even though the existence of a monastery here in 6th century is not certain, it has been found by the burial of Patriarch Germanos who died in 740 here. Maria Dukaina, the mother-in-law of Emperor Aleksios Komnenos (1081-1118) had the ruined monastery repaired and rebuilt again at the end of 11th century. After a short while, the younger son of Aleksios, Isaakios Komnenos had the church rebuilt all over again in a larger size and had a grave place prepared for himself at narthex section.

Main area.

Kariye that became a religious center that the emperors paid attention to due to its close location to Blakhernai Palace, achieved its look today with a major repair that Theodoros Metokhites, a pioneering official of the period, had made between 1315 and 1321. Its dome that was collapsed was made again additions were made such as the outer narthex, additional

Plan of Chora Museum

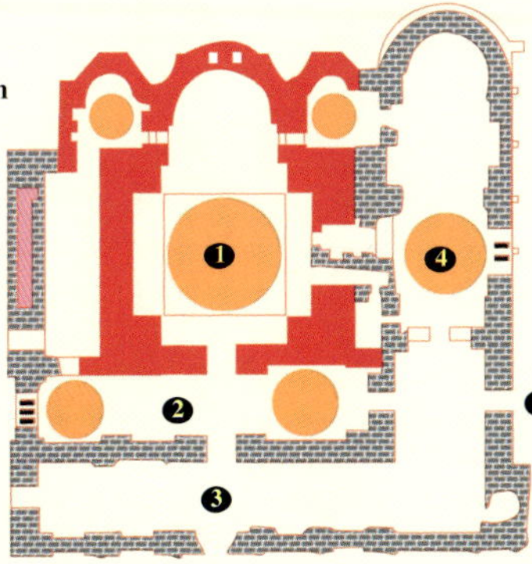

1- *Main area,* 2- *Inner narthex,* 3- *Outer narthex,* 4- *Parecclesion,* 5- *Gate to Museum.*

Virgin Mary and Child Jesus.

General view of Parecclesion, covered with frescoes.

structure on its north and parecclesion on its south. In its last years, Metokhites who retreated to Chora Monastery was buried here when he was dead in 13th March, 1332.

After the conquest of Istanbul by Ottomans in 1453, the church remained empty for a while and then a single serefe minaret was added to its southwest by Grand Vizier Atik Ali Pasha in 1511 and it was turned into a mosque.

As of architecture, it has a lively look with the lines of stone-brick that is often seen in Byzantine churches. The main location with square shape is mostly illuminated with the windows lined in the tambour of the dome. In its west, there are inner and outer narthexes.

At the first half of 14th century, parecclesion which was added to the south of the structure by Theodor Metokhites, united with outer narthex in the west and surrounded the main location in "L" shape. In the middle of this additional structure that was a chapel of graveyard, there is the high tambourine dome with a diameter of 4,5 meters. From here, there is another outer place that opens to the inner narthex.

Ornaments: The mosaics and frescoes at Kariye Museum together with Fethiye Museum are among the most beautiful examples of 14th century which is the last period of Byzantine art. The emphasis of the body

Mosaic of Christ Pantocrator on the door.

with its plastical values, the face expressions of the figures and the technique that is used are signs that a new art tradition started at Byzantine.

The mosaics and frescoes at the narthex and parecclesion were made during the repair of Theodor Metokhites. At the outer narthex, there are scenes of Jesus and at the inner narthex; there are scenes from Mary's life. **Pantocrator Jesus** strikes attention on the door that passes from the outer narthex to the inner narthex. At this section, there are scenes such as Dream of Jacob, Going to Bethlehem, counting of population, birth of Jesus, Kana wedding miracles, Multiplying bread and Murder of Children.

At the inner narthex there are scenes of Birth of Mary, scenes on childhood of Mary, Mary buying wool, scenes about Jacob and Mary as well as Herald and healing miracles. On the door of entrance to the main location, Jesus is shown in the middle and Theodor Metokhites repairing the church is shown on the left as if presenting the model of the church.

Very few mosaics at the main location have survived until today. Here, there is the scene of **Mary's Last Sleep** which is one of the most important ones of Kariye Museum as well as mosaics of Jesus, Mary and Child Jesus. At the main location, ornaments and dome mosaics over the beautiful and colorful wall cover marbles have not survived until today.

All of parecclesion is ornamented with frescoes. The scene of **Resurrection (anastasis)** at the apse is a masterpiece. The depiction of judg-

Anastasis fresco in Parecclesion.

ment day on the vault covering the East side of parecclesion is very much detailed and worth seeing. These two powerful scenes are suitable to the function of the cemetery chapel. In the middle of the parecclesion dome, Mary and Child Jesus are depicted, 12 angel figures are depicted on dome sections and the authors of the Bible are depicted on pendantives.

Mary's Last Sleep.

On the marble head pieces of the columns at the west edge of the structure, head angel busts are engraved. Between 1948 and 1958, as a result of the work carried out by American Byzantine Institute, all the mosaics and frescoes have been brought to light. Thus Kariye was opened to visitors as a museum.

From Kariye to Tekfur

Kariye Museum is within five minutes distance from Tekfur Palace. Follow the Kariye Mosque Street that ascends from Kariye. At the end of the street it will intersect with Vaiz Street which connects with Fevzi Paşa Avenue. At this intersection point you can see Kariye Museum on north and Mihrimah Sultan Mosque on south. On north, bulwark walls attract attention. Walk to the walls and follow down Hoca Çakır Avenue which is parallel to the walls. At the end of the avenue you will see the south façade of Tekfur Palace next to the **Tekfur Palace** Park *(See page 104 for map)*.

MİHRİMAH SULTAN MOSQUE 7

(MİHRİMAH SULTAN CAMİİ)
Fevzi Paşa Avenue No: 355
Edirnekapı

It is located at Edirnekapı, right inside the land city walls. Mihrimah Sultan, the daughter of Kanuni Sultan Süleyman and Hürrem Sultan had the mosque built to Mimar Sinan. Its construction date is unknown as it does not have an epigraph; however, it is assumed that it was completed around 1560. Its main location has a size of 28 x 40 meters with a linear rectangular plan. The middle section is covered with a dome with a diameter that exceeds 20 meters and the side naves are covered with three small domes. The central dome is dominant in the location because the naves are not very high. The four feet carrying the dome are hidden inside the inner place and emphasized outside. The embellishments belong to the restoration of 1957. Güzel Ahmet Pasha, the son-in-law of Mihrimah Sultan is buried at the tomb of the mosque. Mihrimah Sultan is buried at Süleymaniye Mosque, next to Kanuni.

Tekfur Palace gravure.

TEKFUR PALACE 8

(TEKFUR SARAYI)
Şişhane Avenue No:100
Edirnekapı

It is between Eğrikapı and Edirnekapı. From Blakhernai Palace complex used at the last period of Byzantine, only Tekfur pavilion at its south has remained today. It is assumed that it belongs to 13th century. On the East-West direction, only the body walls remain of the palace with a rectangular plan and adjacent to the walls. Its front side overlooks a courtyard at the direction of the Golden Horn.

With its architectural structure and window orders, it is understood that it had three floors. The first floor is the entrance floor that is higher than the other floors and that opens to the courtyard with four vaults. It is divided by three columns in two lines of which only the base remains today.

The window arches of the structure are its ornamentation with the red brick and white stone mixture. The front of the courtyard is bonded with stone and bricks and the south front it is bonded with cut stone. At its south front, there are only the windows of the highest floor and it strikes attention with its balcony that bulges outside.

Southern wall of Tekfur Palace.

We mentioned that the route separates into two at Zeyrek. Thus we finished our tour around the hillsides of Fatih district of Golden Horn. The structures we are going to check over now belong to the other route. They are the structures on the coast of Golden Horn. Therefore alignment from Zeyrek side of Golden Horn is taken into account. The districts on this coast are neighbors and very close to each other. It is suitable for touring on foot.

GÜL (ROSE) MOSQUE 9
(Saint Theodosia Church)

(GÜL CAMİİ)
Vakıf Mektebi Street No: 16
Ayakapı

The structure that is located at the point where Şerefiye Street and Şair Nevi Street intersect at the back street of the Golden Horn is an old Byzantine church and was constructed during the period of Basileios I (867-886). Saint Theodosia, to whom the church was dedicated, was killed during Iconoclasm period (726-843) when she was trying to prevent others who tried to bring down Jesus icon on Halke Door of Grand Palace next to Hagia Sophia square and she was exalted to the title of saint. Since the relics of the saint were placed at the church, it was continuously visited by pilgrims and travelers who came to Istanbul.

The time when the church was turned into a mosque is controversial. The fact that this place was named as "Gül Mosque" in the Vakıflar Tahrir Defteri (the notebook for records) in 1546 show that it was turned into a mosque before this date. The mosque that was greatly damaged in the fire of 1633 was repaired during the period of Mahmut II (1808-1839).

The middle section of the closed cross plan structure is covered with a dome and the arms of the cross are covered with vault. The main location covered with a dome sitting on four large feet with pendantives is reached by gallery floors in "U" shape at both sides and at the entrance side. The semidome of the apse and the dome are ornamented with motifs. The side fronts of the structure as well as the large carrier arches and main dome were renewed in Ottoman period.

FENER GREEK ORTHODOX PATRIARCHATE 10

(FENER RUM ORTODOKS PATRİKHANESİ)
Sadrazam Ali Paşa Avenue
No: 19 Fener

It is located at Fener on Sadrazam Ali Paşa Street which is a back street of the Golden Horn. After Constantine the Great moved the capital of Rome to Istanbul, the church here was elevated to the level of primacy. During the 1st Council of Istanbul in 381, it was decided that Istanbul bishop shall have equal rights with the bishop in Rome. After this council, Rome, Istanbul, Alexandria, Antakya and Jerusalem were accepted as the centers of the Christian world. The religious conflict between the Eastern and Western Churches resulted in a certain separation of the two churches in 1054 with the names Orthodox and Catholic. Thus the pope at Rome Church became the leader of the Catholics and the Patriarch at the head of Orthodox Church in Istanbul became the head of Orthodox people. When Istanbul was conquered by the Ottomans, the last patriarch Athanasios II left his post because he opposed the unification of the two churches and no other person was appointed after him. After Fatih Sultan Mehmet took Istanbul in 1453, he paid close attention to the Patriarchate and found it suitable that a patriarch shall be at the head of Greek society and had an election made for a new patriarch. In 1454, Georgios Kortesios Skholarios became the patriarch with the title Gennadios II. The patriarchate settled in historical order to Havariyyun Church (1453-1455), Pammakaristos Monastery (1455-1586), Panagia Church in Fener (1587) and then Hagios Dimitrios Church in Ayvansaray (1597) and eventually to Hagios Georgios Church in 1602 at Fener and then continued its activities here. At the second half of 19th century, nationalism that started to develop among Orthodox people influenced patriarchate negatively. When Greece won its independence on 3rd, February 1830, Greek Church declared its independence in 1833. In 1865 Romania, in 1870 Bulgaria and in 1879 Serbia churches became independent.

Fener Greek Orthodox Patriarchate.

After the foundation of the Turkish Republic, the patriarchate lost all its privileges from Ottoman State and turned into only a religious institution. The fact that many Greek people in Turkey immigrated to Greece decreased the number of people that belonged to Fener Patriarchate.

HAGIOS GEORGIOS PATRIARCHATE CHURCH 11

(HAGİOS GEORGİOS PATRİKHANE KİLİSESİ)

The Patriarchate Church located in the courtyard of Greek Orthodox Patriarchate was built in 1720 over the old church. The

Hagios Georgios Patriarchate Church.

Fener Greek High School.

church has three naves and the middle nave is covered with vaults and side naves are covered with plain ceiling. At the west of the main location, the gallery over the narthex bulges to the main location over side naves.

Iconostasis, ambon and the throne of the patriarch covering three naves is ornamented with engravings and reliefs. Icons and sacred goods from other churches were collected here since it was the patriarchate church.

For this reason, it is a church rich in icons. The stone that is believed to have been used to flaggelate Jesus, the most important one of the sacred goods was brought here from Jerusalem and placed at the south section of Iconostasis.

Also, the three coffins of the relics that belong to Saint Eufemia, Teophano and Solomoni are located at the south nave.

FENER GREEK HIGH SCHOOL (12)

(FENER RUM LİSESİ)

Sancaktar Yokuşu Street No: 36 Fener

The glorious school building at the high sections of Fener built in 1880 is among the symbols of the Golden Horn with its red color and dome architectural structure. It is also named as "Red High School" because it was made with red bricks. Its architect is Dimadis.

PANAGIA MUHLIOTISSA (Mother Mary) CHURCH (13)

(PANAGİA MUHLİOTİSSA *'Meryem Ana'* KİLİSESİ)

Firketeci Street No: 1 Fener

You may reach the church right beside Fener Greek High School across the west door by turning around the high school. Maria, the daughter of Emperor Michael Palaiologos VIII (1261-82) had it built on her own land in 13th century. It is the only church that was built during Byzantine times and still functions today. It was damaged by the fires in 1633, 1640 and 1729 and as a result of the repairs, its West and South were extended. The middle of the church with a plan of a clover is covered by a high tambourine dome with bricks on it. Other arms of the clover are covered with low half domes. The wooden iconostasis on the East of the main location, despot chair and ambon are ornamented with herbal motifs in engravings and reliefs. The icons at the lower line of the iconostasis are silver covered works that were ornamented as reliefs in 1884.

SVETİ STEFAN (14) BULGARIAN CHURCH

(BULGAR KİLİSESİ)

Mürsel Paşa Avenue, Fener

By the shore of the Golden Horn, it is founded in the middle of the courtyard covered with bars. It is among the most interesting churches in Istanbul as of architecture and it was made completely out of cast-iron. When the previous small wooden church the Bulgars had here was not sufficient anymore, decision was made to build a new church. Architect Hovsep Aznavur, considering that the construction area is filled soil which would make it unsafe, suggested to build it from mountable steel profiles. Cast-iron skeleton method was preferred instead of armored concrete because it was much lighter. The pieces produced at Viena were carried by ship to Istanbul in 1896 through Danube River and Black Sea. In 1898, after a work of 1,5 years, the church was placed to its loca-

Sveti Stefan Bulgarian Church.

tion today. The carrier profiles of the church were made of steel and it was covered with sheet and cast plates.

On the six bells of Sveti Stefan Church that was constructed in Neogothic style, it is written that they were prepared in the city Yaroslavl. There are gallery floors in "U" shape over two naves and that start over the narthex. The iconostasis is ornamented with icons depicting the scenes Saint Stephan, Saint Petrus, Baptist Yahya, Mary and Child Jesus. The grave of the first Bulgarian Patriarch is carefully kept at the church used by the Bulgarians living in Istanbul.

ATİK MUSTAFA PASHA MOSQUE

(ATİK MUSTAFA PAŞA *'Hazret-i Cabir'* CAMİİ)
Çember Street No: 4 Ayvansaray

Further down Balat hospital, it is on Çember Street that is connected with the shore. This historical structure, named as Cabir Mosque with the belief that Hazret-i Cabir was buried there, is an old Byzantine church that was turned into a mosque in 1490. The construction date of the church is unknown. Some claim that it used to be dedicated to Petrus and Marcus and then that it

Atik Mustafa Pasha Mosque.

was a church where Thekla, the daughter of Emperor Theophilos (829-842) retreated but none of these have been proved. The building was damaged in 1894 earthquake and was left empty until 1906 and continued to function as a mosque after it was renewed.

The central dome of the structure with a closed cross plan that sits on a low tambour has the Turkish architectural style and it was made in the place of the original dome. Its southeast wall consists of three apses that bulge to the outside. In the apse on the south, there is the post of Cabir bin Abdullah el-Ensari among the sahabas (people who have seen the prophet) of Prophet Muhammed. In 1957, American Byzantine Institute brought to light the frescoes of Kosmas and Damianos among the saints of medicine origin and Prime Angel Michael from under the paint in the south front of the structure. These frescoes are covered with wood.

When we complete our tour in Ayvansaray, Golden Horn Bridge connecting two sides of Golden Horn comes out before us. Our tour route separates into two here. We enter the borders of Eyüp attending the bridge, following the coast. There is **Eyüp Sultan Mosque** and **Mausoleum** which is mostly the visiting place of Muslim community. The road heading south from Golden Horn Bridge is connected with Edirnekapı and Topkapı. Eğrikapı is located on the high sections of Ayvansaray. You will reach the cemetery in five minutes if you follow the walking-track near the avenue. You will see Eğrikapı, one of the gates of Istanbul here. Enter from Eğrikapı and you will reach Tekfur palace by following the ascent parallel to the walls and Şişhane Avenue. Kariye Museum is just five minutes away from Tekfur Palace. Check the "from Kariye to Tekfur" titled subject for this *(p. 109)*.

Interior view of Eyüp Sultan Mosque.

EYÜP SULTAN MOSQUE

(EYÜP SULTAN CAMİİ)
Kalender Hane Avenue
No: 12 Eyüp

It is at the point where Kalender Hane Street and Camii Kebir Street intersect. Ebu Eyyüb El-Ensari (Halid Bin Zeyd) who joined the siege of Istanbul in 7th century with Emevi army was buried upon his will at the point where the armies could proceed the furthest. He welcomed Hz. Muhammed to his home in 622 when he was immigrating to Medina and then did not leave him and joined wars as his flag man. After the conquest of Istanbul by the Ottomans, it is claimed that Akşemsettin found the

grave and upon this Fatih Sultan Mehmet had the mosque and tomb built here between 1458 and 1459.

The outside courtyard including the mosque and the tomb can be entered from two doors in southeast and southwest. The southeast door opens to the platform that goes up to royal loge of the mosque. In the middle of the outside courtyard, there is a marble fountain.

The mosque became ruined also due to the effect of 1766 earthquake and Selim III (1789-1807) had the building torn down except for the minarets and had today's mosque built in its place between 1798 and 1800. Octagon plan with a central dome supported by tromp l'oeils was applied when the mosque was built. Its inner courtyard has a rectangular plan. The main location covered from its three sides with gallery floors is covered with a dome with a diameter of 17,5 meters that sits on six independent columns and two arches buried in the wall of the *mihrab*.

Located in the inner courtyard of the mosque, across the last congregation place, **Eyüp Sultan Tomb** is among

Entrance to the Tomb.

the most visited tombs of Istanbul since it is covered with tiles inside. It achieved today's form as a result of the repairs made by Ahmet I (1603-1617). Selim III had the silver gridiron made with a rich ornamentation surrounding the sarcophagus.

Eyüp Sultan Mosque gravure.

Eyüp Sultan Mosque and its fountain.

MİNİATÜRK

İmrahor Avenue, Sütlüce
It can be visited between 09:00-17:00

Miniaturk across the shore of the Golden Horn where we visited the historical structures was opened in 2003. It is the museum where important places and historical works in Turkey are exhibited as well as a model of the Ottoman geography.

With an area of 60.000 sqm, over 100 models are displayed.

General view of Miniatürk.

HOTELS

TURİNG AYASOFYA KONAKLARI

Soğukçeşme Street 34400, Sultanahmet
☎ **+90 (212) 513 36 60 (12 Lines)**
€€€
www.ayasofyapensions.com
✉ info@ayasofyapensions.com

YEŞİL EV HOTEL

Kabasakal Avenue No: 5 Sultanahmet
☎ **+90 (212) 517 67 85 (4 Lines)**
€€€€
www.yesilev.com.tr
✉ info@yesilev.com.tr

AND HOTEL ★★★☆☆

Yerebatan Avenue Cami Çıkmazı No:36-40 Sultanahmet €€ www.andhotel.com
☎ **+90 (212) 512 02 07**

HOTEL GOLDEN HORN

Binbirdirek Mah. Binbirdirek Square Street No: 1 Sultanahmet
☎ **+90 (212) 518 17 17**
€€
www.goldenhornhotel.com
✉ info@goldenhornhotel.com

ACROPOL HOTEL

Akbıyık Avenue No: 25 Sultanahmet
☎ **+90 (212) 638 90 21**
€€€
www.acropolhotel.com
✉ info@acropolhotel.com

ARENA HOTEL

Küçükayasofya Mah. Şehit Mehmet Paşa Yokuşu, Üçler Hamam Street No: 13-15 Sultanahmet
€€
☎ **+90 (212) 458 03 64**
www.arenahotel.com
✉ info@arenahotel.com

ARMADA HOTEL ★★★★☆

Ahırkapı Street No: 24 Sultanahmet
€€
☎ **+90 (212) 455 44 55**
www.armadahotel.com.tr
✉ info@armadahotel.com.tr

SULTANAHMET SARAYI

Torun Street No: 19 Sultanahmet
☎ **+90 (212) 458 04 60 (Pbx)**
€€€€
www.sultanahmetpalace.com

VALİDE SULTAN KONAĞI

Cankurtaran Mah. İshakpaşa Avenue Kutlu Gün Street No: 1 Sultanahmet
☎ **+90 (212) 517 65 58 (Pbx)**
€€
www.hotelvalidesultan.com
✉ vsultan@hotelvalidesultan.com

BLUE HOUSE HOTEL ★★★☆☆

Dalbastı Street No: 14 Sultanahmet
☎ **+90 (212) 638 90 10 (Pbx)**
€€€
www.bluehouse.com.tr
✉ info@bluehouse.com.tr

CELAL SULTAN HOTEL ★★☆☆☆

Yerebatan Avenue Salkımsöğüt Street No: 16 Sultanahmet
€€€
☎ **+90 (212) 520 93 23-24**
✉ info@celalsultan.com
www.celalsultan.com

ERESİN CROWN HOTEL

Küçükayasofya Avenue No:40 Sultanahmet
+ 90 (212) 638 44 28
€€€
www.eresincrown.com.tr
✉ eresin@eresincrown.com.tr

FOUR SEASONS ★★★★★

Tevkifhane Street No: 1 Sultanahmet
€€€€€
☎ **+90 (212) 402 30 00**
www.fourseasons.com/istanbul

HOTEL PİERRE LOTİ ★★★☆☆

Piyerloti Avenue No: 5 Çemberlitaş
☎ **+90 (212) 518 57 00**
www.pierrelotihotel.com
✉ info@pierrelotihotel.com

HOTEL ARCADİA

Dr.İmran Öktem Avenue No:1 Sultanahmet
☎ **+90 (212) 516 96 96**
€€
www.hotelarcadiaistanbul.com
✉ info@hotelarcadiaistanbul.com

HOTEL MEGARA PALACE

İshakpaşa Avenue No: 8 Sultanahmet
☎ **+90 (212) 518 36 56**
€€
www.megarahotel.com
✉ info@megarahotel.com

KALYON HOTEL ★★★★☆

Sahil yolu No: 34 Sultanahmet
☎ **+90 (212) 517 44 00**
€€
www.kalyon.com
✉ kalyon@kalyon.com

€ **Up to 50 Euros.** €€ **Between 50 and 100 Euros.** €€€ **Between 100 and 150 Euros.**

HOTELS

TASHKONAK HOTEL

Küçük Ayasofya Avenue Tomurcuk Street No: 5 Sultanahmet
☎ **+90 (212) 518 28 82 (Pbx)**
€
www.hoteltashkonak.com
✉ info@hoteltashkonak.com

HOTEL YUSUF PAŞA KONAĞI

Cankurtaran Avenue, No: 34 Sultanahmet
☎ **+90 (212) 458 00 01 (Pbx)**
€€
www.yusufpasakonagi.com
✉ info@yusufpasakonagi.com

SARNIÇ HOTEL

Küçükayasofya Avenue No.26 Sultanahmet
☎ **+90 (212) 518 23 23**
www.sarnichotel.com
✉ info@sarnichotel.com

HOTEL AMBER

Çifte Gelinler Avenue No: 3 Kumkapı
☎ **+90 (212) 518 48 01**
www.hotelamber.com
✉ info@hotelamber.com

AMBASSADOR HOTEL

Divanyolu Ticarethane Street No: 19 Sultanahmet
☎ **+90 (212) 512 00 02**
€€
www.hotelambassador.com

AZİYADE HOTEL ★★★★☆

Piyerloti Avenue No: 62 Gedikpaşa-Sultanahmet
☎ **+90 (212) 638 22 00 (pbx)**
€€
www.aziyadehotel.com
✉ info@aziyadehotel.com

ORSEP HOTEL

Nöbethane Avenue No : 10 Sirkeci
☎ **+90 (212) 511 85 85**
€€
www.orseproyalhotel.com
✉ info@orseproyalhotel.com

SERES HOTEL

Hüdavendigar Avenue 49 Sirkeci
☎ **+90 (212) 519 30 20**
€€
www.sereshotel.com

YAŞMAK HOTEL ★★★★☆

Ebusuud Avenue 14-20 Sirkeci
☎ **+90 (212) 528 13 43**
€€
www.hotelyasmaksultan.com

BEYAZ SARAY THE HOTEL

Yeniçeriler Avenue No: 85 Beyazıt
€€€
☎ **+90 (212) 458 98 00**
www.beyazsaray.com
✉ info@beyazsaray.com

ANTİK HOTEL ★★★★☆

Ordu Avenue Sekbanbaşı (Darphane) Street No: 10 Beyazıt
☎ **+90 (212) 638 58 58**
www.antik-hotel.com
✉ info@antikhotel.com

BARIN HOTEL ★★★☆☆

Fevziye Avenue No: 7 Şehzadebaşı
☎ **+90 (212) 513 91 00 - 513 13 33**
€€
www.barinhotel.com
✉ info@barinhotel.com

HOTEL ERBOY ★★★☆☆

Ebusuud Avenue No: 32, Sirkeci
☎ **+90 (212) 513 37 50 - 513 37 51**
€€
www.erboyhotel.com
✉ erboy@erboyhotel.com

ERESİN TOPKAPI HOTEL

Millet Avenue No: 186 Topkapı
☎ **+90 (212) 631 12 12**
€€€€€
✉ eresintopkapi.res2@barcelo.com

AKGÜN HOTEL ★★★★★

Adnan Menderes Bulvarı Topkapı
☎ **+90 (212) 534 48 79 (20 lines)**
€€
www.akgunhotel.com
✉ info@akgunhotel.com

HOLIDAY INN İSTANBUL ★★★★☆

Millet Avenue No: 189 Topkapı
☎ **+90 (212) 530 99 00**
€€€€
www.hiistanbulcity.com
✉ info@hiistanbulcity.com

KARİYE HOTEL

Kariye Camii Street No. 6 Edirnekapı
☎ **+90 (212) 534 8414**
€€
www.kariyeotel.com
✉ info@kariyeotel.com

€€€€ **Between 150 and 200 Euros.** €€€€€ **250 Euros and more.**

WHAT TO EAT AND DRINK?

After your visit to Sultanahmet, you shouldn't leave without eating **Sultanahmet Köftesi** *(Sultanahmet meatball)* at the **Tarihi Sultanahmet Köftecisi** (Historical Sultanahmet Meatball Restaurant). You can prefer *Piyaz* (cold dish made with dried beans) and *İrmik Helvası* (dessert made of semolina, oil and sugar) and also *Shish kebab* (meat on skewers) with meatball. The various restaurants in **Yeşil Ev** and **Soğuk Çeşme Sokağı** (Soğuk Çeşme Street) offer you different options. When you go downwards from the Ahmet III Fountain, which is in front of the Topkapı Palace, the second street on your right (*Akbıyık Avenue*) is completely full of tourist hotels, restaurants and bars. The **fish restaurants** in **Kumkapı** serve dishes of sea food and Traditional Turkish Cuisine. Turkish and foreign tourists usually go to Kumkapı to eat fish and remove the fatigue of the day with a few glasses of alcohol. In Kumkapı, while you are having your dinner you can enjoy yourself with the music of amateur street musicians and watch the *Oriental Dance Shows* at the following hours. You can have your meal and drink something looking at the view of the Golden Horn and the Bosphorus in the fish restaurants and cafes of **Galata Bridge** in Eminönü. Moreover, you can taste **balık ekmek** *(fish served in bread)* which are prepared and served on the boats on the shore of Eminönü.

In the **Gar Restaurant** at Sirkeci Train Station, you can find a wide range of Turkish Cuisine dishes. Just on the top of the street you can taste the dishes of Turkish-Ottoman Cuisine in **Konyalı** and the desserts of **Bolulu Hasan Usta**, also try the products of fast-food shops and *simit (savory roll covered with sesame seed)* shops.

Hamdi Restaurant at Eminönü Meydanı (Eminönü Square) offers you not only dishes of the Turkish Cuisine, but also the oriental dishes. The historical **Pandeli Restaurant** in the **Mısır Çarşısı** (Spice Bazaar) offers only lunch and it is a nice restaurant with traditional dishes. This restaurant, the authentically decorated walls of which are furnished with photographs witnessing famous people tasting their meals, must definitely be visited.

There are many restaurants in Sultanahmet and in its neighborhood. In the pide (pita with various ingredients) shops and buffets in Cağaloğlu, you can eat cheaper meals, and you can also find products more familiar to you at the fast-food restaurants, bakers and pizza restaurants on Divanyolu Street, which goes to Beyazıt. You can have a rest and take a tea-coffee break at **Bedestan Cafes** in **Kapalıçarşı** (Grand Bazaar). If you are tired after your trip, having a break at historical places will help you relax. On the part of Divanyolu Street, which reaches to Beyazıt, at **Çorlulu Ali Pasha Madrasah** on the right, you can have a tea-coffee break and savor the pleasure of *nargile* (hubble-bubble, a type of smoking pipe used in eastern countries in which the smoke is filtered through a water pipe before reaching the inhaler pipe). Another alternative is **Darüzziyafe**, which offers service at the soup kitchen of Süleymaniye Mosque's *Complex*, complex of buildings adjacent to a mosque, in Süleymaniye neighbourhood and carries on the Ottoman dining culture with its historical texture.

Eminönü.

RESTAURANTS-CAFES

AYASOFYA KONAKLARI
Soğukçeşme Street 34400, Sultanahmet
☎ **+90 (212) 513 36 60 (12 Lines)**
www.ayasofyapensions.com

YEŞİL EV
Kabasakal Avenue No: 5 Sultanahmet
☎ **+90 (0212) 517 67 85 (4 hat)**
www.yesilev.com.tr
✉ info@yesilev.com.tr

AND RESTAURANT
Yerebatan Avenue 36-40, Sultanahmet
☎ **+90 (0212) 512 02 07**

HOUSE OF MEDUSA
Yerebatan Avenue No: 19 Sultanahmet
☎ **+90 (0212) 511 41 16**
www.medusarestaurant.com
✉ info@medusarestaurant.com

SULTANAHMET KÖFTECİSİ
Divanyolu Avenue No. 12, Sultanahmet
☎ **+90 (0212) 513 64 68 - 520 05 66**
www.sultanahmetkoftesi.com

ORIENT EXPRESS
İstasyon Avenue Sirkeci Train Station No. 2, Sirkeci
☎ **+90 (0212) 522 22 80**

EROL RESTAURANT
Çatalçeşme Street No.3 Cağaloğlu
☎ **+90 (0212) 511 03 22**

KARADENİZ SOFRASI
Divanyolu Avenue Dr. Eminpaşa Street No. 16 Sultanahmet
☎ **+90 (0212) 526 72 02-03**

BALIKÇI SABAHATTİN
Seyit Hasan Kuyu Street Cankurtaran Mah. Sultanahmet
☎ **+90 (0212)** 458 18 24

VONALI CELAL
Kennedy Caddesi Sahil Yolu No: 40/1 Ahırkapı / Cankurtaran
☎ **+90 (0212) 516 18 93 - 517 68 84**
www.vonalicelal.net
✉ vonali@vonalicelal.net

BEDESTEN CAFE & PATISSERIE
Bedesten Cafe & Patisserie Cevahir Bedesteni No: 143-151 Kapalıçarşı
☎ **+90 (0212) 520 2250**
www.cafebedesten.com
✉ bedesten@cafebedesten.com

ŞARK KAHVESİ
Yağlıkcılar Avenue 134 İşbank yanı Kapalıçarşı
☎ **+90 (0212) 512 11 44**
www.sarkkahvesi.com
✉ info@sarkkahvesi.com

YENGEÇ BALIK RESTAURANT
Telli Odalar Street No: 6 Kumkapı
☎ **+90 (0212) 516 32 27**
www.yengecrestaurant.com
✉ info@yengecrestaurant.com

HAMDİ ET LOKANTASI
Tahmis Avenue Kalçın St. No. 17 Eminönü
☎ **+90 (0212) 528 03 90**
www.hamdirestorant.com.tr

DARÜZZİYAFE
Şifahane Street No: 6 34430 Süleymaniye
☎ **+90 (0212) 511 84 14**
www.daruzziyafe.com.tr
✉ daruzziyafe@daruzziyafe.com.tr

KABURGA SOFRASI
Şekerci Street No: 8 Aksaray
☎ **+90 (0212) 532 73 73**
www.kaburgasofrasi.com

EROL TAŞ KÜLTÜR MERKEZİ RESTAURANT
Cankurtaran Square No: 18
☎ **+90 (0212) 518 12 57 (3 Hat)**

PUDDING SHOP LALE RESTAURANT
Divanyolu Avenue No: 6, Sultanahmet
☎ **+90 (0212) 522 29 70 - 511 05 39**
www.puddingshop.com

SULTAN PUB RESTAURANT
Divanyolu Avenue No: 2 Sultanahmet
☎ **+90 (0212) 528 17 19 (pbx)**
www.sultanpub.com.tr
✉ sultanpub@sultan pub.com.tr

KÖR AGOP RESTAURANT
Ördekli Bakkal Street No. 7 Kumkapı
☎ **+90 (0212) 517 23 34**

YENGEÇ RESTAURANT
Çaparikız Street Kumkapı
☎ **+90 (0212) 516 32 27**

BUHARA OCAKBAŞI
Nuruosmaniye Avenue No.7/A Cağaloğlu
☎ **+90 (0212) 527 51 33**

SHOPPING

Rich varieties of the Spice Bazaar (Mısır Çarşısı).

Mosque Lamp.

Hand-made decorated plate in Kütahya.

If shopping is mentioned, what comes to mind first at the Historical Peninsula are the historical bazaars. **Grand Bazaar**, which is the most popular among them, offers a wide range of alternatives with thousands of shops if you want to buy jewellery and souveniers. It is possible to find different examples of Turkish arts from carpets to jewellery embroidered richly, silver, copper, ceramic souvenirs and leather products. After you do your shopping, you can have a rest at the cafeterias and restaurants in the bazaar. The bazaar where bargaining is a part of tradition is *open from 7 a.m. to 7 p.m. except Sundays.* Spice, dried fruits, delight, delicatessen and marriage portions for those to get married are sold in the **Spice Bazaar** in Eminönü. You can buy fresh ground Turkish Coffee from the famous **Kurukahveci Mehmet Efendi** opposite the western door. Like Grand Bazaar, Spice Bazaar is closed on Sundays as well. Various plants and pets are sold at **Çiçek Pazarı** (Flower Market) just by the Spice Bazaar. There are shops that sell various jewellery, carpets and souvenirs on Nuruosmaniye Street. It is possible to find souvenir shops at and around Sultanahmet Square, at **Sipahi (Arasta) Bazaar**. You can find all kinds of textile products on and around the Mahmutpaşa Yokuşu (Muratpaşa narrow climbing street) between the Grand Bazaar and the Spice Bazaar.

Carpet.

Shopping at Atmeydanı.
HIPPODROME
Atmeydanı Street No.15-17
Sultanahmet.

Turkish Delight.

Ceramic Ewer.

TRANSPORT

Kabataş-Zeytinburnu line tramway.

Transport within the region:

It is always practical to use the tramway when you go to the other neighbourhoods from Sultanahmet. You can go on foot to Çemberlitaş, Beyazıt, Süleymaniye, Aksaray regions, which are close to Sultanahmet.

From Sultanahmet to Eminönü: From Sultanahmet, you can go to Eminönü either by tramway or you can go to Sirkeci and Eminönü on foot by following the tramway route or through the Bab-ı Ali Avenue, which starts at Mahmut II's Tomb.

Yedikule Fortress-Kariye (Chora): You can get on the public buses which leave from Eminönü and Beyazıt to see Yedikule Hisarı (Yedikule Fortress) and Kariye. You can also go to Yedikule Fortress by Sirkeci-Halkalı train.

Fener-Balat: You can go to Fener-Balat by Fener-Balat public buses that depart from Eminönü.

Tourist City Tour: Travel buses that depart from Sultanahmet Square do city tour around the Historical Peninsula and Beyoğlu. Moreover, you can have a nostalgic tour on phaetons at the square.

Transport to Outside of the Region:

Taksim-Istiklal Avenue: There are different ways to go to Taksim and Istiklal Avenue:

1) *The first route is using the Kabataş-Zeytinburnu tramway and funicular system.* Tramway takes you to Kabataş. From Kabataş you can get to Taksim Square in three minutes with the Kabataş-Taksim subway line that works with funicular system.

2) *The second route is by tramway, but this time by using the Tunnel.* You should get off at Karaköy stop of the tramway. By getting on the Tunnel subway in Karaköy, you can get to Tunnel Square, the end of Istiklal Avenue in a short time.

3) *If you are in Aksaray (Atatürk Boulevard) or Eminönü,* you can get to Taksim by public buses.

4) *If you are in Eminönü,* another alternative is walking. Go to Karaköy by walking over Galata Bridge. You can get to Tunnel Square by following the Yüksek Kaldırım Avenue.

On this route are the **Galata Tower** and **Galata Mevlevihanesi**.

Dolmabahçe Palace: The palace is a short distance after Kabataş, which is the last stop of the tramway. You can walk to **Beşiktaş** from there, but if you want to go to **Ortaköy**, you should get on the buses that go from Kabataş towards the Bosphorus.

Transport from Eminönü on Ferry Boat: There is a pier where there are ferryboats going to three different directions; they are **Üsküdar**, **Kadıköy**, **Bosphorus** lines. Üsküdar and Kadıköy ferries are every 20 minutes. The Bosphorus line provides you with the possibility to see the Bosphorus by stopping off at various ferry boat piers. Moreover, you can have a one and half hour Bosphorus cruise on the ferry boats departing from Eminönü.

Ferry boats of city lines, which have an important role in public transport.

Transport by Train: From Sirkeci Train Station, there are train services to various European cities, and also the Sirkeci-Halkalı train service works in the city.

This train that departs from Sirkeci Station reaches at Halkalı by going along the Marmara shore of the Historical Peninsula.

See the general Transport part (page 193) for the tramway routes, and some bus routes in Eminönü and Beyazıt.

ATTENTION!

The tramway that offers service on Kabataş-Zeytinburnu-Airport route works between 6 a.m. and 12 p.m.

THE FORMATION OF MODERN ISTANBUL FROM GALATA TO PERA (BEYOĞLU)

Bas-reliefs on the doors of Rumeli Inn.

The Genoans who settled in the shores of the Golden Horn with the privileges they gained from Byzantines in the period of Manuel Komnenos I (1143-1180) lost their place to Venetians when the Latins invaded Istanbul in 1204. For this reason they started to settle in the land across to Galata. They continued their free commerce in Galata as a result of the agreement they made after Byzantine state took Istanbul back in 1261.

When the Byzantine became weaker, the borders of Genoa extended to Galata Tower on the north, Azapkapı and Tophane in the shore of the Golden Horn.

Until 16th century, today's Beyoğlu was covered with grass and groves. When the rule of a permanent embassy practice started in 1535, the first embassy buildings started to be built here. During the period of Kanuni Sultan Süleyman, as a result of good relations with France, permission was given for the French embassy to be founded outside of Galata, to Pera that would develop in the future. This area of today's French Palace is at Nuri Ziya Street surrounded by court walls. After this first embassy that was founded, Venetian and British embassies and Denmark Embassy at the beginning of 17th century settled at this area, however, still it only remained as a small population. The settlement at this period was at the section from Galata until Galatasaray Square.

The important event for Beyoğlu to form its identity today is the **Tanzimat Fermanı** (Reform Decree) declared in 1839. With this declaration, the foreigners had more assurances and had the right to own a property. Then with their financial abilities, came a period when they constructed buildings in the style that they want.

On **Istiklal Avenue** as its name today and on the streets that open to it, a small formation emerged similar to European cities with buildings, passages, hotels, theatres, night clubs and bookstores. The bridge for pedestrians opened in 1838 between Unkapanı-Azapkapı and Galata Bridge opened in 1845, and thus two main centers of the city were connected to each other.

When the fire in Beyoğlu destroyed the wooden structures in 1870, new buildings were made in their places with engravings and reliefs on their fronts.

In the 19th century, Pera's population consisted mostly of Levantines, Greek, Armenian and Jewish minorities who were in good condition economically. The region enabled people of different culture mosaic with Ottoman citizenship to live together for long years. There were many churches and synagogues in the region due to the abundance of foreigners and minorities. Ten thousands of Russian people who flew away from Russia with the revolution of 1917 were added to this interesting population mosaics.

After Republic was declared, with the taxes applied to non-Muslims in 1942, many wealthy merchants and businessman left Istanbul. Greek population decreased with insecurities and with the foundation of Israil state, most of the Jewish went there. Thus in the second half of the 20th century, the population structure of Beyoğlu changed in favour of Turks.

Today, with the transformation of commercial activities to various regions of the city aiming higher income groups, the area became a center where commercial and entertainment places aims middle income groups. It is still the most interesting place in Istanbul due to the entertainment and culture life that is intense in Istiklal Avenue which is closed to vehicle traffic.

Santa Maria Inn.

European *(Avrupa)* Passage, or arcade with mirrors where souveniers are sold.

Monument of Republic at Taksim Square.

İSTİKLAL AVENUE EXTENDING TO TUNNEL (GALATA) TAKSİM SQUARE

İstiklal Avenue and nostalgic tramway.

Taksim Square is at the start of Istiklal Avenue and it crowns with a Monument of Republic. The monument made by Italian sculptor Pietro Canonica was placed to its place in 1928 after a work of 2,5 years. It is 11 meters high and one face of it represents Republic period and the other represents War of Independence. On its south front, there are depictions of Mustafa Kemal Atatürk with civil clothes, his friends İsmet İnönü, Fevzi Çakmak and the people. On its north front, there is Atatürk with his military clothing as the leader of armies of men and women. At the West and East of the monument, soldiers are depicted with flags in their hands.

On the north of Taksim Square, there is a park named *Taksim Gezi* and the building rising behind it is Ceylan Inter-Continental. Behind Continental, Hilton Hotel is within a large garden. At the east of Taksim Square, there

Atatürk Cultural Center.

Etap Marmara Hotel.

is metro station that goes between Levent and Kabataş and at the east end of the square, there is **Atatürk Cultural Center** (A.K.M.) and The Marmara Hotel. A.K.M. is a multi functional culture center used for music, exhibition and conferences. The road that goes down next to it is İnönü Avenue and it goes to the place of Dolmabahçe Palace.

On the south of the square, there is Sıra Selviler Avenue reaching German Hospital and parallel to it, there is Istiklal Avenue. The nostalgical tramvay that turns around the Monument of Republic serves until the Tunnel throughout Istiklal Avenue. Before the tramway, there were tramways with two floors on horse. Istiklal Avenue is one of the liveliest streets of Istanbul with the stores and passages, movie theaters and theaters, bookstores, café, restaurants in two sides of the road and bars on intersecting roads and a crowd that never ends until after midnight. At the start of the street, on the right, there is the French Consulate. Meşelik Street that is on the left goes to **Hagia Triada Church** that can also be seen from the square.

Taksim Square gate to Taksim-4.Levent and Taksim-Kabataş subways.

Subway line stop.

Taksim-Kabataş Funicular stop.

Polis Police
Hastane Hospital
Cami Mosque
Kilise Church
Otel Hotel
PTT PTT
Sağlık Ocağı Health Clinic
Saray-Kasır Palace-Summer Palace
Surlar City Walls
Tarihi Anıt Historical Monument
Türbe Tomb
Tramvay Durağı Tramway Stop
Tramvay Hattı Tramway Line
Tren Yolu Train Line
CAD. Avenue
Sk. Street
Taksim
Eminönü
Üsküdar
Taksim Square 1 (Taksim Meydanı)
İstiklal Avenue 2 (İstiklal Caddesi)
Hagia Triada Greek Church 3 (Hagia Triada Rum Kilisesi)
Ağa Mosque 4 (Ağa Camii)
Galatasaray High School 5 (Galatasaray Lisesi)
Flower Passage 6 (Çiçek Pasajı)
European Passage 7 (Avrupa Pasajı)
Pera Palace 8 (Pera Palas)
Saint Antonio Church 9 (Saint Antonio Kilisesi)
Santa Maria Church 10 (Santa Maria Kilisesi)
Tunnel 11 (Tünel)
Galata Mevlevi Lodge 12 (Galata Mevlevihanesi)
Galata Tower 13 (Galata Kulesi)
Galata Bridge 14 (Galata Köprüsü)
Arap Mosque 15 (Arap Camii)
Unkapanı Bridge 16 (Unkapanı Köprüsü)
Yeraltı Mosque 17 (Yeraltı Camii)
Surp Krikor Lusavoriç Church 18 (Surp Krikor Kilisesi)
Kılıç Ali Pasha Mosque 19 (Kılıç Ali Paşa Camii)
Tophane Fountain 20 (Tophane Çeşmesi)
Nusretiye Mosque 21 (Nusretiye Camii)

TOMTOM
EVLİYA ÇELEBİ
ŞAHKULU
HACIMİMİ
EMEKYEMEZ
BEREKETZADE
MÜEYYEDZADE
KEMANKEŞ KARAMUSTAFA PAŞA
ARAP CAMİ
MECLİS-İ MEBUSAN CAD.
KILIÇALİ PAŞA CAD.
KEMERALTI CAD.
LÜLECİ HENDEK CAD.
YÜKSEK KALDIRIM CAD.
GALİP DEDE CAD.
SERDAR-I EKREM CAD.
BÜYÜK HENDEK CAD.
KÜÇÜK HENDEK CAD.
İLK BELEDİYE CAD.
ŞAİR ZİYA PAŞA CAD.
OKÇU MUSA CAD.
PERŞEMBE PAZARI CAD.
BANKALAR CAD.
TERSANE CAD.
YOLCUZADE İSKENDER CAD.
SADİ KONURALP CAD.
YELKENCİLER CAD.
FERMENECİLER CAD.
MAKARACILAR CAD.
KARAKÖY CAD.
KEMANKEŞ CAD.
RIHTIM CAD.
MUMHANE CAD.
MALİYE CAD.
NECATİBEY CAD.
LÜLECİLER CAD.
KARABAŞ CAD.
SANATKARLAR CAD.
TERSANE KAVŞAĞI
Tünel
Şişhane
Karaköy
Tophane
Nusretiye Camii
Nusretiye Kasrı
Amerikan Pazarı Sk.
T.D.İ. İst Salı Pazarı Terminali
Karaköy İDO Deniz Otobüsü İskelesi
Karaköy Vapur İskelesi
Karaköy İDO Şehir Hatları İskelesi
Galata Kulesi
Beyoğlu Belediye Başkanlığı
Galip Dede Türbesi
Perşembe Pazarı Parkı
Sokullu Mehmet Paşa Camii
Azapkapı Çeşmesi
Kılıç Ali Paşa Camii
Karaköy Karakolu
Alman Galata Polikliniği
Yeraltı Camii
Mimar Sinan Üniversitesi Kültür ve Sanat Merkezi
Tarık Zafer Tunaya Kültür Merkezi
Özel Alman Lisesi
Özel Saint Benoit Fransız Lisesi
Sen Piyer Kilisesi
Okçumusa Camii
Modern Palas
Makbul İbrahim Paşa Camii
Türkiye Denizcilik İşletmeleri Hastanesi
Beyoğlu Hastanesi

HAGIA TRIADA GREEK CHURCH ③

(HAGİA TRİADA RUM KİLİSESİ)
Meşelik Street No: 7

At the location of the church, there used to be Greek cemetery. At this cemetery, there was also a wooden church that was dedicated to Hagios Georgios. After Tanzimat Fermanı (Reforms Decree) was declared, the Patriarchate that took the permission to make a church, built Zapyon Girls School in the place of the wooden church and removed some parts of the cemetery and built Hagia Triada Church. Architect Vasilaki Ioannidi started to build it in 1867 and then it was opened to worship thirteen years later on Sunday, 14th September, 1880. Hagia Triada is within a large courtyard that is surrounded by high walls. In the courtyard, there are dormitories and official buildings that belong to the church as well as a holy spring dedicated to Hagios Georgios. The structure constructed as a basilica with a dome carries the characteristics of European eclectical architecture. The apse behind the marble iconostasis is covered with a half dome and can be ascended with three steps. At the fronts of the galleries stretching in two sides of the galleries, there are icons. Hagia Triada Church exhibits a rich look as of its motifs, frescoes and relief techniques.

Hagia Triada Greek Orthodox Church.

AĞA MOSQUE ④

(AĞA CAMİİ)
Mahyacı Street No: 2

The only mosque over Istiklal Avenue is on the right section within a courtyard separated from the street with its dome. It is at the point where Sakızağacı Avenue intersects with Istiklal Avenue. Its main entrance is on Mahyacı Street but it also has an entrance from Istiklal Street. It was built by Galatasaray Ağası Hüseyin Ağa in 1594 and repaired in 1834.

The roof of the small structure with a rectangular plan and without a dome as well as the sides of its windows, is ornamented with classical pen crafts. At the entrance section, there is women's mahfil. The fountain in its courtyard was brought from Sinan Pasha Mosque built by Mimar Sinan in Kasımpasa and that did not reach today.

Ağa Mosque.

Post office building (PTT) is directly at the opposite of Galatasaray High School. Yeni Çarşı Avenue descending from here joins with Boğazkesen Avenue and comes out to Tophane the district where **Kılıç Ali Pasha Mosque** is (*See page 126-127 for map*).

GALATASARAY HIGH SCHOOL ⑤

(GALATASARAY LİSESİ)
İstiklal Avenue,
Galatasaray Square

Devshirme boys brought to Istanbul were trained at Galata Palace School founded during the period of Bayezid II (1481-1512). Until 19th century, it kept its identity of being a preparation school for candidates of Enderun which is the palace school. Along with its dormitory, it had a mosque, hammam and *dar al-shifa*. When it was damaged in Tophane fire, Mahmut II had it repaired in 1820. After Janissary School was aban-

A store selling books and technologic products on İstiklal Avenue.

Galatasaray High School.

doned in 1826, its function to train *içoğlanı* (Enderun student) ended in 1834.

In 1838, it passed to medicine school and in 1865, it passed to preparation school for military schools and then started to function as Galatasaray High School with the name Mekteb-i Sultani on 1st September, 1868.

ÇİÇEK (FLOWER) 6, EUROPEAN 7 AND ASLI INN PASSAGES

(ÇİÇEK, AVRUPA 'AYNALI' VE ASLI HAN 'KREPEN' PASAJLARI)

Before exiting to Galatasaray Square, at the right on the point where Solakzade Street and Istiklal Avenue intersect, you will see **Tokatlıyan Han** opened in 1897 in the place of the famous hotel of the past. The building that needs repair is now used by various shops. **Flower Passage** is at the line of Tokatlıyan and it strikes attention with its front architecture and forms an important piece of Beyoğlu's historical and entertainment life. It was made in the place of Naum Theatre that was destroyed in Beyoğlu fire in 1870 and where there were three floors and a capacity of one thousand five hundred people and the new building was opened in 1875 with the name *Cite de Pera*.

İstiklal Avenue gate to Çiçek (Flower) Passage.

Its front that overlooks Istiklal Avenue has a striking look with its half columns, reliefs and the clock at its upper floor. Because of the flower selling people during war years, its name was turned into Flower Passage. Its identity of beer house and *meyhane* starting with 1930's stays permanent and attracts a vast customer potential. In 1950s when the flower selling people left the passage, new *meyhanes* were opened in their places. Today Flower Passage is among the places that attracts most of the tourists.

Following Flower Passage, Sahne Street starts where there is also Fish Bazaar. Here, there are shops that sell *kokoreç* and mussels. Further down Sahne Street that also has an entrance to Flower Passage, **Nevizade Street** on the right has locations that have the atmosphere of the passage. Another passage that opens to Fish Bazaar is European Passage on the left and it is connected with Meşrutiyet Avenue. Here you may find interesting products at the shops in two lines that sell various souvenirs. Between

Interior view of Çiçek (Flower) Passage.

Bas-reliefs on the facade of the passage.

the shops, there are giant mirrors and on the upper floors, there are women statues embedded in niches. At Aslı Han Passage parallel to the passage, there is sahaflar bazaar. The shops mainly sold clothes at its opening years and then *meyhane*s were settled in the area and now it has the identity of being a Sahaflar Bazaar where old magazines and books are sold. European Passage and Aslı Han passage parallel to

Nevizade Street.

each other open to Meşrutiyet Avenue where you may see British Consulate. Following this street, there is The Marmara Pera and historical **Pera Palas** Hotels where Odakule is connected to Istiklal Avenue.

PERA PALAS 8

(PERA PALAS)
Meşrutiyet Avenue

Despite many hotels at Beyoğlu that could not reach today, Pera Palas is outside of this group. Istanbul became livelier after the railway system extension at the end of 19th century and the city needed more comfortable hotels. Pera Palas was built in

A bookstore on İstiklal Avenue.

European Passage, or arcade with mirrors.

order to meet this need and opened for service in 1895.

The most famous train that carries passengers to Istanbul through railways was **Orient Express**. During its first years in lines between Paris-Istanbul, it started to serve with a transfer from ships between 1883 and 1977. Orient Express becoming a topic of many writers such as *Graham Greene* and *Agatha Christie* caused the train to be very famous worldwide.

The design of Pera Palas belongs to Alexandre Vallaury. The structure which is among the most beautiful examples of 19th century has nine floors along with basement floors. With classical elements, Art Nouveau style also ornaments the architecture. Among the guests of the hotel that welcomed many famous people, there were *Mustafa Kemal Atatürk, İsmet İnönü, Agatha Christie and Ernest Hemingway.*

SAINT ANTONIO CHURCH 9

(SAİNT ANTONİO KİLİSESİ)
İstiklal Avenue No: 171

At the left side of the avenue after Galatasaray Square, Saint Antonio which is a Catholic Church having the largest

Mosaic of Saint Antonio Church.

Saint Antonio Church.

caboodle in Istanbul is open to visitors. The ferroconcrete apartments in the atrium of the Church restrict the view of the church from the avenue because the atrium becomes narrow through the gates. It was build in place of Concordia Theatre which was damaged by fire, between 1906 and 1912. Architects of the building is Giulio Mongeri and Edoardo De Nari who are Italians born in Istanbul. They have built the church in Italian Neo-gothic style.

St. Antonio was depicted with *Virgin Mary, Infant Jesus and St. Francesco* in the mosaic boards that are over three entrance doors. The Church having a Latin cross plan is 20x50 meters. The building which is separated into three naves by thick buttresses is covered with squinches.

The three abscissas are four stairs higher than the naos. Stained glass windows on the north, south and east facades lighten up the church.

The sculpture of Jesus on the Cross and the timber and gold leaved sculpture of St. Antonio were made by Luigi Bresciani. There are two mosaic boards in the side abscissas depicting baptism and supper scenes. Buttresses which are connected to each other with sharp archways and form the bearing system

Nostalgic Tramway connecting Taksim Square to the Tunnel.

Facade of Santa Maria Church.

of the structure have caps adorned with large leaf patterns. The Church is administrated by Italian priests.

SANTA MARIA DRAPERIS CHURCH ⑩

(SANTA MARİA DRAPERİS KİLİSESİ)

İstiklal Avenue No: 215

Santa Maria Draperis Church is also emplaced on the left side close to the Tunnel. It sits under the avenue because it is built on a slope area. The Santa Maria Inn and public housings in between form a complex by connecting with the church. At the gates of the Santa Maria Inn which was built for making income, a Virgin Mary Statue placed in a niche attracts attention.

After the burn out of the Santa Maria Church which was built on Galata Mumhane Avenue in 1584, it was build again on the area of the house which Madame *Clara Bratola Draperis* donated and because of this, "Draperis" word was added to its name. It came through many fires, on 1769 it moved into its today's location, but the fires carried on. The building was built again and used for other purposes, then renewed and turned into a church with the permission of Abdülhamit II on 1904. There is a Virgin Mary mosaic over the entrance gate.

TUNNEL ⑪

(TÜNEL)

İstiklal Avenue ends when we arrive at the Tunnel. Tunnel is a 573 meters long historical underground public transportation system which connects Beyoğlu and Karaköy. It is important because it is the second oldest underground public transportation system.
Construction of the Tunnel started in 1871 and opening was on 18th January, 1875.

The subway connecting Tünel Square to Karaköy.

You can go down to Karaköy using the metro line on Tunnel or choose walking down from Galip Dede Avenue which is not very long. You can directly go down to Karaköy from Galip Dede Avenue which is parallel to the Tunnel passing through various music stores. There are important historical structures on this avenue. First of them is **Galata Mevlevihanesi** (Mevlevi Lodge) on the start of the avenue. When you follow the avenue down Şahkapı Street having stairs, will bring you an important historical treasure of Istanbul: **Galata Tower** (*See page 126-127 for map*).

KALE
KALE
KİLİT
KALEÇELİKKAPI
KALEÇELİKKASA
Güvenlikte Son Nokta...
www.kalecelikesya.com
KALE
ÇELİK
EŞYA
Türk Milleti'nin karakterine ve
adetlerine en uygun olan idare,
Cumhuriyet idaresidir.
İSTANBUL BÜYÜKŞEHİR BELEDİYESİ

Galata Tower, one of the symbols of Istanbul.

Entrance to Galata Mevlevi Lodge.

MEVLEVİ LODGE ⓬

(GALATA MEVLEVİHANESİ)
Galip Dede Avenue No: 15
Except Tuesdays between 09:30-16:30

It is the first *Mevlevihane* that was built in Istanbul. It is also known as *Kulekapısı* (Tower gate) *Mevlevihanesi* because it is just outside the *Kulekapısı* near the Galata Tower. It was built on the hunting ranch of Iskender Pasha, Vizier of Beyazid II at ridges of Galata in 1491. *Mevlevihane* consists of mausoleums of *Mevlevi* dervishes, library, public fountain, water tank and *semahane* (whirling place). Interior of the *semahane* is adorned with rich decorations and has an artistic atmosphere. The gallery floor carried by buttresses and columns surrounds the ceremony place of the square planned *semahane*, in an octagonal form. Top of the middle part is covered with a timber dome. *Mevlevihane* was in service until the confinement of all the lodges in Republic period in 1925. It serves as **Divan Literature Museum** affiliated to Cultural Ministry nowadays. Whirling *dervishes* make whirling ceremonies a few times a month.

GALATA TOWER ⓭

(GALATA KULESİ)
Galata Kulesi Street No: 2
Kuledibi-Galata

It was built in place of another tower by Genoese who started settling in Galata from 13th century in 1348. It serves as a head tower, forming the verge of Galata walls in this section which guards Genoese. Along with the raising of the walls in 1446 the tower was also raised. It was collapsed until the level of the brick bands that can be seen on the body during the intense earthquake in 1509. Architect Murat bin Hayrettin renovated the tower, therefore upper parts from 13th meter belongs to Turkish period. Galata Tower which served as a dungeon in the reign of Kanuni (1520-66) and a watch tower in the reign of Murat III (1574-95), witnessed an interesting event in Murat IV (1623-40); Hezarfen Ahmet Çelebi flied from the Tower to Doğancılar in Üsküdar by using the wings he made.

Height of the tower is over 60 meters and its base diameter is 16,45 m. Thickness of the body wall which was built by rubble stones is 3,75 m.

Top floor started to serve as a restaurant after the addition of an elevator during the renovation in between 1964-67. Nowadays many domestic and foreign tourists visit the Tower because of both the historical importance and its position that dominates the panoramic views of Golden Horn, Bosphorus and Marmara.

◄ **Galata Bridge, and Galata Tower.**

FROM KARAKÖY TO YILDIZ

Karaköy district (Galata) became an active place after 13th century when Genoese settled around here and started commercial businesses. Nowadays this district is still an active place because it is one of the important Commercial Centers. Galata Bridge connects Karaköy and Eminönü which is one of the central points of the Historical Peninsula and at the opposite of Karaköy. The subjects we will be discussing in this section reach from the shores till Beşiktaş. **Istanbul Modern Art Museum** which is on Tophane, exhibiting in modern and contemporary art, is also an educational and cultural center.

ARAP MOSQUE 15

(ARAP CAMİİ)
Galata Mahkemesi Street
No: 10-14 Galata

Nafe Street which is between Karaköy and Azapkapı and connects to Tersane Avenue takes you to Arap Mosque. Even if there are some thoughts that it was built by the Arabs during the blockade, the predominant thought is that it was a Genoese mosque transformed into a mosque in the reign of Fatih in the name of Galata Mosque. After the emplacement of exile Andalusia Arabs who came from Spain in 1492, its name changed into Arab Mosque. A large number of Genoese grave stones were found in the renovations made in 1913 and put into Archaeology Museum.

Tower of Arap Mosque.

The open roof of the square planned building was closed with timber during the renovations. Its tower serves as minaret. Timber gallery floors having a large area surround the whole place from outside of the *mihrab* wall. Windows were emplaced in harp arched niches.

Yeraltı (Underground) Mosque.

YERALTI MOSQUE 17

(YERALTI CAMİİ)
Kemankeş Avenue No: 23
Karaköy

It is on the avenue at the back of the pier of Karaköy Seaport. This building was the cellar of the tower serving as a fortress controlling the entrance of the Golden Horn during Byzantium period. It was used as an ammunition store after the conquest of Istanbul and transformed into a mosque in the reign of Mahmut I (1730-54). Its main area has a limited view because of the low ceiling and 54 symmetrical buttresses.

SURP KRİKOR LUSAVORİÇ CHURCH 18

(SURP KRİKOR LUSAVORİÇ KİLİSESİ)
Sakızcılar Street No: 3 Karaköy

It is in between Karaköy and Tophane, north wall facing Kemeraltı Avenue. The

Surp Krikor Lusavoriç Church.

first mosque which was built in 1431 was completely demolished during the extension of Kemeraltı Avenue in 1958. The Church which was

General interior view of Kılıç Ali Pasha Mosque.

built according to the plans prepared by Architect Bedros Zobyan, made open for prayer by Patriarch Şınorhk Kalustyan in August 1965.

Surp Krikor Lusavoriç Church has the characteristics of Armenian Architecture as distinct from the first church which has he characteristics of Byzantine Architecture. Main area is reached after passing the entrance next to the bell tower of 10 x 14 meters. Dome sitting on archways and pendants has a high embroidery frame and 23 meters high from the ground. Top of the abscissa is covered with roof tiles.

KILIÇ ALİ PASHA MOSQUE 19

(KILIÇ ALİ PAŞA CAMİİ)
Ali Paşa Medresesi Street, Tophane

It is between Ali Pasha Medresesi Street which connects with Kemeraltı Avenue and Kılıç Ali Pasha Avenue. It was constructed in 1580-81 with its complex buildings by Architect Sinan on behalf of the famous seaman Kılıç Ali Pasha. The complex buildings are; mosque, mausoleum, madrasah, public fountain and single Turkish bath. A lead coated roof cover a part of the atrium including the last gathering area. Window tops of the last gathering area are decorated with triangular tiles. The dome of the rectangular planned mosque is supported by two semidomes on the axis of kiblah *(kıble)*. Three pews that surrounds the building from three directions are separated from the main area as in Hagia Sophia. The archways that carry the 12,70 m dome sits on four buttresses on four corners.

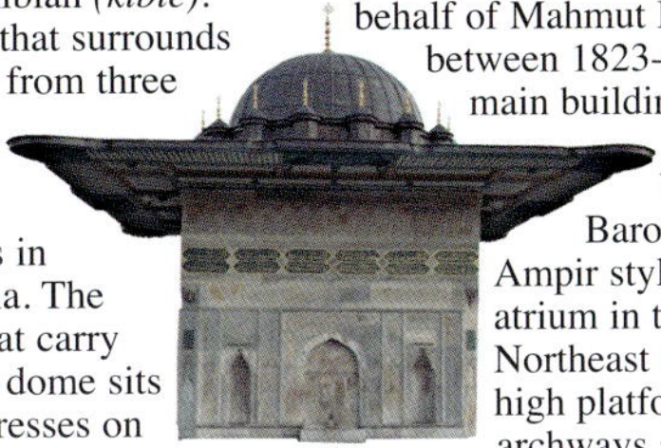

Tophane Fountain.

Building is supported with buttresses having archways distinctive from the exterior. Tiled boards that adorn the lower window tops of the Mosque and the triangular stained windows on top of the two boards enrich the place.

TOPHANE FOUNTAIN 20

(TOPHANE ÇEŞMESİ)
Tophane Square

Tophane fountain which attracts attention with its large fringe and rich embossments is emplaced at the north of Kılıç Ali Pasha Mosque. It was built in the reign of Mahmut I in1732. Environment of fountains which are placed in sharp arched niches has rich decoration with branch, leaf and flower in vase figures.

NUSRETİYE MOSQUE 21

(NUSRETİYE CAMİİ)
Meclisi Mebusan Avenue No: 4
Tophane

It is a little further from Kılıç Ali Pasha Mosque. Nusretiye Mosque which reflects the gratefulness of the palace by its exterior was built by Krikor Balyan on behalf of Mahmut II in between 1823-26. The main building enriched by Baroque and Ampir styles and its atrium in the Northeast is on a high platform. The archways and buttresses that support the dome covering the main area take attention with their reflection on the exterior view. The square planned main area that is covered with a single dome having a diameter of 7,5 m extends through northwest with the last gathering place. The frontals of the lower windows in the distinctive area which is illuminated through a large number of windows are adorned with leaf patterned embossments. Upper windows are accentuated with geometric patterned borders. Sultan's Kiosk at the

Nusretiye Mosque reflecting the elegance of palace.

Dolmabahçe Mosque seen from the Bosphorus.

Dolmabahçe Mosque ❶ *(Dolmabahçe Camii)*
Dolmabahçe Clock Tower ❷ *(Dolmabahçe Saat Kulesi)*
Dolmahçe Palace ❸ *(Dolmahçe Sarayı)*
Naval Museum ❹ *(Deniz Müzesi)*
Yıldız Mosque ❺ *(Yıldız Camii)*
Yıldız Palace ❻ *(Yıldız Sarayı)*
Yıldız Park ❼ *(Yıldız Parkı)*
Malta Kiosk ❽ *(Malta Köşkü)*
Çadır Kiosk ❾ *(Çadır Köşkü)*
Çırağan Palace ❿ *(Çırağan Sarayı)*

right of the mosque entrance is connected with the Sultan's Pew which juts out from the Southwest wall of the main area by a cage. Interior view of the Pew from the main area is restricted by the metal network implemented on the cage.

DOLMABAHÇE MOSQUE ❶

(DOLMABAHÇE 'BEZM-İ ALEM VALİDE SULTAN' CAMİİ)
Meclisi Mebusan Avenue, Dolmabahçe

Its construction which started in the south of Dolmabahçe Palace by Bezm-i Alem Valide Sultan (1807-53), mother of Abdülmecit, and after the death of the mother completed by his son Abdülmecit (1839-61). The construction of the mosque started in 1852 and it opened for praying in 1855. The double floored Sultan's Kiosk which is adjacent to the entrance facade gives the impression as if it was a building separate from the mosque. Sultan's Mosque juts out to the avenue from its two corners and minarets rise from these sections.

Body of the main mosque is square planned and covered by a single dome. Its dome adorned

Dolmabahçe Clock Tower.

with engravings is without embroidery frame and window and has a chandelier in the middle of it. The big windows on the lower line having archways illuminate the area.

DOLMABAHÇE CLOCK TOWER ❷

(DOLMABAHÇE SAAT KULESİ)

It is in front of the monumental entrance gates of Dolmabahçe Palace. It is built by Abdülhamit II (1876-1909) in between 1890-94 and reflects architectural style of the palace. Tower having an 8.5 x 8.5 meters basement becomes narrow while rising through the upper floors and is 30 meters high. The sides of the windows on the ground and first floors are enriched by double columns and on the third and fourth floors columns leave their places to pilasters. On the entrance floor there are barometers inside the archways of doors and windows. Clocks brought from France are emplaced on the four facades of the third floor.

DOLMABAHÇE PALACE MUSEUM ❸

(DOLMABAHÇE SARAYI MÜZESİ)
Dolmabahçe Avenue, Dolmabahçe-Beşiktaş
Tel: (0212) 236 90 00 (20 lines)

The area where Dolmabahçe Palace is present today was a small bay. In the first half of the 17th century it was filled and timber kiosks were built by various Sultans. These kiosks were demolished and renewed many times and Dolmabahçe was

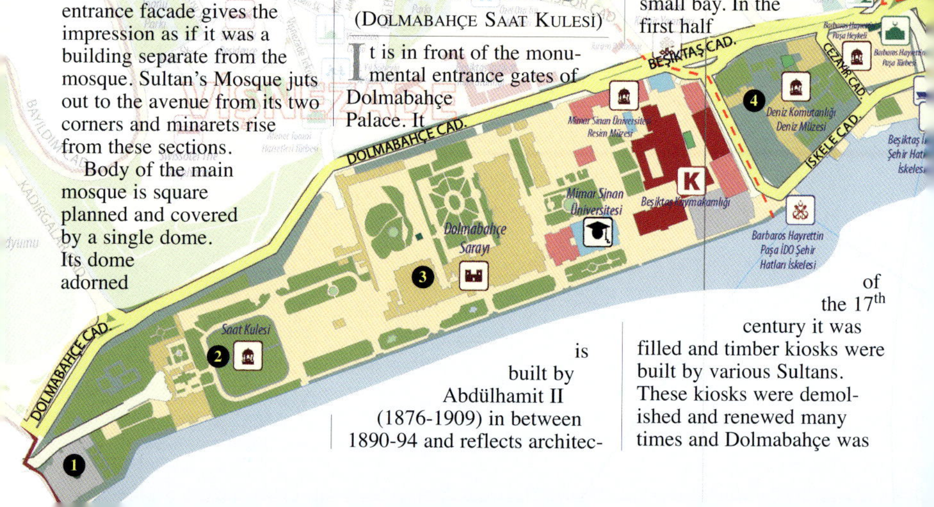

transformed into Privy Garden where Sultans use for entertainment and relaxation. There was Beşiktaş Palace with its large number of rooms in this area, before the present palace was built. Abdülmecit, who lived for many years in this palace and some of whose children were born here, wanted to transfer the Topkapı Palace where various sweet and bitter incidents took place in the history to these shores in 19th century when the influence of Europe was being perceived widely. Beşiktaş Palace was demolished and foundation of a bigger palace was laid. Dolmabahçe Palace was built by Garabet and Nikogos Balyan who are from Balyan's, a famous architect family of the period, in between 1843-56

The longer arm of the Palace built on "L" shape plan lies parallel to the Bosphorus, short arm lies through the land. Landside of the palace is surrounded by high atrium walls.

Neo-classic, baroque and ampir architectural designs were mixed with Ottoman culture and art values in the construction of the palace. **Mustafa Kemal Atatürk** also lived in this palace which hosted many famous guests, in the late period of his illness and died on 10 November 1938 in his room with a sea view. The palace which survived well preserved till today holds a rich collection of: wall and ceiling paintings, crystal chandeliers and candlesticks, Yıldız, Europe, China and Japan porcelains, over 900 paintings made by foreign and domestic painters, carpet made in Hereke specially for the palace which cover 4454 m^2 area and various other valuable good. There are 285 rooms, 44 saloons, 68 toilets and 6 Turkish baths in the Dolmabahçe Palace.

Touring the Palace: *Dolmabahçe Palace is open for visit except Mondays and Thursdays: between 09:00-15:00 in between October 1st*

Selamlık (the quarters reserved for the men) entrance of Dolmabahçe Palace.

Crystal Stairs.

and February 28th *and between 09:00-16:00 in between March* 1th *- September* 30th. The ones who want to visit the *Harem* section have to buy additional ticket.

We can analyze Dolmabahçe Palace in three sections: **Selamlık** (*Mans Quarters or Mabeyn-i Hümayun*), **Muayede** (Feast) **Saloon** which can be visited with Selamlık and **Harem** *(Women's Quarter or Harem-i Hümayun)*. Palace is visited with a tour guide. Selamlık tour starts with *Medhal Saloon*. Government ambassadors and foreign guests were hosted in the rooms of this saloon that have sea view. The landside rooms on the left side were used by the Grand Vizier and other ministers. The hallway separated from the right side of the Saloon was used by the clerks for Palace correspondence. It was called *Clerical Department* or *Tile Saloon*. On the right wall of the hallway there is the biggest painting of the Palace which depicts the Sürre Regiment (the caravan that moves off to Mecca for the sacred pilgrimage) painted by Italian artist Stefano Ussi. Following that *Binek (access-exit) Saloon* and the exhibition where special goods and writing sets used by the sultan and members of the dynasty are exhibited.

Gate of the Museum.

When the tour in the protocol entrance finishes, you continue to the sovereign floor; the importance of this floor is that the scarecrows were made from crystal. Because of this it is also called *Crystal Stairs*. This section is the most illuminated area of the Palace because its roof is closed by windows. Further on the tour, there is *Süfera (Ambassador) Saloon*, one of the most luxurious saloons of the Palace. Saloon has a rich decoration due to its functioning as a saloon for official receptions and meetings. The fireplaces on the four corners of the saloon are coated with English porcelains. At two corners of the saloon; there is the room for the guest waiting for getting audience to the Sultan and the ambassador acceptance room that these meetings took place, also called the red room.

Zülvecheyn Saloon is also one of the important saloons of the Selamlık Section. In the saloon, daily works and acceptances of the Sultan and also the *iftar* (Ramadan breaking dinner) invitations took place. There is a library, a relaxation room and a hammam around the saloon.

Paintings of Abdülmecit, his father Mahmut II, Abdülaziz and Mehmet Reşat attract attention in the *Hatıralar (Remembrance) Saloon*. The following hallway that connects *Selamlık and Harem* looks like an art gallery. There is the *Hünkar's (Sultan's) Apartment* at the end of this hallway connecting Selamlık to Harem. After this place, *Hünkar Room, Harem Binek (access-exit) Saloon and Exhibition Saloon of Valuable Goods* where tea-coffee sets, gold and silver dinner services exhibited is toured and then comes **Muayede** *(Feast)* **Saloon**, the most grandiose saloon of the palace. Feast Ceremonies and various official acceptances with ministers and officials of the government were set here.

Muayede Saloon with its magnificant decoration.

The sloped roof is 36 m high and is covered with a dome having a diameter of 25 m from inside. The large archways that are opened from the four sides of the dome enrich the area with their adornments. Four sides of the saloon are surrounded by gallery floors. The biggest and most grandiose chandelier of the Palace which was manufactured in England in 1853 and weights 4,5 tons is in this saloon.

Harem: Harem section of Dolmabahçe consists of places for: the sultan, valide sultan (sultan's mother), wives of sultan, Shehzades (princes) and lady sultans (princesses). The celebration and meeting saloons, apartments, hammams of the Harem members and the study room of Mustafa Kemal Atatürk and the room that he died are the places to visit in this section. In saloon called *Mavi (Blue) Saloon* valide sultan, or the mistress in absence of her, hosts wives of foreign presidents. In the *Pembe (Pink) Saloon*, valide sultan or the mistress in absence of her, hosts the special guests; also some family meetings were made here. The most interesting painting adorning the saloon is the portrait of Dürrüşşehvar Sultan who is the daughter of Ottoman Caliph Abdülmecit Effendi who is also the painter of this painting.

Atatürk's room, where he passed away in 1938.

NAVAL MUSEUM ④

(DENİZ MÜZESİ)

Beşiktaş Avenue, Beşiktaş

Tel: (0212) 327 43 45

Museum is open for visiting between 09:00 and 17:00 except for Mondays and Tuesdays.

Naval Museum which was built in 1897 and served on various locations was transferred to its current location in 1961. Valuable goods from Turkish marine history, ship models, and marine paintings are exhibited in this

Naval Museum.

museum. There are many valuable boats in the **Historical Boats Exhibition** in another building near it. The galley of Mehmet IV (1648-87) and other sovereignty galleys form a rich collection in here.

IHLAMUR QASR

(IHLAMUR KASRI)
Ihlamur Road, Beşiktaş
Tel: (0212) 259 50 86

Entance to the Tomb of Barbaros Hayrettin Pasha.

Against the Naval Museum, if you follow Ortabahçe Avenue connecting Beşiktaş Avenue, in a fifteen minutes walk you will arrive at Ihlamur Qasr. The area of Ihlamur Qasr was a promenade area known as Hacı Hüseyin Vineyards in 18th century. In the reign of Ahmet III (1703-30), it was transformed into relaxation and entertaining area of the Palace members. It was also

Monument of Barbaros Hayrettin Pasha at Beşiktaş Square.

used by the following Sultans. Abdülmecit (1839-61) hosted French poet Lamartine in here. In the promenade where Abdülmecit himself also frequently visited for relaxation, **Merasim Kiosk** *(Ihlamur Qasr)* and **Maiyet Kiosk** were built in place of Hacı Hüseyin Vineyard Kiosk in between 1849-55 by Nikogos Balyan. Merasim Kiosk which was designed for ceremonies and official businesses and Maiyet Kiosk which was used by attendants of the Sultan were built in an eclectic design.

They are surrounded by walls and in a pooled garden. Especially Merasim Kiosk attracts attention with its façade which has bilateral stairs adorned with rich architectural patterns. Inside it consists of an English fireplace, Hereke carpet and ceiling decorations adorned with golden leaf. Maiyet Kiosk has a more simple decoration. A cafeteria gives service in the garden of the Qasrs.

YILDIZ (HAMİDİYE) MOSQUE 5

(YILDIZ CAMİİ)
Yıldız Avenue,
Yıldız-Beşiktaş

It was built near Yıldız Palace with the order of Abdülhamit II (1876-1909) in between 1885-86. It is an interesting example that reflects the last period of Ottoman Architecture. Monumental façade views were accentuated in the direction of entry and on the *mihrab* wall. Rectangular planned apartments adjacent to the northeast and southwest walls are similar with last period *selatin* mosque examples. The pew of the mosque is in the entrance section. The middle of the rectangular planned place is covered with embroidery framed dome and other parts with flat ceiling. Interior of the dome attracting attention with its blue color is adorned with golden gilded stars. Two elegant columns reach the embroidery frame of the dome both in entrance and *mihrab* directions. Interior was decorated rich and care-

There is the **Mausoleum of Barbaros Hayrettin Pasha,** the Great Admiral on one end of the Naval Museum and **Barbaros Monument** on the other. Architect Sinan built the mausoleum with octagonal body of which entrance is with stoa in 1541. The mausoleum which is closed for visiting only opens for special days like 1st of July Coasting Feast and 4th of April Commemoration Day of Sea Martyrs. Barbaros Monument was built by bronze smelting in 1942 *(See page 136-137 for map).*

Ihlamur Qasr with its rich embroidery.

fully, illuminated by neo-gothic style sharp arched windows. The crossbeam surrounding from the middle separates the main place into two horizontally, this two parts are decorated in two different styles. The timber balconies of two apartments adjacent to the northeast and southwest walls, opening to the main place are jut out like a cage. There is a clock tower constructed in 1890 in the atrium entrance in the north of Yıldız Mosque.

YILDIZ PALACE 6

(YILDIZ SARAYI)
Yıldız Avenue,
Yıldız-Beşiktaş
Tel: (0212) 258 30 80

It is the last example of Turkish-Ottoman Palace architecture. Kiosks, qasrs ad pavilions which were built by different Sultans in the area that have been used as hunting area starting from the reign of Kanuni (1520-66), forms the palace. The area where the first building was built by Ahmet I, stayed as a forest till the beginning of 19th century. This place is known as "Yıldız" because of the kiosk built by Selim III (1789-1807) for his mother Mihrişah Valide Sultan in between 1804-05 in the name of "Yıldız". Abdülmecit built a new kiosk for his mother Bezm-i Alem Valide Sultan by demolishing existing kiosks. Abdülaziz (1861-76) who usually came here in summer months built Great Mabeyn Kiosk, Çit Qasr and Malta and Çadır Kiosks in the outer garden. The main evolution of the palace occurred during the reign of Abdülhamit II (1876-1909). Also government was trans-

Yıldız (Hamidiye) Mosque.

ferred from Dolmabahçe Palace to here because of safety matters.

Yıldız Palace which is surrounded by high walls consists of three parts. **Selamlık** which includes official apartments and service buildings, **Harem** which includes *Hasbahçe* (privy garden) and the buildings of Sultan and his family, and the outer garden **Yıldız Park** *(page 155)*, on the hillside between Beşiktaş and Ortaköy which is open for public nowadays.

Hasbahçe (privy garden) which starts from in front of the Harem apartment and ends at Cihannüma Kiosk, is one of the most stunning places of Harem. A pool looking like a natural river having 300 m length was formed in the garden and a small island was put in the middle. **Great Mabeyn Kiosk**, the most sumptuous building of the palace was built by Agop and Sarkis Balyan in 1865-66. Government was prosecuted here in the reign of Abdülhamit. **Çit Qasr,** having thin and long plan is the kiosk were foreign government agents waited and had meetings with Sultan. On the right of the entrance from Harem, there is **Small Mabeyn Kiosk** built in 1901 and used by the Sultan as working and relaxing area. The cute **theater** built by Abdülhamit II has importance because it is the only palace theater that survived till today. **Cihannüma Kiosk**, at the southeast end of the *Hasbahçe*, was used as a relaxation and watch kiosk because of its view that is open through Marmara and Bosphorus.

There are **Şale Kiosk, Çadır Kiosk, Malta Kiosk** which serves as restaurant and cafe and **Yıldız Tile Factory** in Yıldız Park, the outer garden of the palace.

Yıldız Palace is open for visiting from 09:30-16:00 except Mondays and Thursdays. But most of the parts are closed due to restorations.

HOTELS

BEST WESTERN ERESİN TAKSİM
Topçu Avenue No: 16 Taksim
☎ **+90 (212) 253 22 47**
€€€
www.eresintaxim.com.tr

BÜYÜK LONDRA OTELİ
Meşrutiyet Avenue No: 53 Beyoğlu-Taksim
☎ **+90 (212) 249 10 25**
€
www.londrahotel.net
✉ londra@londrahotel.net

CARTOON HOTEL
Tarlabaşı Bulvarı No: 36 Taksim
☎ **+90 (212) 238 93 28**
€€
www.cartoonhotel.com

CEYLAN INTERCONTINENTAL
Askerocağı Avenue No: 1 Taksim
☎ **+90 (212) 368 44 44**
€€€€€
www.intercontinental.com.tr

DİVAN TAXIM SUITES
Cumhuriyet Avenue No: 2
Elmadağ-Taksim
☎ **+90 (212) 315 55 00**
€€€€
www.divan.com.tr
✉ info.divanistanbul@divan.com.tr

EURO PLAZA
Tarlabaşı Bulvarı No:292 Tepebaşı-Taksim
☎ **+90 (212) 254 59 00**
€€
www.europlazahotel.com
✉ info@europlazahotel.com

GEZİ HOTEL
Mete Avenue No: 42 Taksim
☎ **+90 (212) 251 74 30**
€€
www.hotelgezi.com
✉ info@hotelgezi.com

HILTON
Cumhuriyet Avenue Harbiye-Taksim
☎ **+90(212) 315 60 00**
€€€€€
www.hilton.com.tr

GRAND HYATT ISTANBUL
Taşkışla Avenue Taksim
☎ **+90 (212) 368 12 34**
€€€€
www.istanbul.grand.hyatt.com
✉ istanbul.grand@hyatt.com

LARES PARK HOTEL
Topçu Avenue No: 23 Taksim
☎ **+90 (212) 313 51 00**
€€€
www.laresparktaksim.com

LUSH HOTEL
Sıraselviler Avenue No: 12 Taksim
☎ **+90 (212) 243 95 95**
€€€€€
www.lushhiphotel.com

THE MARMARA TAKSİM
Taksim Square
☎ **+90 (212) 251 46 96**
€€€€€
www.themarmarahotels.com
✉ taksim-info@themarmarahotels.com

POINT HOTEL
Topçu Avenue No: 2 Taksim
☎ **+90 (212) 313 50 00**
€€€€
www.pointhotel.com
✉ info@pointhotel.com

RICHMOND HOTEL
İstiklal Avenue No: 227 Beyoğlu-Taksim
☎ **+90 (212) 252 54 60**
€€€
www.richmondhotels.com.tr
✉ info@richmondhotels.com.tr

TAXIM HILL HOTEL
Sıraselviler Avenue No: 5 Taksim Square
☎ **+90 (212) 334 85 00**
€€
www.taximhill.com

THE MARMARA PERA
Meşrutiyet Avenue Tepebaşı-Taksim
☎ **+90 (212) 251 46 46**
€€€€
www.themarmarahotels.com
✉ Pera-info@themarmarahotels.com

ANEMON GALATA
Bereketzade Mah. Büyükhendek Avenue
No: 11 Kuledibi
☎ **+90 (212) 293 23 43 (Pbx)**
€€
www.anemonhotels.com
✉ info@anemongalata.com

ANSEN SUİT HOTEL
Meşrutiyet Avenue No: 70
Tepebaşı/Tunnel-Taksim
☎ **+90 (212) 245 88 08**
€€€€
www.ansensuites.com
✉ info@ansensuites.com

€ **Up to 50 Euros.** €€ **Between 50 and 100 Euros.** €€€ **Between 100 and 150 Euros.**
€€€€ **Between 150 and 200 Euros.** €€€€€ **250 Euros and more.**

RESTAURANTS

DİVAN TAKSİM
Cumhuriyet Avenue No: 2 Taksim
☎ +90 (0212) 231 41 00

FERAYE
İstiklal Avenue Balo Street No:1-1 Taksim
www.feraye.net
☎ +90 (0212) 244 74 72

GALATA TOWER
☎ +90 (0212) 293 81 80
www.galatatower.net
✉ info@galatatower.net

İKİNCİ BAHAR
Çiçek Pasajı Beyoğlu
☎ +90 (0212) 244 50 20

MAHZEN
Çiçek Pasajı Beyoğlu
☎ +90 (0212) 249 03 29

İMROZ
Balık Pazarı Nevizade Street No: 24 Beyoğlu
☎ +90 (0212) 249 90 73

CUMHURİYET MEYHANESİ
Balıkpazarı Sahne Street No: 47 Beyoğlu
☎ +90 (0212) 243 64 06

BONCUK
Nevizade Street No: 19 Beyoğlu
☎ +90 (0212) 243 12 19

MERİH RESTORAN
Balık Pazarı Beyoğlu
☎ +90 (0212) 245 43 25

ALEM RESTAURANT
Nevizade Street No: 8 Beyoğlu
☎ +90 (0212) 293 40 40

DEMGAH
Nevizade Street Balık Pazarı No: 18 Beyoğlu
☎ +90 (0212) 245 09 64

ASIR RESTAURANT
Kalyoncu Kulluk Avenue No: 94 Beyoğlu
☎ +90 (0212) 256 34 38
www.asirrestaurant.com

KALLAVİ 20
İstiklal Caddesi Kallavi Street No: 20 Beyoğlu
☎ +90 (0212) 251 10 10

TERAS 6
Meşrutiyet Avenue Çavuşoğlu İş Merkezi No. 131, Kat: 6 Beyoğlu
☎ +90 (0212) 245 97 98

SOHO
Meşelik Street No: 14 Beyoğlu
☎ +90 (0212) 245 01 52

PIERO CAFE
İstiklal Avenue Fuat Özkınay Street No: 3 Beyoğlu
☎ +90 (0212) 252 51 19

NICE ISTANBUL BISTRO
İstiklal Avenue İmam Adnan Street No: 16 Beyoğlu
☎ +90 (0212) 252 65 01

ÇETİN GURME
İstiklal Avenue No. 10/C Beyoğlu
☎ +90 (0212) 245 56 56

ŞEYHBENDER
Asmalımescit Şeyhbender Street No: 14/1 Beyoğlu
☎ +90 (0212) 292 73 14

YAKUP
Asmalımescit Street No: 35/37 Tünel
☎ +90 (0212) 249 29 25

AFACAN
İstiklal Avenue No. 86 Beyoğlu
☎ +90 (0212) 245 42 41

BONSOIR RESTAURANT BAR
Fransız (Cezayir) Street No. 4 - Beyoğlu
☎ +90 (0212) 249 55 65 / 75

BARCELONA PATISSERIE
İstiklal Avenue No: 246 Beyoğlu
☎ +90 (0212) 292 43 21

ASMALIMESCİT BALIKÇISI
Asmalımescit Mah. Sofyalı Street No: 5/A Tünel
☎ +90 (0212) 251 3939 - 245 7467

PEHLİVAN
İstiklal Cad. No. 5 Taksim
☎ +90 (0212) 252 15 80

General interior view of the historical Flower Passage.

Nevizade Street in Fish Market.

WHAT TO EAT AND DRINK?

As ten thousands of people come to Taksim and Istiklal Avenue every day, every corner is full of restaurants and cafes. The places on the street have reasonable prices. The little buffets that are placed along the Sıraselviler Avenue near the square offer cheap and filling food like doner (pressed lamb roasted on a large vertical spit). You can also taste "wet hamburger" sold at these buffets. On Istiklal Avenue there are fast-food and pizza restaurants, cafes, bakers and self-service restaurants lined up next to each other. You can buy Turkish delight from **Hacıbekir** on the left before the Galatasaray Square. You can taste the *döner kebab* and famous bread *kadayıf* (similar to a bread pudding and not containing kataif pastry. It is served with *kaymak,* a kind of clotted cream) at **Saray Muhallebicisi** (literally Saray Rice Pudding) on the same row, and the famous profiterole of **İnci Pastanesi** (İnci Patisserie) on the right.

At Galatasaray Square, near the Fish Market, the restaurants of **Çiçek Pasajı (Flower Passage)** and **Nevizade Street** where you can drink alcohol are the most attractive restaurants in the evening. You can have fried

Shop vindows in Beyoğlu offer many alternatives.

mussels, *kokoreç* (roasted sheep's intestines), and iced almond with beer, and you will be surprised by the rich varieties of appetizers that you can have with your *raki*. You shouldn't leave Beyoğlu without visiting the Historical **Cumhuriyet Meyhanesi** (literally Republic Tavern) at the Fish Market.
The historical Russian restaurant **Rejans** (Olivya Arcade, Galatasaray) is unique with its appetizers and special vodkas. Although the Historical Lebon Patisserie at the corner of the Kumbaracı Street is not open anymore, the **Lebon** patisserie and café carries on its name. **Markiz Arcade**, which is one the stable elements of patisserie culture, opposite Lebon is one of the indispensables of Beyoğlu.

The **Cezayir (Fransız) Sokağı** (Algerian (French) Street) is a good choice to be away from the crowd of Istiklal Avenue. This street

Entertainment at Beyoğlu. Belly-dancer Princess Banu.

ARAF
İstiklal Avenue Balo Street No: 32/5 Beyoğlu
☎ +90 (0212) 244 83 01
www.araf.com.tr
✉ info@araf.com.tr

AURA PERA
İstiklal Avenue Balo Street No: 24 Beyoğlu
☎ +90 (0212) 245 56 16
www.aurapera.com
✉ info@aurapera.com

HAYAL KAHVESİ
Büyük Parmak Kapı Street Afrika Han, No: 19, Beyoğlu
☎ +90 (0212) 244 25 58
www.hayalkahvesibeyoglu.com
✉ info@hayalkahvesibeyoglu.com

BABYLON
Şehbender Street No: 3 Asmalımescit, Tunnel-Beyoğlu
☎ +90 (0212) 292 73 68
www.babylon.com.tr

SHAMAN WORLD MUSIC CLUB
Jurnal Street No: 5/2 Tünel-Beyoğlu
☎ +90 (0212) 249 96 06
www.shaman.com.tr

has a decent atmosphere with two rows of cafes and restaurants. To go to this street, go along Yeniçarşı Avenue next to Galatasaray High School. Take the first turning on your left into Hayriye Avenue. The climbing street with steps on the right is the Algerian (French) Street. The cafes rowed one by one opposite Ali Pasha Mosque in Tophane are nice places where you can have pleasure drinking tea and coffee, and smoking nargile.

ENTERTAINMENT

Beyoğlu is a popular district in Istanbul with its cinemas, theatres, bookstores, cafes and night clubs. Cinemas and theatres are on the Istiklal Avenue, cross streets and in the Arcades. Every corner is a cafe, a restaurant, a bookstore or a store. The bars and night clubs are crowded until dawn. Besides these, it is the busiest center in Istanbul in cultural activities.

SHOPPING

On Istiklal Avenue, shopping means mostly textile products of the stores that are lined along the street. The stores Benetton, Adidas, Kiğılı, Collezione, Lacoste, Levi's, Çetinkaya are on the street. The other shopping items are

European Passage.

the products of book stores, technology stores and shops that sell some souvenirs. Besides the famous brand textile stores which are lined until Galatasaray Square, you can find sports wear and some stand accessories in *Halep Pasajı* and *Atlas Pasajı (Halep* and *Atlas Arcades)*, which are after the Greek Consulate; and you can buy souvenirs in

Textile shop windows of Beyoğlu are rich.

Stop of Taksim-Darüşşafaka subway service.

Avrupa Pasajı (European Arcade), which has a door to the street where the Fish Market is located. There are sellers of second hand books in *Aslı Han Pasajı* parallel to *Avrupa Pasajı*. You can buy different women-men clothes in *Örs İş Merkezi* (Örs Business Center) opposite *Çiçek Pasajı* (Flower Passage) and *Beyoğlu İş Merkezi* (Beyoğlu Business Center) opposite Odakule. There are shops that sell different sound systems and musical equipments at the beginning of Galip Dede Street that stretches from Tunnel Square to Karaköy. While Istiklal Avenue can satisfy you with shopping, you can also prefer the luxurious stores of Nişantaşı and large shopping centers. The Taksim-Darüşşafaka subway station at the Taksim Square helps you get to some shopping centers and Nişantaşı. Get off at Osmanbey, stop to go to Nişantaşı, use the Nişantaşı-Rumeli Avenue exit. Turn to Rumeli Avenue ahead the exit, and visit the stores of Nişantaşı. **Cevahir** and **Kanyon** shopping centers, which have a large capacity with their hundreds of stores, restaurants, cafes and cinemas that are directly connected to the subway line.

You should get off at Şişli stop to go to Cevahir, and at 1. Levent stop to go to Kanyon. There is **Metrocity** shopping center next to Kanyon.

Escalator in subway station.

Nostalgic Tramway of Taksim-Tunnel line.

TRANSPORT

You can see the information about how to go to Taksim from the Historical Peninsula on the related part *(page 121)*. Although the **Nostalgic Tramway** offers service between the Taksim Square and the Tunnel, you should prefer walking. The public buses departing from Taksim Square have services to a wide range of directions.

See the general Transport part *(page 191)* for the bus services departing from there. Let me explain you shortly how to go to many directions from Taksim.

Taksim-Darüşşafaka Subway Line: There are the Large Shopping Centers of Istanbul on the route of the subway line. Cevahir Shopping Center is located at the exit of the Şişli subway station. Metrocity and Canyon Shopping Centers are located at the exit of the Levent subway station.

Taksim-Dolmabahçe Palace: If you want to go to the Dolmabahçe Palace from Taksim, you can use the *Taksim-Kabataş* funicular system. The Palace is just ahead of the Kabataş stop. You can also get to the Dolmabahçe Palace after a short walk from the front of *Atatürk Kültür Merkezi* (Atatürk Cultural Center) through the İnönü Avenue.

Taksim-Bosphorus line: If you wish to see the Bosphorus, you can prefer the buses departing from Taksim Square. If you are near the Dolmabahçe Palace, you can use the public buses that depart from Kabataş bus stops and go towards that direction.

Taksim-Sultanahmet: Use the *Kabataş-Zeytinburnu* tramway line. Get on the tramway either at Kabataş or Karaköy tramway stops.

Tunnel connectig İstiklal Avenue to Karaköy.

Taksim-Kabataş: You can get to Kabataş in two-three minutes by the *funicular system* that connects Taksim Square and Kabataş

Tünel-Karaköy: You can get to Karaköy in two or three minutes through the Tunnel that connects the Tunnel Square and Karaköy.

Tünel-Karaköy walking path: You can walk to Karaköy along Galip Dede Avenue that is connected to the Tunnel Square. You can also visit **Galata Mevlevihanesi** (Mevlevi Lodge) and **Galata Tower** on that street.

Funicular system of Taksim-Kabataş line.

Karaköy-Tophane: After the tramway line, the walking path between Karaköy and Tophane is short. You can see **Kılıç Ali Paşa Mosque** and **Nusretiye Mosque**. You can prefer getting on the tramway at Karaköy and get off at Tophane one stop later.

Galatasaray Square-Tophane: You can get to Kılıç Ali Pasha Mosque by walking through Yeni Çarşı Avenue that goes downwards from Galatasaray High School, or you can get to Galatasaray Square by going up Boğazkesen Avenue from Tophane.

Karaköy-Kadıköy: There are services to Kadıköy from the pier in Karaköy in short intervals.

From Kabataş to Üsküdar-Leander's Tower: There are frequent ferry boat services to *Üsküdar* and Kız Kulesi (Leander's Tower) from Kabataş. The ferry boat services from Kabataş to *Adalar* (Princes' Islands) and *Kadıköy* are less frequent.

From Beşiktaş to Kadıköy-Üsküdar: There are ferry boat services from Beşiktaş to *Kadıköy* and *Üsküdar* in short intervals.

The *Beşiktaş-Küçüksu* ferry boats, and the ferry boats on *Boğaz Hattı* (Bosphorus Line), which go to different piers, go to Beşiktaş as well. You can have the complimentary booklets available at the piers.

BOSPHORUS

Istanbul Bosphorus, which forms a natural border between Asia and Europe and connects Black Sea with Mediterranean, is an important sea passage. Even if religious buildings and Palaces were built in Byzantines' strong period, only small agricultural and fisherman villages remained in guarded bays in its last period. Intensive settlement was prevented because of the unsafe atmosphere and inclined slopes that limits the coastline. Anatolian and Rumeli Fortress which were built by Ottoman Empire in order to control the strategic importance of Bosphorus gave Turks the chance to settle around before the conquest.

Leander's Tower.

The population density which started to increase in 16th century, due to the increase of well-endowed classes interest and reconstruction activities, was grazed from its rural identity. Bosphorus lived its most shiny period due to the intense structuring in 18-19th centuries when large meadows became the excursion and picnic areas of public. There were waterside palaces, kiosks and mansions on the shores, villages sustaining their production on the bays and valleys, hunting kiosks on the hillsides. The propertied class formed by the governing class prefers to come here mostly in summer, but the villages formed by lower classes were resi-

dential areas both in summer and in winter. Rumeli (European) Side was like a summer resort starting from the waterside palace of the Sultan on Beşiktaş, waterside palaces of the women members of the dynasty and high level governor agents on Ortaköy-Kuruçeşme, mansions of governor agents descended from Byzantine bloodline on Arnavutköy and summerhouses of ambassadors and mansions of foreigners on Tarabya-Büyükdere. On the Asian (Anatolian) Side there were rare settlements of lower level officials. Emigration movement to Istanbul that started from 1950's, provided a natural increase in the population of the Bosphorus. Large forest areas turned into residential areas. Some waterside mansions were demolished due to the expansion of the coastline and construction of new roads, then new buildings were constructed on their gardens. High parts of the hillside were expanded by settlements of villas. Fish restaurants, cafes and parks on the coastline of both sides are places where visitors can enjoy themselves.

Küçüksu Summer Palace.

Fatih Sultan Mehmet Bridge connecting the European and Asian Parts.

Fatih Sultan Mehmet Bridge.

Two Towers of Rumeli Fortress.

Historical structures on Arnavutköy coast line.

Start of the traditional Eurasia Marathon from the Bosphorus Bridge.

Ortaköy Mosque.

Waterside mansions lined along the coast seen from Kanlıca Ferry Boat Pier.

Anatolian Castle seen from the Bosphorus.

Küçüksu Qasr.

Kuleli Military High School.

Beylerbeyi Palace.

Leander's Tower.

Sadberk Hanım Museum.

Surp Boğos Armenian Catholic Church.

Tarabya Bay.

Yellow Kiosk (Sarı Köşk) in Emirgan Forest.

Genoese (Yoros) Castle.

A waterside mansion in Bosphorus.

Çengelköy Ferry Boat Pier.

Hıdiv Qasr on the ridges of Kanlıca.

Çırağan Palace.

ÇIRAĞAN PALACE
(ÇIRAĞAN SARAYI)
Çırağan Avenue No: 32

Marble columned timber waterside mansions that were here before the Palace and made by Mahmut were demolished by Abdülmecit in 1857; but project was postponed due to financial matters. After the death of Abdülmecit his brother Abdülaziz took his place and made Sarkis and Agop Balyan built the Çırağan Palace in between Beşiktaş and Ortaköy in between 1863-1871. Unfortunately only the body walls of the magnificent building that was endowed with valuable goods produced specially for the palace remained after the fire in January 1910. The other adjacent buildings of the palace that were spread through Beşiktaş and Ortaköy, were assigned to schools in the Republic Period and are serving for this purpose now. The main palace building which waited as a ruin for long years, was rented to a foreign investor with a contract signed in 1986. A new hotel building was constructed in its garden; the interior of the burned palace was renewed and used as the ballroom, ceremony saloons and restaurants of the hotel.

◀
Shores of Bosphorus from Kuruçeşme to Rumeli Fortress.

YILDIZ PARK
(YILDIZ PARKI)
Çırağan Avenue

The passageway near *Small Mecidiye Mosque*, across the Çırağan Palace reaches the entrance of Yıldız Park. This Mosque was built by Gabaret Balyan in 1848-49 on behalf of Abdülmecit. It has a single domed main area and large last gathering place. It attracts attention with its red porphyry pulpit, sliced *mihrab* and gothic style minaret.

Yıldız Forest, covering the hillside between Beşiktaş and Ortaköy is now connected to Çırağan Palace by a bridge over Çırağan Avenue.

The peaceful area which was also called Mabeyin Garden at those times was open for the Sultan, his relatives, and also the harem members with the permission of the Sultan.

When Abdülhamit II settled in Yıldız Palace for security matters, he included the forest into the border of the palace. After the nationalization, forest area was expanded through Ortaköy. In this period foreign specialists were brought to organize the garden befitting the exterior garden of the Palace.

The forest which is known as Yıldız Park nowadays is a relaxing area for the people who want to move away from the noise of the city. **Şale Kiosk, Malta Kiosk** and **Çadır Kiosk** which are buildings of Yıldız Palace, are on the higher parts of the forest. While Restaurants and cafeterias are in service at Malta and Çadır Kiosks, Şale Kiosk serves as a museum open for visiting except Mondays and Thursdays. Also the pool with a giant fountain near the Çadır Kiosk makes the area even more attractive.

Malta Kiosk.

Çadır Kiosk.

Ortaköy and its neighbourhood.

Bosphorus Bridge seen from Ortaköy.

ORTAKÖY 1

At the end of the Çırağan Avenue where you walk from Beşiktaş, you reach Ortaköy which is one of the most beautiful districts of Bosphorus. *Ortaköy Mosque, Hagios Fokas Greek Church* which is on the Muallim Avenue and *Etz Ahayim Sinagogue* being very close to each other, is a good example showing how different cultures live in peace here. The district is a living place with its bars, cafes, stands which are mostly selling jewelry set on the streets at weekends, baked potato and *gözleme* (pancake) shops spread around Ortaköy Square on Bosphorus shores.

Ortaköy Square having a small pier has a wonderful view with; the *Ortaköy Mosque* on the east, *Bosphorus Bridge* running along to Anatolian Side and *Beylerbeyi Palace* just under the bridge. You reach the ruins of the mansion of Esma Sultan, daughter of Abdülhamit I (1774-89) if you continue in front of Ortaköy Mosque. It is now a lovely restaurant after the renovation. If you head to the main avenue you live see the baked potato and *gözleme* (pancake) shops on the east of the Greek Church and at the other side of the avenue the Ortaköy *Hammam* (Turkish bath), a 16th century work of Architect Sinan which is not in service nowadays. If you follow Muallim Naci Avenue through the bridge, you will reach another ruined mansion. This Mansion is Naime Sultan Mansion which was used as Gaziosmanpaşa Junior High School and burned in 2002.

ORTAKÖY MOSQUE 2

(ORTAKÖY 'BÜYÜK MECİDİYE' CAMİİ)
Ortaköy Square

It as built by Nikogos Balyan on behalf of Abdülmecit (1839-61) over

Famous *kumpir* and *gözleme* shops of Ortaköy.

Ortaköy Mosque and Bosphorus Bridge in the background.

Bosphorus Bridge, which connects the European and Asian parts, at night.

the area jutting out to the Bosphorus on the east of the square in 1853. It consists of a double floored, "U" planned Sultan's apartment and a single domed main building. Being built on a location dominating the Bosphorus and having an exterior view built with palace peevishness gives a symbolic meaning to the building.

Facades of the Mosque, sliced by sepulture columns and enriched by carved and embossed decorations exhibits an active view. Double lined large arched windows provide good illumination. Its dome which hasn't got an embroidery frame, sitting on the hanging archways and renewed in renovations, is adorned by hand-carvings.

BOSPHORUS BRIDGE 3

(BOĞAZİÇİ KÖPRÜSÜ)

The first bridge that connects Europe and Asia coasts of Istanbul is

Galatasaray Island near Kuruçeşme.

Bosphorus Bridge. The construction of the bridge started in 1970 and it opened on 29th, October, 1973 which is the 50th year of the Republic. The hanging bridge that lies between Ortaköy and Beylerbeyi has 1560 m total length and the highest part is

Bosphorus.

64 m higher from Bosphorus. It is 1074 m between the two towers supported by carrier cables having 165 m height. Bridge consists of two towers on both sides and an apron stretched between them hanged on two main cables with hanging cables.

KURUÇEŞME 4

There are famous night clubs on the coast side of the avenue though Kuruçeşme after leaving Ortaköy. Kuruçeşme which was adorned by the mansions of famous people once, took its name form the fountain on the roadside façade of

Tezkireci Osman Efendi Mosque. Galatasaray Island which can be reached by a boat rented from coasts of Kuruçeşme has a restaurant and a beautiful pool which opens in summer. *Kuleli Military High School* attracts attention on the other side.

There are two churches on the Kırbaç Street which crosses the coast avenue. *Surp Haç Greek Church* which was built in place of a timber church in 1834 and *Hagios Dimitros Greek Church* which was built in 1820 takes place in this street.

Coast houses of Arnavutköy.

ARNAVUTKÖY

Arnavutköy which is one of the oldest settlements in Bosphorus was a well-kept and lovely Greek village until the middle of 19th century. Constantine built Hagios Mikhail Church here, and in the reign of Justinian, the church was renewed. When the Church was ruined after being despoiled in Latin occupancy, its stones were used in the construction of Rumeli Fortress. The water-side mansions of Sultan's wives spread from Ortaköy-Kuruçeşme to these parts from mid 18th century and beginning of 19th century. In the period when the Muslim population was rare, a mosque in 1832 and a police station which is also in use today in Akıntıburnu district that forms the border with Bebek. *Taksiarhis Greek Church* which was built in the second half of 19th century is on Satış Meydanı Street. Fisherman from all over Istanbul surrounds the coasts of Arnavutköy on weekends. Arnavutköy which is among the most beautiful places of Bosphorus, even if it is covered by structures and apartments contravening with the historical atmosphere, preserves its charm with the luxurious restaurants, bars, night clubs and cafeterias.

Bebek Mosque.

BEBEK

There were gardens of the Sultan in Bebek Bay which was covered with greenery till 18th century and it was not a desired place for settlement. Its population started to increase after the construction of *Bebek Qasr, Bebek Mosque* and various buildings in the reign of Ahmet III (1703-30). From the mid 19th century, Bebek,

General view of Arnavutköy.

Bebek Bay.

which was used as a summer resort, became a constant settlement area after steamboat and tram transportations reached this section. *Bebek Qasr* which was settled parallel to the Bosphorus and was a beautiful example of Turkish civilian architecture with its 110 m length was demolished by Abdülmecit in 1846. *Bebek Mosque* built near Bebek Qasr was demolished in 1913 and the present mosque was built by Kemalettin Bey in its place. It was built in National Architectural Style I and consists of; a square place covered with single dome and a last gathering stoa. The beautiful building across the mosque is a summerhouse of *Egyptian Consulate*.

It was built by Hidiv family in the beginning of 20th century in place of the mansion of Grand Vizier Ali Pasha.

Rumeli Fortress.

Many apartments have built rapidly in Bebek after it became one of the outstanding districts of modern

Egyptian Consulate in summer in Bebek.

Bosphorus. At the end of the bay on the other side of Bosphorus *Küçüksu Qasr* with its wonderful façade attracts your attention.

RUMELİHİSARI

Rumelihisarı which took its name from the fortress built by Fatih is the first settlement area of Turks on this side of the Bosphorus. As opposed to the other districts examined till here, it was settled in 1450s and became a Muslim village. Coastline of Rumelihisarı is covered with mansions of famous people. Shantytowns grew up on the higher parts of the district after the increase of emigration after 1950s.

FORTRESS OF RUMELİ ❶

(RUMELİ 'BOĞAZKESEN' HİSARI)
Yahya Kemal Avenue No: 42
Rumelihisarı

Mehmet, the Conqueror built the Fortress of Rumeli to take the control of the narrowest point of the Istanbul Bosphorus before the conquest of Istanbul. With the *Fortress of Anatolia* on the other side, it was intended to shut out the aids that could come to Byzantium through the Bosphorus. The historical heritage that survived from 15th century till today was built in a short time like four months on the hillside which lies perpendicular to Bosphorus. It is estimated that Architect Muslihuddin Aga drew the plan of the fortress. The Fortress was used as a prison after losing its importance by completion of the conquest.

The fortress consists of three large fortress on three sides and walls and towers in between them. These three fortress has the names of three viziers who took care of the construction: the one on the seaside is called *Çandarlı Halil Pasha Tower*, the one on the south, on Bebek side was called *Zağanos Pasha Tower* and the one on the north was called *Sarıca*

EMİRGAN
BALTA LİMANI
RUMELİ HİSARI
Emirgan Korusu
İstinye Koyu
FATİH SULTAN MEHMET KÖPRÜSÜ
İSTİNYE BAYIRI CAD.
BOĞAZİÇİ CAD.
MUVAKKITHANE CAD.
SEZAİBEY CAD.
HEKİM ATA CAD.
ÇAKIRPINARCI CAD.
BALTALİMANI ÇAYIR CAD.
BALTALİMANI HİSAR CAD.
BALTA LİMANI-HİSARÜSTÜ YOLU
KENAN EVREN CAD.
HİSARÜSTÜ NİSPETİYE CAD.
YAHYA KEMAL CAD.
MASLAK CAD.
Rumeli Fortress 1 (Rumeli Hisarı)
Fatih Sultan Mehmet Bridge 2 (Fatih Sultan Mehmet Köprüsü)
Balta Limanı 3 (Balta Limanı)
Emirgan Forest 4 (Emirgan Korusu)
İstinye Bay 5 (İstinye Koyu)
Polis Police
Hastane Hospital
Cami Mosque
Kilise Church
Otel Hotel
PTT PTT
Sağlık Ocağı Health Clinic
Saray-Kasır Palace-Summer Palace
İDO İskele Pier
Tarihi Anıt Historical Monument
İDO Feribot İDO Ferry boat
Türbe Tomb

Istanbul Bosphorus looks magnificant from the walls of Rumeli Fortress.

Pasha Tower. Other than these big towers, there are 13 more small towers adjacent to the walls.

The fortress which was renovated by Selim III (1789-1807) after it was on fire was left by itself and the housing around it became a district because of negligence.

These settlements were removed after the big renovation and the historical heritage was saved by building a museum.

The minaret body seen in the atrium of the fortress remained from the mosque built in the reign of Fatih and demolished in 1907. This place was formed as an amphitheatre by taking advantage of the sloping area. There is also a cistern under the platform.

Amphi Theater stage where concerts are organized in summer.

Fortress of Rumeli is open for visiting as a museum in between 09:00-16:30 except Wednesdays.

The Magnificent view of Istanbul Bosphorus can be watched on the roads over the walls which can be climbed from the stairs in the atrium.

FATİH SULTAN MEHMET BRIDGE 2

(FATİH SULTAN MEHMET KÖPRÜSÜ)

It is the second hanging bridge which connects the European and Asian coasts of Istanbul. The construction of Fatih Sultan Mehmet Bridge started in 1985 and it opened for traffic on July, 3rd 1988. The Bridge connecting *Kavacık* and *Hisarüstü* is 1510 m in length, the distance between two carrier towers is 1090 m and the highest point is 64 m. It has the same construction technique with Bosphorus Bridge, only differs in the vertical arrangement of the hanging cables which connects the main cables with the apron and their being double line.

Fatih Sultan Mehmet Bridge.

FROM THE FORTRESS TO RUMELİ KAVAĞI

After the Fortress of Rumeli and Fatih Sultan Mehmet Bridge, you reach the **Baltalimanı** which took its name from Baltaoğlu Süleyman Pasha, the naval commander of Fatih. The clough where Baltalimanı Valley pass was a famous resort. The building used as *Osteopathic Hospital* which is at the coast before the *Baltalimanı* valley, was a masonry Palace built by Sarkis Balyan on behalf of Mustafa Reşit Pasha, one the preliminaries of the Tanzimat Fermanı (Reforms Decree). **Boyacıköy (Dyers Village)** which is subsequent to Baltalimanı took its name after the settlement of a large family of master fabric dyers called Kafkaryadi whom Selim III (1789-1807) brought from Kırklareli. Due to its expansion by disorganized structuring, it connects with Emirgan.

There were only the kiosk, hunting kiosk and gardens of Nişancı Feridun Bey who took a large area as a present in **Emirgan** where no settlements were seen till the mid 16th cen-

Yellow Kiosk *(Sarı Köşk)* in Emirgan Forest.

A waterside mansion in İstinye.

rebuilt by Mahmut II in 1838. The large forest covering the hillside of Emirgan was given first to Nişancı Feridun Bey then to Yusuf Pasha by Murat IV in 1635, then to Egypt Khedive Ismail Pasha by Abdülaziz. The Municipality of Istanbul bought this place and opened for public use in 1943. *Yellow, White and Pink Kiosks* that Egypt Khedive Ismail Pasha built are also in here. Nowadays "Tulip Feast" is being organized every year by the Municipality of Istanbul in *Emirgan Forest* which is one of the most beautiful touring, relaxation and entertainment places of Bosphorus.

As opposed to the other bays of the Bosphorus **İstinye Bay** served as a base and bunker for Byzantine, Genoese an Ottoman navies, due to its deep and guarded structure like the Golden Horn. It was used as a ship-yard starting from Ottoman period because of its natural harbor characteristic and this function of the bay ended in 1991.

After surpassing the İstinye Bay you reach **Yeniköy** which is one of the most pop-ular places that well-endowed

tury. The importance of the area increased after the con-struction of a mosque, a square fountain, a Turkish bath and shops on behalf of Abdülmecit I in between 1779-81. Emirgan Mosque was

İstinye Bay.

GORENLER
II

communities esteem in Bosphorus. The historical and modern mansions lined side by side through the coastline displays this condition.

Following the line of mansions, out of settlement area of **Kalendar Bay** which is exposed to heavy storms of the Bosphorus comes. *Austrian Consulate* is emplaced at the beginning of the bay and *Kalendar Kiosk* built for Ahmet III (1703-30) by Damat İbrahim Pasha takes place further away from it. This kiosk was rebuilt in the reign of Abdülaziz. Construction of the place that is owned by the Austrian Consulate was started on the land of Mıgırdiç Cezayirliyan but couldn't be completed. The land of Mıgırdiç was nationalized after his death by Abdülhamit II and given to Australian's as a sign of amity. The construction of the palace was completed in 1898. One of the most

beautiful bays of the Bosphorus, **Tarabya Bay** starts after Kalendar Bay. **Tarabya** which is one of the most favorite districts of Bosphorus is settled here.

Fishing boats in Yeniköy.

Selim II (1566-74) built a kiosk in this area and then it transformed into village settlement. Popularity of Tarabya increased more and more due to its becoming the most popular summer resort in 18th century. Some of the consulates owned summer kiosks in here in 19th century. Mansions at the coastline, kiosks and villas at the inner parts of Tarabya displays its being one of the most attractive districts of Bosphorus.

Before entering Tarabya Bay you see the *Huber Kiosk* one of the most grandiose structures of Bosphorus. August Huber, Ottoman representative of a weapon company built the main building and additional buildings in a large garden. Main building which is parallel to the coastline was built in the end of 19th century, its additional building was built in 20th century. The architect of the main building is unknown but the architect of the additional buildings was Italian Raimondo d'Aranco, master of Art Nouveau. The complex which changed hands many times is now used as *Presidential Palace*. There are buildings of *German Consulate* following the Huber Kiosk.

Luxurious fisher restaurants, night clubs and taverns are in service at the coastline of Tarabya Bay which is used as a marina. In pursuit of the bay summer kiosks owned by *French, English and Italian* consulate takes place.

A large bay covering **Kireçburnu, Cumhuriyet, Çayırbaşı** and **Büyükdere** starts after leaving Tarabya behind. This place was a fisherman village formed by houses lined around the valley pouring out through the bay. After the conquest it couldn't move forward on account of settlement, but it was one of the most favorite resorts of Istanbul owing to its wonderful meadow where the valley pours through and being close to the *Belgrad Forests* which has rich water sources. **Büyükdere**, which covers the northern parts of the bay and has a predominant population of Greek and Armenian minorities, was an attractive settlement area in 19th century. The excess minority and foreign popula-

Kalender coast on the Tarabya road.

Sadberk Hanım Museum established in the Historical Azaryan Kiosk.

Büyükdere.

Armenian Catholic Church.

tion during the Ottoman period gathered some churches around here. The first of thee churches is *Surp Hripsimyantz Armenian Gregorian Church* is on the staked road side of Büyükdere Avenue which is parallel to the coastline. Other churches are very close to each other: *Santa Maria Italian Catholic Church* on the Azatlı Street, *Hagios Paraskevi Greek Church* on Danişment street, *Spanish*

Sarıyer, one of the most crowded places of Bosphorus.

Embassy further away on the avenue and *Surp Boğos Armenian Catholic Church* which attracts attention with its architecture, at the corner where staked road connects the avenue. Summer mansions owned by the Russian Consulate are also in this area.

At the end of the district, the historical *Azaryan Mansion* which is on Piyasa Avenue and has a different façade execution is open for visiting as **Sadberk Hanım Museum** nowadays.

Museum can be visited between 10:00-17:00 except Wednesdays.

Azaryan Mansion was built by Bedros Azaryan in place of an older mansion which burned in a fire in the beginning of 20th century. Collections arranged by the family are exhibited in the building bought by the Koç family. Various Turkish porcelains, İznik tiles, examples of Ottoman women clothing, examples of calligraphy, bejeweled goods, Turkish handiwork and Turkish traditions are exhibited in the rooms. In the *Sevgi Gönül Building* which is near the historical mansion and owned by the museum is where important Archaeological works are exhibited in. Works, coins, metallic, glass and ceramic objects of early Anatolian Civilizations and rich collections of Byzantine and Roman periods are worth seeing.

Sarıyer due to being near to the Belgrad Forest of which some parts are in its border has preserved its characteristic of being a resort in all periods. However it did not have an intense settlement till recent times. Rapid emigration to Istanbul after 1950s and intense settlement of Bosphorus area throughout 1980s prepared negative expansion of Sarıyer. If you visit Sarıyer, you shouldn't leave before eating its pastry, ice cream and milk pudding.

The following district **Rumeli Kavağı,** opposite of the active atmosphere of Sarıyer, is a modest fisherman village which is famous with its restaurants. **Anadolu Kavağı** and *Ceneviz (Genoese) Fortress* which are on the other side of the Bosphorus where it connects with Black sea appear tremendous form here.

Telli Baba Mausoleum which is on the Sarıyer-Rumeli Kavağı road is visited by youth who wants to marry for finding a partner, and by married ones for having a long marriage. They take wedding dress threads from the mausoleum and pray for their wishes to realize. After the realization of their wishes, they come back and leave some wedding dress threads on the mausoleum, so that the wedding dress threads never lack around the mausoleum.

Fishing boats in Rumeli Kavağı.

Coast of Rumeli Kavağı.

Anadolu Kavağı.

ANADOLU KAVAĞI

It is a lovely fishermen village across the Rumeli Kavağı on the Anatolian side of Istanbul Bosphorus. It was endowed with castles due to its strategically important position near the connection point of the Bosphorus and Black Sea. The most important one of these is the **Yoros Castle** settled over a hill dominating Anadolu Kavağı. The castle which was built by Byzantines was captured by Ottomans in 1305 with the weakening of Byzantium and their being

Genoese (Yoros) Castle.

condemned to the historical peninsula, but Ottoman couldn't hold it for a long time. The castle was then patronized by Genoese who were holding the commercial roads of Black Sea in 1348. It was also known as *Genoese Castle* due to the additions made in Genoese period.

It was again gained to the control

of Ottoman by Yıldırım Beyazıt (1389-1402) in 1391. A Mosque, a Turkish bath and a fountain was built in the castle which continued to be used after the conquest of Istanbul. It was abandoned to its faith in 19th century.

The other castle built on the coast of this hill on Anadolu Kavağı was *Kavak Castle* which was built by Murat IV in 1694, but it couldn't survive till today. Anadolu Kavağı is a touristic district with the castle on the hill and fishermen restaurants and cafeterias on the coast.

Kanlıca coasts.

Hıdiv Qasr.

FORTRESS OF ANATOLİA ❷

(ANADOLU HİSARI)

It is in the district where it gave its name and is on the place where Göksu River pours into the Bosphorus which was once one of the most famous resorts of Istanbul. It was built by Yıldırım Beyazıt who was intending to conquer Istanbul like Fatih in between 1394-1395. This first square planned building consisted a 25 m long four floored tower and walls surrounding it. Later when Mehmet, the Conqueror was building the Fortress of Rumeli, he also surrounded this fortress by larger walls and towers to increase its attacking power. It was used to stop the 17th an 18th century Kazak raids after the conquest. It lost its function with the construction of new fortifications on the north of the Bosphorus. The Fortress of Anatolia which was neglected through 19th century had some damage and roads were passed from its borders. The castle which was bonded to the Management of Fortresses Museum in Republic period is closed for visiting.

KÜÇÜKSU QASR ❹

(KÜÇÜKSU KASRI)

Küçüksu Avenue, Anadoluhisarı

Küçüksu Qasr which is near the Fortress of

Anatolia Fortress at the side of Göksu River.

Göksu River.

Anatolia was built by Nikogos Balyan on behalf of Abdülmecit in between 1856-57, in place of the timber kiosk built in the reign of Mahmut I (1730-54). It was built double floored over the basement, and has an active view with its baroque-rococo style facades. The façade parallel to the Bosphorus has convex protrusions on both sides and has a grandiose stairway in the middle. The basement was separated for cellar, kitchen and servants, upper floors was arranged as a saloon and four corner rooms. There are no bedrooms because the structure was used only for one day for relaxation and hunting purposes. The table in the saloon of the second floor that can

Küçüksu Qasr with its rich facade bas-reliefs.

Kuleli Military High School.

be ascended by the baroque stairs, which Abdülhamit II made when he was a shehzade (prince) attracts attention. The rug on this floor is an Iranian rug adorned with various animal figures. Küçüksu Qasr reflects last period Ottoman taste with its valuable art works adorning the saloon and rooms, rugs, furniture brought from Europe and fire places.

The Qasr which was used for governmental receptions in Republic period was opened for visiting as a museum in 1983.

It can be visited between 09:30-17:00 (16:00 in winter season) except for Mondays and Thursdays.

BEYLERBEYİ PALACE 6

(BEYLERBEYİ SARAYI)
Abdullahağa Avenue,
Çayırbaşı Beylerbeyi
Tel: (0216) 321 93 20-21

It consists of a waterside palace parallel to the coastline in a large garden and adjacent kiosks. *İstavroz Garden* around the palace which used to cover a larger area was a resort where Sultans gave importance. Architect Krikor Balyan built a timber waterside palace on behalf of Mahmut II in between 1829-32 which was called "Yellow Palace" because of its yellow color. Abdülaziz (1861-76) after he succeeded the crown demolished this palace and made architect brothers Sarkis Balyan and Agop Balyan built Beylerbeyi Palace in between 1861-65. Palace was used mostly on summer months and for hosting foreign presidents. Abdülhamit II dethroned and exiled to Salonika in 1909, settled in Beylerbeyi Palace in 1912 and stayed there till his death in 1918. The nacreous furniture placed in the palace which he made by himself are interesting examples showing his carpentry ability. Nevertheless handmade *Hereke* weaved curtains, handmade *Hereke* carpets, porcelain vases, English and French crystal chandeliers,

Beylerbeyi Palace.

paintings of Şeker Ahmet Pasha and various other famous painters forms the rich collection of the palace. The floor of the palace is covered with reeds resistant to humidity that are brought from Egypt.

The building which was built double floored over a high basement has an approximately 65 x 40 m rectangular plan. It was separated into two main parts: Southern part *Selamlık (Mabeyn)* and Northern part *Harem*.

The entrance of **Selamlık** is adorned with Sevr Vase and Bohemia Crystal Chandelier and floor is covered by *Hereke* carpet. There is a beautiful double sided stairway going up to the upper floor. Following the adjutant and guest rooms on the waterside, there is the largest saloon of the first floor having a large pool in the middle. This pool was designed to chill the place hot summer days. The bronze statue of Sultan Abdülaziz on a horse at the other side of the pool also attracts attention. **Harem** section which starts with a saloon consists of; rooms of Abdülhamit II and his wives, on the upper floor, study room of Abdülhamit II, the bedroom of Valide Sultan (Sultan's Mother), reception room, *Sedefli Saloon* which enchants the observers with their beautiful decorations.

Following the upper *Harem* section comes *Mavi (Blue) Saloon,* the most grandiose saloon of the palace. The interiors of the blue columns of this saloon which was used for ceremonies are timber. The bedroom of Abdülaziz which was used by guest bedroom afterwards, the waiting room, ministers room of which walls were covered with timber, are richly decorated places suited to the magnificence of the saloon.

There are kiosks and a large pool in the garden of the palace which was organized by sets due to its slope. *Yellow Kiosk* and *Marble Kiosk* which was built in the reign of Mahmut II are placed around the large pool. Two waterside kiosks built with the new palace, one for *Harem* and one for *Selamlık* attracts attention with their different designs. There are stoas covered by many little domes at the entrances of the kiosks which are formed by a main area long at the Bosphorus and a service room. Top of the main area is also covered by a sliced dome. The ceiling of the kiosk of *Selamlık* is adorned with animal figures, the ceiling of the kiosk of *Harem* is covered with flower patterns.

Beylerbeyi Palace which is open for visiting *can be visited between 09:30-17:00 (16:00 in winter period) except for Mondays and Thursdays.*

Beylerbeyi Palace.

ÜSKÜDAR ❶

Pier and dockyard of Khalkedon (Kadıköy) which was founded in 7th century B.C. takes place in Üsküdar or Khrysopolis (Golden City) as it was called in ancient times. It was called Golden City because taxes were stored in a treasury here. It was taken under protection of various governments many times and it sustained its existence as an important settlement during Byzantine period. Also, Üsküdar was the starting point of many revolutions in which emperors were changed during Byzantine period. Orhan Gazi (1324-60), the second sultan of Ottoman Empire took control of Kadıköy and Üsküdar, one century before Ottoman's conquest Istanbul. Mehmet,

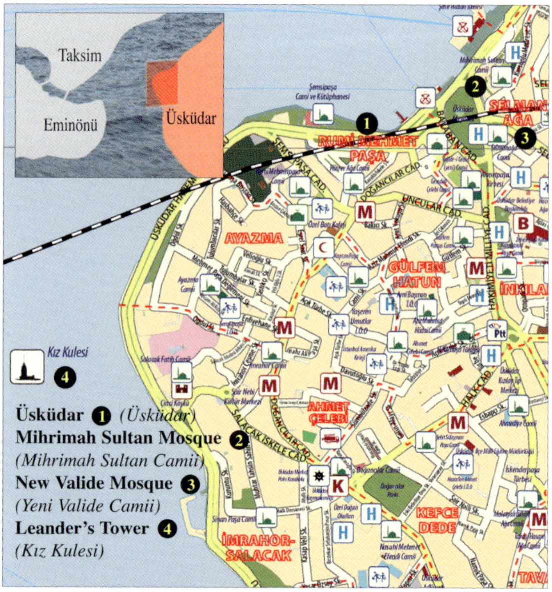

Aerial view of the Leander's Tower and coasts of Üsküdar.

Ayazma Mosque.

the Conqueror placed Muslims he brought from various places into Üsküdar after the conquest of Istanbul. Many complexes *(külliye)* were built in Üsküdar which was one of the important districts of the city in Ottoman period: **Mihrimah Sultan Complex (külliye)** takes place on the center near **Ahmet III fountain**, **New Valide Complex** on Hakimiyet-i Milliyet Avenue in the south of the center, **Şemsi Pasha Complex** which was built by Architect Sinan on the foreland jutting out to Bosphorus, **Ayazma Mosque** on a higher

Çinili Mosque.

level across the **Leander's Tower**. There are two more complexes other than these inside the districts of Üsküdar. **Çinili Complex** where interior walls are covered with tiles, is at the end of Çavuşdere Avenue which connects to Dr. Fahri Atabey Avenue with Sansar Street. Çinili Camii Street which is near Çinili Complex and connects to Çavuşdere Avenue opens to **Atik Valide Complex** which was built by Architect Sinan on behalf of Nurbanu Sultan, mother of Murat III, wife of Selim II in between 1570-79.

Mihrimah Sultan Mosque 2

(Mihrimah Sultan Camii)
Üsküdar Square

The complex buildings which are in Üsküdar

Mihrab of the Çinili Mosque.

Square across the pier were built by Architect Sinan and completed in 1548 on behalf of Mihrimah Sultan, daughter of Süleyman the Magnificent. The last gathering place with double stoa and a part of the atrium placed on a high platform is covered by a lead roof in a setting peculiar to Sinan. The main area, except the entrance side, expands in width by the three semi domes supporting the central dome. The dome and semi-domes are adorned with blue and red handiworks. Windows that illuminate the place are also elements that enrich the main area. While the lower windows are rectangular framed and have simple characteristics, the ones over them are in triangular form and have stain glass windows and the ones over the triangles are circular stained glass windows which are attractive with their emplacement and beauty. The flanks of lower windows,

Mihrimah Sultan Mosque.

Mihrab of the Atik Valide Mosque.

Ceramic tile board.

marble *mihrab* and pulpit are products of fine workmanship.

NEW VALİDE MOSQUE ③

(YENİ VALİDE CAMİİ)
Hakimiyet-i Milliye Avenue, Üsküdar

It is in the south of Mihrimah Sultan Mosque, at the other side of the square. It was built by Gülnuş Emetullah Valide Sultan, mother of Ahmet III in between 1708-1710. The timber Hünkar Kiosk was added to the mosque which was formed according to Classical period architecture in continuum of westernization. It has an inner atrium having a şadırvan (water-tank with a fountain) surrounded with stoas. The center of the rectangular in width planned

Beylerbeyi Mosque.

New Valide Mosque.

main area was covered by a large dome and its pews are covered with mirrored squinches.

Elegant columns connected by sharp archways carry the pews. Corner transitions of the square planned middle area which is covered by the dome were lightened by squinches, the section where the dome sits over the body walls was enriched with stalactite stuffing.

The mausoleum of the Valide Sultan who built the complex is on Hakimiyet-i Milliye Avenue.

Leander's Tower, and Hagia Sophia, Sultanahmet Mosque and Topkapı Palace in the background.

Selimiye Mosque, Harem.

LEANDER'S TOWER 4

(KIZ KULESİ)
Tel: (0216) 342 47 47

At the offshore of Salacak, close to Üsküdar, Leander's Tower is the guardian of the point where Bosphorus meets Marmara Sea. Tower took its name from the legend that tells a Byzantine Emperor who sealed his daughter into the tower. Emperor Manuel Komnenos (1143-80) built guard tower here in 12th century and it has been used as a

Coasts of Üsküdar and Şemsi Pasha Mosque.

customs station and traffic control office. It is said that the emperor stretched a chain from another tower near Sarayburnu for the security of Istanbul.

Mehmet, the Conqueror built a new tower here after the conquest of Istanbul. The tower which demolished in the earthquake of 1509 was renovated with the order of Yavuz Sultan Selim (1512-20). After 16th century in which Ottoman Empire was very powerful, the tower stopped being used as a watch tower and became a lighthouse to guide ships. When the timber tower built during the reign of Yavuz destroyed in the fire of 1719, it renewed in between 1725-26, a glass kiosk placed on it and its dome covered with lead. It became the station of quarantine in the cholera epidemic of 1829 and in 1832, it was transferred to management of lighthouses. Leander's Tower took its current form due to the renovation made in the reign of Mahmut II (1808-39).

You can reach Leander's Tower by boats departing from Salacak, Ortaköy and in weekends, Kabataş. You can just go there to see its wonderful view or to breathe its mystical atmosphere in its cafeteria that is open in daytime or restaurant in nighttime.

KADIKÖY

The mythical history of Kadıköy goes back to Megarians who settled here in 680 B.C. and founded Khalkedon. As being one of the important centers it made hosting for the Khalkedon Council that gathered in 451.

Haydarpaşa Train Station.

However it became a village that earns its living with agriculture and fishing after abasement of Byzantium. Its name was thought to have changed into Kadıköy after Mehmet, the Conqueror gave the district to Hızır Bey, kadı (Muslim judge) of Istanbul after its conquest. Until 19th century, Kadıköy and its region was a resort consisting kiosks of high level governor agents. Otherwise there was a Greek fishermen village and some Turkish farmer villages at the interior parts. When the organized steamboats voyages reached Kadıköy, it became an exclusive housing area for the middle and higher income groups and non Muslims. In the last period of Ottoman, it became one of the most developed districts which had constant settlement besides being a resort. The exposure of Istanbul to migration in 1950s accelerated the enlargement of Kadıköy into large areas which became a district in Republic period. Nowadays Kadıköy is one of the most attractive places of Istanbul with its implements that can provide shopping, culture and entertainment needs alongside being a housing area where middle and higher income groups live. The *large coastline* that opens to Marmara, *Kadıköy Bazaar* with its bookstores, cafes, fishers, restaurant and patisseries and *Bahariye Avenue* and region with its movie theatres, culture and shopping centers have always been a visiting place for the people in Istanbul.

PRINCES' ISLANDS
(ADALAR)

Islands which are one hour away from the Historical Peninsula and are suburbs of Istanbul consist of 9 islands which are in Marmara Sea at the offshore of the coastline between Bostancı and Kartal. Following are the ones that are suitable for settlement: *Büyükada* (5,4 km^2), *Heybeliada* (2,3 km^2), *Burgazadası* (1,5 km^2), *Kınalıada* (1,3 km^2) and *Sedefadası* (0,157 km^2), and others are *Yassıada* (5,2 hectare), *Sivriada* (4,5 hectare), *Tavşanadası* (1 hectare) and *Kaşıkadası* (0,8 hectare). They were known as Prince Islands because they were used as a place of exile for the Palace members, princes, patriarchs and emperors who were kept in the prisons and dungeons here. Monasteries and churches built over the ruins of Roman temples starting from the Byzantium period caused the religious region characteristic of the area to be dominant till mid 19th century. Some of these monasteries and churches are in service today. Together with the steamboat voyages which started in 1846, islands attracted Turks and became a relaxation and entertainment place for spring and summer months with their rich natural beauty and kiosks, schools and hotels were built. Islands which Istanbul people visit also today during summer months host thousands of visitors with their beaches, green picnic areas, fish restaurants and entertainment places. Phaetons and bicycles are used for touring because motor-vehicles are not allowed. The largest ones, Büyükada and Heybeliada are among the places that most of the Istanbulite show interest in especially in weekends. *Hagios Georgios Monastery and Church* which are placed over the 203 m high Yücetepe in Büyükada are popular with their lively feast ceremonies and being an offering place.

Kınalıada.

Burgazada.

Heybeliada.

Büyükada.

Büyükada.

HOTELS

SWISSÔTEL

Bayıldım Avenue No: 2 Maçka
☎ +90 (212) 326 11 00
€€€€€
www.swissotel.com.tr
✉ istanbul@swissotel.com

PARKSA HILTON

Bayıldım Avenue No: 12 Maçka
☎ +90 (212) 310 12 00
€€€
www.istanbul-park.hilton.com
✉ sales.parksa@hilton.com

CONRAD HOTEL

Barbaros Bulvarı Saray Avenue No. 5 Beşiktaş
€€€€
☎ +90 (212) 310 25 25
www.istanbul.conradmeetings.com
✉ istanbulinfo@conradhotels.com

ÇIRAĞAN PALACE HOTEL KEMPINSKI

Çırağan Avenue No:32 Beşiktaş
☎ +90 (212) 326 46 46
€€€€€
www.kempinski-istanbul.com
✉ ciraganpalace@kempinski.com

THE PLAZA HOTEL

Barbaros Bulvarı No: 165 Balmumcu-Beşiktaş
☎ +90 (212) 370 20 20
€€€€€
www.theplazahotel.com.tr
✉ info@theplazahotel.com.tr

DEDEMAN HOTELS & RESORTS INTERNATIONAL

Yıldız Posta Avenue No: 52 Esentepe-Beşiktaş
☎ +90 (212) 337 39 00
€€€
www.dedeman.com
✉ hotels@dedeman.com

DIVAN CITY İSTANBUL

Büyükdere Avenue No: 84 Gayrettepe-Beşiktaş
☎ +90 (212) 337 49 00
€€€
www.divan.com.tr
✉ info.divancity@divan.com.tr

RESIDENCE GAYRETTEPE

Rüştübey Street No: 2 34349 Gayrettepe
☎ +90 (212) 288 95 90 (Pbx)
€€€€
www.residencegayrettepe.com
✉ info@residencegayrettepe.com

İSTANBUL SÜRMELİ

Prof. Dr. Bülent Tarcan Street No: 3 Gayrettepe
☎ +90 (212) 272 11 61
€€€
www.surmelihotels.com
✉ info@surmelihotels.com

GRAND CEVAHİR OTEL

Darülaceze Avenue Okmeydanı Şişli
☎ +90 (212) 314 42 42
www.grandcevahirhotel.com
✉ info@gch.com.tr

RESİDENCES ASTORİA

Büyükdere Avenue No:127 Esentepe
☎ +90 (212) 370 00 00
€€€€€
www.kempinski-astoria.com
✉ info.astoria@kempinski.com

NİL HOTEL

Tavukçu Fethi Street No: 25 Osmanbey
☎ +90 (212) 230 29 69
www.nilhotel.net
✉ reservation@nilhotel.net

MÖVENPICK HOTEL

Büyükdere Avenue 4. Levent (Metro çıkışı)
☎ +90 (212) 319 29 29
€€€€€
www.moevenpick-hotels.com
✉ hotel.istanbul@moevenpick.com

HOTEL İSTANBUL SHERATON

Büyükdere Avenue No. 233 Maslak
☎ +90 (212) 335 99 99 (Pbx)
€€€€€
✉ info@sheratonistanbulmaslak.com
www.sheraton.com/istanbul

PRINCESS ORTAKÖY

Dereboyu Avenue No: 10 Ortaköy
☎ +90 (212) 227 60 10
€
www.ortakoyprincess.com
✉ info@ortakoyprincess.com

THE ISTANBUL EDITION

Büyükdere Avenue No. 136 1. Levent
☎ +90 (212) 287 28 72
www.editionhotels.com
✉ iereservations@editionhotels.com

€ Up to 50 Euros. €€ Between 50 and 100 Euros. €€€ Between 100 and 150 Euros.

HOTELS

HOTEL LES OTTOMANS

Muallim Naci Avenue No: 68 Kuruçeşme
☎ +90 (212) 359 15 00
€€€€€
www.lesottomans.com
✉ info@lesottomans.com

BEBEK HOTEL

Cevdetpaşa Avenue No: 34 Bebek
☎ +90 (212) 358 20 00 (Pbx)
€
www.bebekhotel.com.tr
✉ bebekhotel@bebekhotel.com.tr

THE MARMARA ÇAMLICA

Atıf Bey Street No: 67-69 Acıbadem
☎ +90 (216) 362 10 10
€€
www.themarmarahotels.com
✉ residence-info@themarmarahotels.com

RADISSON BLU BOSPHORUS HOTEL

Çırağan Avenue No: 46 Ortaköy
☎ +90 (212) 310 15 00
€€€€
www.radissonblu.com

KALE HOTEL ★★★☆☆

Kale Avenue No: 78 Kilyos
☎ +90 (212) 201 18 18
www.kilyoskalehotel.com
✉ info@kilyoskalehotel.com

ADEN HOTEL ★★★★☆

Rıhtım Avenue Yoğurtçu Şükrü Street No. 2 Kadıköy
☎ +90 (216) 345 10 00 Pbx
€€
www.adenotel.com
✉ info@adenotel.com

THE MARMARA SUADİYE

Bağdat Avenue No: 435 Suadiye
☎ +90 (216) 362 10 10
€€€
www.themarmarahotels.com
✉ residence-info@themarmarahotels.com

BOSPHORUS PALACE

Yalıboyu Avenue No : 64 Beylerbeyi
☎ +90 (216) 422 00 03 (9 hat)
€€€€€
www.bosphoruspalace.com
✉ info@bosphoruspalace.com

THE GREEN PARK HOTELS

Temenye Mevkii Eski Ankara Avenue No. 200 Pendik
☎ +90 (216) 491 72 72
€€€€
www.thegreenpark.com

SUMAHAN

Kuleli Avenue No: 51 Çelgelköy
€€€€€
☎ +90 (216) 422 80 00
www.sumahan.com
✉ info@sumahan.com

VILLAGE PARK COUNTRY HOTEL

Ayazma Mah. No: 19
İshaklı Köyü-Beykoz
☎ +90 (216) 434 59 31-32
€€€
www.villagepark.com.tr
✉ info@villagepark.com.tr

ÇIRAĞAN PALACE HOTEL

Çırağan Avenue No: 32 Beşiktaş
☎ +90 (212) 326 46 66
€€€€€
www.ciragan-sarayi.kempinski.com

AJİA HOTEL

Ahmet Rasim Paşa Yalısı, Çubuklu Avenue No: 27 Kanlıca
☎ +90 (216) 413 93 00
€€€€€
www.ajiahotel.com
✉ info@ajiahotel.com

ŞİLE KLAS OTEL

Kordonboyu Avenue Ayazma Mevkii No:7 Şile
☎ +90 (216) 711 53 67
€€€

ŞİLE RESORT HOTEL

Balıbey Mah. Ağlayan Kaya Avenue No: 33 Uzunkum-Şile
☎ +90 (216) 711 36 27-28
€€
www.sileresorthotel.com
✉ sileresort@sileresorthotel.com

KLASSIS RESORT HOTEL

Karga Burun Mevkii, Silivri
☎ +90 (212) 727 40 50
€€
www.klassisotel.com.tr
✉ resort.operasyon@klassis.com.tr

€€€€ **Between 150 and 200 Euros.** €€€€€ **250 Euros and more.**

RESTAURANTS

ZİYA RESTAURANT

Muallim Naci Avenue No. 109/1 Ortaköy
☎ **+90 (212) 261 60 05**

A LA CREPE RESTAURANT

Salhane Street No: 2 Ortaköy
☎ **+90 (212) 258 83 36**

ALA TURCA RESTAURANT

Cami Square, Hazine Street 8, Ortaköy
☎ **+90 (212) 258 79 24**

ALARGA RESTAURANT

Kuruçeşme Avenue No: 19 Beşiktaş
☎ **+90 (212) 358 31 57**

HEMERA RESTAURANT

Princess Hotel, Ortaköy - Beşiktaş
☎ **+90 (212) 227 60 10**

ADEM BABA BALIK LOKANTASI

Satış Meysan Street No: 2 Arnavutköy
☎ **+90 (212) 263 29 33**

COCO PAZZO

1. Avenue No: 62/A Arnavutköy
☎ **+90 (212) 265 21 29**

ALESTA BOAT RESTAURANT

Çamlıbahçe Mevkii Bebek
☎ **+90 (212) 257 97 97**

BALIKLAMA RESTAURANT

Köybaşı Avenue No: 10 Yeniköy
☎ **+90 (212) 262 00 71**

SANDAL BALIK EVİ

Köybaşı Avenue No. 211 Yeniköy
☎ **+90 (212) 262 36 43**

BAY BALIKÇI RESTAURANT

Kireçburnu Avenue No: 14 Kireçburnu
☎ **+90 (212) 262 22 94**

AMBASSADEURS BALIK LOKANTASI

Bebek Oteli Cevdet Paşa Avenue No: 34 Bebek
☎ **+90 (212) 358 20 00**

BEBEK BALIKÇISI RESTAURANT

Cevdet Paşa Avenue No: 26/A Bebek
☎ **+90 (212) 263 34 47**

ALTINKUM DİCLE RESTAURANT

Plajyolu, No: 8, Rumelikavağı
☎ **+90 (212) 242 13 93**

AQUARIUS 2

Kefeliköy Avenue No: 172, Tarabya
☎ **+90 (212) 223 87 77**

KIYI BALIK RESTAURANT

Kefeliköy Avenue No: 126 Tarabya
☎ **+90 (212) 262 00 02**

ALİBABA RESTAURANT

Kireçburnu Avenue No: 20-22 - Sarıyer
☎ **+90 (212) 262 08 89**

ARKA BAHÇE RESTAURANT

Kalebahçe No: 10 Rumelihisarı
☎ **+90 (212) 265 38 48**

AYDER RESTAURANT

İskele Avenue, Rumelikavağı
☎ **+90 (212) 218 34 34**

BABA RESTAURANT

İskele Avenue, No:13, Anadolukavağı
☎ **+90 (216) 320 20 47**

ÇAPARİ RESTAURANT

Anadolu Kavağı
☎ **+90 (216) 320 20 06**

BOĞAZİÇİ PAYSAGE RESTAURANT

Hidiv Kasrı Yolu Hakimler Sitesi No:18/A Kanlıca
☎ **+90 (216) 322 00 77**

KORU RESTAURANT

Beykoz Korusu, Beykoz
☎ **+90 (216) 322 29 01**

KIZ KULESİ

Salacak Üsküdar
☎ **+90 (216) 342 47 47**

DİLRUBA RESTAURANT

Fethipaşa Korusu, Fıstıkağacı - Üsküdar
☎ **+90 (216) 492 15 00**

İNCİ RESTAURANT

Salacak Sahil Yolu, No:25, Üsküdar
☎ **+90 (216) 310 69 98**

AŞIYAN RESTAURANT

Kalamış Yat Limanı - Kalamış- Kadıköy
☎ **+90 (216) 349 55 69**

ÇİYA SOFRASI RESTAURANT

Caferağa Mah. Güneşlibahçe Street No: 48-B Kadıköy
☎ **+90 (216) 330 31 90**

WHAT TO EAT AND DRINK?

The Bosphorus with its long shores is famous for its waterside mansions and fish restaurants. You can savour the pleasure of non-alcoholic restaurants at **Çadır** and **Malta** manor houses in **Yıldız Forest** which has a royal garden, and open buffets at the weekend in forest. You can see the magnificent view of Ortaköy Mosque, Bosphorus Bridge and Beylerbeyi Palace from the cafeterias at Ortaköy Square. Ortaköy is famous for its **kumpir** (stuffed baked potatoes) and **gözleme**s (savory pancakes). The night clubs between Ortaköy and Kuruçeşme are frequently visited places in summer with many restaurants inside. You can prefer the restaurant of **Galatasaray Adası (Galatasaray Island)** which has a magnificent view.

The other districts after Ortaköy are calmer. The fish restaurants in Arnavutköy spread from the coast to inwards and get smaller and cheaper. **Emirgan Forest** is one of the important places with tables where the people of Istanbul go to picnic at the weekends. The historical **Sait Halim Paşa Yalısı (Sait Halim Pasha Waterside Mansion)** now hosts many receptions and luxurious restaurants. The taverns and casinos in Tarabya are some of the places where people go for enjoying themselves. You can taste the ice-cream, famous milk pudding, pastry with raisin and walnut in **Sarıyer**, which is more crowded in comparison to the other districts of the European Part of Istanbul. There are fish restaurants in **Rumeli Kavağı,** where the prices are more reasonable like Sarıyer. The prices in fish restaurants on the Sarıyer-Rumeli Kavağı road and those in Rumeli Kavağı are moderate. In the Asian part of Istanbul, **Üsküdar** and **Kadıköy** are popular places. There are beer houses and alcoholic restaurants lined on the Kadıköy pier. On the **Leander's Tower** near Üsküdar, you can watch Istanbul with a view of 360 degrees; eat, and drink alcohol in its restaurant. By the way, in this part of the city Kanlıca is famous for its yoghurt.

SHOPPING

In Bosphorus, you can't see the activity you see in the other districts. It is difficult to find even somewhere to shop in some less developed small districts. The accessories stands that are built in Ortaköy at the weekends have always been attractive with their modest souvenirs.

You can give a hand-made souvenir you buy from here to someone as a gift. A shopping center we can recommend is **Istinye Park** on İstinye Bayırı Avenue which is inwards. As it is near Maslak, you should get on the public buses or mini buses passing by İstinye Bay and Maslak.

İstinye Park.

The Tersane (shipyard) stop is more convenient to get on İstinye buses. After you leave İstinye Park, you don't need to go back to Bosphorus. You can get on Kabataş buses to go to Kabataş or use the Darüşşafaka - Taksim subway to go to Taksim.

TRANSPORT

You can get to this side of the Bosphorus by buses. The buses from Kabataş, Beşiktaş or Taksim offer service. There are enough bus services to the long coast that stretches from *Ortaköy* to *Rumeli Kavağı*. The detail that you should take into consideration here is the route of the bus because some buses that go to some districts follow the coastal route or Maslak-Levent route which is inwards from the coast. If Ortaköy is written on the destination sign of the buses, it means that that bus uses the route along the coast. Keep it mind that Sarıyer buses go all along the coast.

From Sarıyer to Rumeli and Anadolu Kavağı on ferry boats: The ferry boats departing from the ferry boat pier from Sarıyer to Rumeli and Anadolu Kavağı. One of the piers, the one in Büyükdere side in the south, offers this service. The ferry boats go to Rumeli Kavağı first and from there to Anadolu Kavağı.

To Rumeli Kavağı by Buses and Mini Buses: From Sarıyer, you can get to Rumeli Kavağı which is famous for its fish restaurants, by public buses and mini buses.

Land Transport in Asian Part of Istanbul: You can get to the coast line from *Kadıköy and Üsküdar to Anadolu Kavağı,* where there are palaces and summer palaces, by public buses, dolmus-minibuses.

See the general Transport section of the book (*page 191*) for lines and departure points.

Ferry Boat: Ferry boat is one of the frequently used means of Transport in Bosphorus. There are ferry boat services from Besiktaş and Eminönü piers to *Kadıköy and Üsküdar* every 20-30 minutes.

The Bosphorus Line that stops off at many piers in Bosphorus has less frequents services.

To have a nice day on **Adalar** (Princes' Islands) use Kabataş-Adalar services that also stop off at Kadıköy.

Bosphorus Tour*:* To tour around the Istanbul Bridge, you can use the 1,5-hour Bosphorus tours that depart from *Eminönü, Besiktaş and Ortaköy*, and *Eminönü-Kavaklar* services.

It is possible to get to **Küçüksu Kasrı (Küçüksu Summer Palace)** on Besiktaş Küçüksu ferry boats; but their services are very rare.

ENTERTAINMENT

Famous night clubs such as **Sortie** and **Reina** on the coast between Ortaköy and Kuruçeşme are very popular in summer.

The Guide

TRANSPORT

Istanbul has a wide local, intercity and international Transport network including land transport, railway, sea transport and airlines. You can get to every region of Turkey and the world from Istanbul.

AKBİL (SMART TICKET)

Pass the electronic on the box.

You can get on the means of transport such as bus, tramway, subway, train, ferry boat without wasting time if you have an '*Akbil*', a magnetic pass with discount, which is accepted on all means of mass transport. Akbil is a smart ticket that is used for all of the public transport means. It is used by pressing the chip at a round but hollow metal casing the size of your chip located on the akbil machines at the front near the driver on buses and on the turnstiles on tramway, subway and ferry boats. Besides this, after your first use, Akbil applies 50% discount for every 5 uses in 2 hours. But this discount is not applicable to the uses done one after one, because there must be at least 10-minute intervals between each use. Double-deckers, Tunnel and IDO Sea Buses don't allow discount. You have to pay a little deposit for Akbil, which you can buy from Akbil Kiosks. You can claim your deposit when you give back the akbil. Akbil operates by credit; you can recharge as many credits as you wish. In each use, these credits get down. On the screen, you can see how many credits you ave used and the credits you have in your akbil. Not to hear the negative signal which happens when you run out of credits, don't forget to recharge your akbil before your credits run out. You can recharge your akbil at an Akbil Sales Point or akbil recharger machines. As your credits gets down 1,65 liras in each use, 20 liras is an average amount for recharging your akbil. You can also use **Istanbulkart** which has the same features with Akbil.

Some Akbil Sales Points: Beyazıt, Eminönü, Taksim, Beşiktaş, Levent, Sarıyer, Üsküdar, Kadıköy.

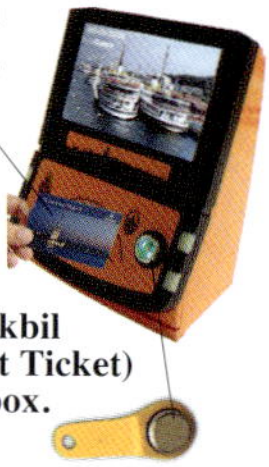

Akbil (Smart Ticket) box.

Get on the vehicle by contacting Akbil with the Akbil hole.

You can also use the coins you will get from this machine to travel in addition to akbil and electronic cards.

ELECTRONIC TICKET

These credit card size cards are valid for five uses and worth the price of five tickets. These cards, which are accepted only on buses for now, are passed through a reader on the top of an akbil machine. When the process is complete it makes a sound and display an illuminated warning. You have to buy a new card when you have completed your five uses. Unlike Akbil, Electronic Ticket doesn't make discount. It is for five-use price.

PUBLIC BUSES AND PRIVATE PUBLIC BUSES (İETT and ÖHO BUSES)

These are crucial for city public transport. There are 2800 İETT buses and 2000 private public buses (ÖHO) administered by IETT (Istanbul Electric Tramway Tunnel Administration). These buses start operating at 05:30 a.m. Services get less frequent after 10.00 p.m and end at 11.00 p.m. We recommend you to use the Akbil system if you travel by bus frequently.

The line number and departure-arrival points are written on the destination signs on the front of buses. On the signs just next to the front doors of buses you can see the route it will follow as well as the departure and arrival points. You need to press the stop button before arriving at the bus stop where you want to get off.

Public Bus: This group which comprises double deckers and green buses as well as the normal buses accept akbil and electronic

Destination sign.

Line number.

Public Bus.

Private Public Bus.

tickets. See the related section for more information about akbil and electronic ticket.

Private Public Bus: While akbil and electronic tickets are accepted on these buses, you can also pay your fare in cash. Pay your fare to the officer on the left of the front door.

Taksim-Tünel line Nostalgic Tramway.

RAILWAY

TRAMWAY AND SUBWAY

Tramway and subway lines contribute to especially the transport in the Historical Peninsula and Taksim area. The **Kabataş-Zeytinburnu, Aksaray-Airport** tramway lines, and **Taksim-Kabataş** subway line which is integrated with Kabataş and **Taksim-Darüşşafaka** subway line are fast. The trains that depart every five minutes offer service from 6 a.m. to 12 p.m. **Tünel-Karaköy** subway line offers service from 6 a.m. to

BUS LINES AND ROUTES

Bus stops in Eminönü are near the Galata Bridge towards Unkapanı direction and on the coast. If you would like to go to Fener-Balat, you can get on a bus on the destination signs on the sides which you see the signs 'Fener' or 'Balat'.

Eminönü-Yedikule 80 *(Eminönü, Karaköy, Azapkapı, Unkapanı, Aksaray, Merhaba, İmrahor, Yedikule)*

Eminönü-Draman 90 *(Karaköy, Azapkapı, Unkapanı, Fatih, Yavuzselim, Nişanca, Çarşamba, Fethiye, Draman)*

Beyazıt bus stops are next to the Beyazıt tramway stop.

Beyazıt-Yedikule 80B - **Beyazıt-Draman 90B**

Vezneciler bus stop is at the beginning of the Şehzadebaşı Street. It is behind the Faculty of Science-Literature next to the tramway road in Laleli.

Vezneciler-Edirnekapı 86V *(Vezneciler, Şehzadebaşı, İtfaiye, Fatih, Yavuzselim, Atikali, Karagümrük, Acıçeşme, Edirnekapı)*

Kabataş bus stops are opposite the Kabataş tramway stop.

Kabataş-İstinye Dereiçi 22 *(Beşiktaş, Ortaköy, Kuruçeşme, Arnavutköy, Bebek, Rumelihisarı, Baltalimanı, Boyacıköy, Emirgan)*

Kabataş-Sarıyer 25E *(Beşiktaş, Ortaköy, Kuruçeşme, Arnavutköy, Bebek, Rumelihisarı, Baltalimanı, Boyacıköy, Emirgan, İstinye, Yeniköy, Tarabya, Kireçburnu, Büyükdere, Sarıyer)*

The last Beşiktaş bus stops are opposite the Üsküdar pier.

To Bosphorus, you can find a bus in a shorter time at the Beşiktaş bus stop on the Beşiktaş-Ortaköy road.

Beşiktaş-Edirnekapı 28 *(Beşiktaş, Kabataş, Tophane, Karaköy, Eminönü, Unkapanı, Fatih, Yavuzselim, Atikali, Karagümrük, Acıçeşme, Edirnekapı)*

Beşiktaş-Topkapı 28T *(Beşiktaş, Kabataş, Fındıklı, Tophane, Karaköy, Eminönü, Unkapanı, Aksaray, Haseki, Çapa, Pazartekke, Topkapı)*

Ortaköy-Yenikapı 30D *(Ortaköy, Beşiktaş, Kabataş, Tophane, Karaköy, Eminönü, Unkapanı, Aksaray, Yenikapı)*

Taksim bus stops are at Taksim Square.

Taksim-Sarıyer 40 *(Gümüşsuyu, Beşiktaş, Ortaköy, Kuruçeşme, Arnavutköy, Bebek, Rumelihisarı, Baltalimanı, Boyacıköy, Emirgan, İstinye, Yeniköy, Tarabya, Kireçburnu, Büyükdere, Sarıyer)*

Taksim-Sarıyer 25T *(Beşiktaş, Yıldız, Zincirlikuyu, Levent, 4. Levent, Maslak, Büyükdere, Sarıyer)*

Taksim-Beyazıt 61B *(Taksim, Tepebaşı, Şişhane, Unkapanı, Aksaray, Laleli, Beyazıt)*

Taksim-Yedikule 80T

Taksim-Topkapı 83

Taksim-Edirnekapı 87

Taksim-Atatürk Airport 96T

Kadıköy bus stops are opposite the Eminönü Pier.

Kadıköy-Üsküdar 12-12A

Kadıköy-Kavacık 14M *(Beylerbeyi, Küçüksu)*

Kadıköy-Beykoz 15F *(Beylerbeyi, Küçüksu, Anadoluhisarı)*

Üsküdar bus stops are opposite the Beşiktaş Pier.

Üsküdar-Beykoz 15 *(Beylerbeyi, Küçüksu, Anadoluhisarı)*

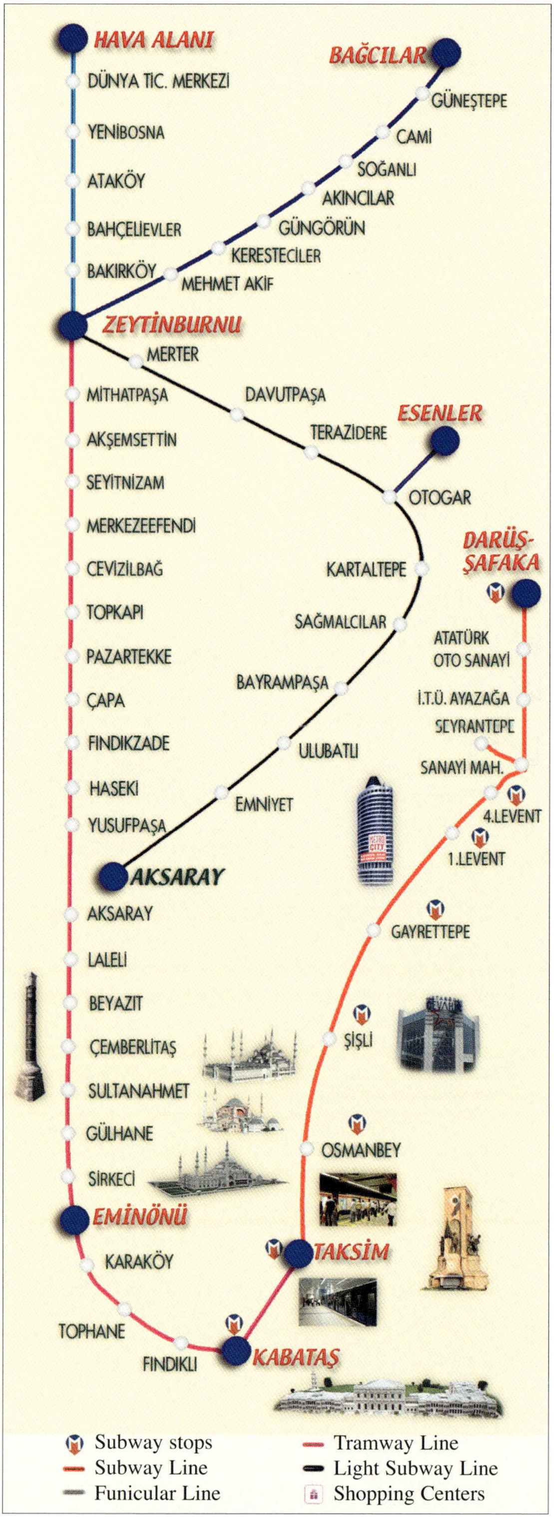

Tramway and Subway route plan.

Tramway.

9 p.m. There are escalators and moving bands, and the art gallery in Taksim, and telephone and lifts designed for disabled people at **Taksim-Darüşşafaka** subway that started operating in September 2000. It is directly connected with *Cevahir* shopping center in Şişli and *Metrocity* and *Kanyon* shopping centers in 1.Levent.

Travelling by *Taksim Square-Tunnel* and *Kadıköy-Moda* nostalgic tramways offer nostalgic service with their short distance lines. *Maçka-Taşkışla* and *Eyüp-Pierre Loti* electric cars offer enjoyable trips with their unique views.

Akbil and tokens are used on tramway and subway lines. There are token sales kiosks at subway stations and busy tramway stops.

4. Levent subway stop.

Tunnel stop.

Funicular system Taksim stop.

SUBURBAN RAILWAY

The suburban railway services of the Turkish Republic State Railways (TCDD) in Istanbul run between **Sirkeci** and **Halkalı,** and between **Haydarpaşa** and **Gebze.** Akbil and tokens sold at the stations are accepted in the city; but tickets should be bought from the ticket sales offices for train services to other cities in the country and abroad.

Sirkeci Garı (Sirkeci Train Station) that provides the connection between Istanbul and Europe was constructed by the German architect August Jasmund between the years 1888 and 1890. Granite marble and stones brought from Marsellie-Aden were used in its construction, and two clock towers were placed in its front. **Haydarpaşa Garı** (Haydarpaşa Train Station), which is the starting point of the suburban railway line of the Asia side and of the railway network that spreads to Anatolia, was constructed with eclectic architecture method, and has a 'U' plan with one side of it longer. It was constructed by the German architects Otto Ritter and Helmut Cuno between 1906 and 1908.

City Lines passenger ferry boats.

SEA TRANSPORT

Ferry boats, motorboats and sea buses which depart from various piers have a big role in transport within the city. Using preferably ferry boats and motorboats for going to the other side of the strait will facilitate your transport. Akbil and tokens which you can buy from pier booths are accepted on city ferry boats and private motorboats. You can get information about departure times from the complimentary booklets you can get at piers. The routes of the ferry-boat and motorboat services we mentioned below may change at the weekend. They operate from 6:30 a.m. to 9 p.m. The privately operated motorboats offer service until later hours. Privately operated motorboats that depart from

Private boats for sea transport are operated in connection with Istanbul Municipality.

SUBURBAN RAILWAY (TRAIN) ROUTES

Sirkeci-Halkalı *(Sirkeci, Cankurtaran, Kumkapı, Yenikapı, Kocamustafapaşa, Yedikule, Kazlıçeşme, Zeytinburnu, Yenimahalle, Bakırköy, Yeşilyurt, Yeşilköy, Florya, Menekşe, Küçükçekmece, Soğuksu, Kanarya, Halkalı)*
Haydarpaşa-Gebze *(Haydarpaşa, Sögütlüçeşme, Kızıltoprak, Feneryolu, Göztepe, Erenköy, Suadiye, Bostancı, Küçükyalı, İdealtepe, Süreyyaplajı, Maltepe, Cevizli, Atalar, Kartal, Yunus, Pendik, Kaynarca, Tersane, Güzelyalı, Aydıntepe, İçme, Tuzla, Çayırova, Fatih, Osmangazi, Gebze)*

FERRY BOAT SERVICES

Eminönü-Kadıköy
Eminönü-Üsküdar
Eminönü-Kavaklar *(Eminönü, Beşiktaş, Kanlıca, Yeniköy, Sarıyer, Rumeli Kavağı, Anadolu Kavağı)*
Eminönü-Bosphorus Line *(Eminönü, Beşiktaş, Ortaköy, Kuzguncuk, Beylerbeyi, Çengelköy, Arnavutköy, Bebek, Kandilli, Anadoluhisarı, Kanlıca, Emirgan, İstinye, Çubuklu, Paşabahçe, Beykoz, Yeniköy, Büyükdere, Sarıyer, Rumeli Kavağı, Anadolu Kavağı)*
Karaköy-Haydarpaşa-Kadıköy
Kabataş-Kadıköy
Kabataş-Üsküdar
Kabataş-Adalar *(The Princes' Islands) (Kabataş, Kadıköy, Kınalıada, Burgazadası, Heybeliada, Büyükada)*
Beşiktaş-Kadıköy
Beşiktaş-Üsküdar
Beşiktaş-Küçüksu
Üsküdar-Eyüp *(Üsküdar, Eminönü, Kasımpaşa, Fener, Hasköy, Ayvansaray, Sütlüce, Eyüp)*
Sarıyer-Rumeli Kavağı-Anadolu Kavağı
İstinye-Çengelköy *(İstinye, Emirgan, Kanlıca, Anadoluhisarı, Küçüksu, Kandilli, Bebek, Arnavutköy, Çengelköy)*

Eminönü, Beşiktaş and Ortaköy offer a one and half hour **Bosphorus Tour** along the shore from and to certain points. **Eminönü-Kavaklar** line operated by IDO takes you to Anadolu Kavağı by stopping off at various piers. You can go back on the same line by learning the departure time.

Taxis offer service for 24 hours.

DOLMUŞ, MINI BUS AND TAXI

The other means of public transport are *dolmuş (share taxi)* and *mini buses*. Cash is accepted on these vehicles, and they are used mostly for travelling to places outside the city center. *Taxis*, which are another important means of transport in the city are operated by private taxi stands and offer service for 24 hours a day. Taxi fares are calculated by taximeter according to the distance of the destination in km.

Shared taxi, mini bus.

ATATÜRK AIRPORT

www.ataturkairport.com

Atatürk Airport in Yeşilköy is the largest airport in Turkey. This airport, which provides transport from Istanbul to many places in the world, is 28 km from Sirkeci. You can prefer airlines not only for international transport, but also for travelling to other cities you can go in Turkey. You can get to the airport by taxi, or by the buses of Havaş (Ground Handling Co.). These buses which are used in exchange for a certain fare depart from **Kozyatağı** *(Derya Street, Moğulkoç İş Merkezi No: 7 / A Sahrayıcedit-Kozyatağı)*, **Taksim** *(Büyükşehir Sanat Galerisi-Metropolitan Art Gallery, just ahead of Turkish Airlines office)* and **Bakırköy** *(Bakırköy Sea Buses Pier)*. The destinations of Havaş services from the airport are again these

points.

If you don't have much luggage, you can use the **Taksim-Atatürk Airport** tram line (96T) which departs from Taksim or **Kabataş-Aksaray-Airport** tramway line.

DOMESTIC AIRLINES

Turkish Airlines (THY)
www.thy.com.tr
☎ +90 (212) 444 08 49

THY Ticket Sales Offices
Cumhuriyet Avenue Gezidükkanları Sok. No: 7 Taksim
☎ +90 (212) 252 11 06
Recep Peker Avenue No: 27 Kızıltoprak-Kadıköy
☎ +90 (216) 418 44 86-87
Atatürk Airport International Terminal
☎ +90 (212) 463 63 63

ANADOLUJET
☎ +90 (212) 444 25 38

ATLAS JET
☎ +90 (216) 444 33 87

PEGASUS
☎ +90 (212) 444 07 37

FREEBIRD AIRLINES
☎ +90 (212) 663 77 77

ONUR AIR
☎ +90 (212) 444 66 87

ESENLER BUS STATION

Transport is provided to all the cities in Turkey from Esenler Bus Station. The buses that depart from this huge bus station where there are hundreds of transport companies go to the Harem Bus Station, which is on the Asia side of Istanbul to take other passengers, and leave Istanbul. You can go to the bus station by different means. You can get on either a taxi or Aksaray-Airport light rail subway line. If you use the subway, you should get off at bus station stop. Another alternative is

Intercity transport is carried out on modern buses.

getting on the public buses, on which your travel lasts more than one hour. Beşiktaş (28O), Mecidiyeköy (75O), Taksim (83O), Eminönü (91O) services go to the bus station.

COMMUNICATION

POST

Postal services in Turkey are operated by PTT (Turkish Republic Post Telephone Telegraph

Administration General Directorate). You can find the closest PTT office by using the maps in this book.
PTT offers the following services: local and international postal services, transfers, foreign exchange, sales of credits for GSM and call cards for pay phones available on the streets, American Express cheque transactions, prepaid telephone services, sales of TCDD (Turkish State Railways) tickets.

If you want to send parcels to other countries, the PTT office in the **Istanbul Adliye Sarayı** (Istanbul Court House-Sultanahmet) accepts the parcels up to two kg. You have to send heavier parcels from **Büyük Postane** (Grand Post Office) in Sirkeci. As the officers have to see what is inside the parcel before sending, you had better leave it open not to waste time. Express Mail Service is more expensive. Don't use this service for sending your valuables. The international cargo companies can be useful as well, but they are more expensive than PTT.

SOME PTT CENTERS

Sultanahmet: *İmren Öktem Avenue,* inside Istanbul Adliye Sarayı building.
Beyazıt: *Mithatpaşa Avenue, İbrahimpaşa Street, No: 19.*
Kapalıçarşı (Grand Bazaar): *Beyazıt Mahallesi, Gani Çelebi Street, No: 1, Kapalıçarşı.*
Sirkeci (Büyük Postane - *Grand Post Office*): *Hobyar Mahallesi, Büyük Postane Avenue, No: 25*
Taksim: Istiklal Street, Galatasaray Square
Taksim Square: Cumhuriyet Avenue No. 2

PAY PHONES

The pay phones are in the booths you see on the streets, and they are available at many places such as streets or squares, hospitals and train stations. The call cards used for these phones are sold in Türk Telecom Offices and Branches, PTT offices and some buffets. The prices of the cards vary depending on the amount of credits in them. Besides using pay phones, you can also call from post offices, Türk Telecom branches and internet cafes.

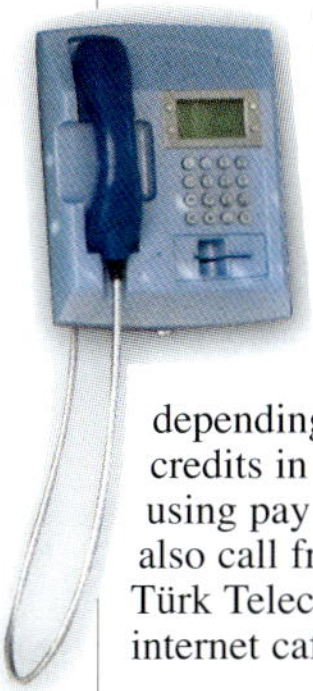

TELEPHONE CODES

In Istanbul, where two different codes are used, you should pay attention to the telephone code while calling the place you want to communicate with. The codes of two sides of the city seperated by a strait are different; the code of **Avrupa Yakası** (European Side) is **(0212)** and the code of **Asya Yakası** (Asian Side) is **(0216).** But if you want to call a place in the side where you are, for example you are in Eminönü and you call Taksim, then you don't need to dial the code; just dial the 7 digit number like xxx-xx-xx. This situation is also valid for two districts of the Asian Side. For example, for calling a place in Üsküdar, which is a district in the Asian side, from Sultanahmet, Eminönü or Taksim, which are the districts of the European side, you should dial 0216 before dialing the seven digit number. Similarly, you should dial the code 0212 first before dialing the seven digit number when you are calling a place in the European side from Beylerbeyi, which is a district in the Asian side.

When you call a phone in Turkey, first you dial 0090, which is the country code of Turkey. Then you shouldn't dial 0 (zero) when you are dialing the area code. For example, if you are calling a place around Sultanahmet from a foreign country, you should dial a number like 0090-212-xxxxxxx. The number changes for the Asian side like 0090-216-xxxxxxx.

Some of the districts in the European side are Sultanahmet, Beyazıt, Eminönü, Beşiktaş, Taksim, Ortaköy, Sarıyer. *Some of the districts in the Asian side are* Kadıköy, Üsküdar, Beylerbeyi, Küçüksu, Anadoluhisarı, Kız Kulesi (Maiden Tower), Adalar *(The Princes' Islands).*

GSM OPERATORS

There are three GSM operators in Turkey. They are **Vodafone, Turkcell** and **Avea**. If you wish to use your personal mobile phone in Istanbul, these lines will help you for your communication both in the country and for calling abroad. You can buy these lines at cheap prices from the shops where you see their emblems. Two different lines are sold; one is invoiced line and the other one is pre-paid line. The pre-paid lines are more suitable for you, and your line starts to operate within 2-3 days after you fill the application form. In the pre-paid lines, your credits get down according to durations of calls. You can easily provide the credits sold in card form from most of the buffets and telephone shops. As these operators have different codes, you should dial the area codes we mentioned in the Telephone Codes section above when calling normal telephones (office and home phones). For example you want to call an office phone in Levent on your mobile phone; then you should dial the area code and the phone number like 0212-xxxxxxx.

Customer Relations Phone Numbers:
Turkcell: **0532 444 0 532**
Vodafone: **0542 444 0 542**
Avea: **0555 444 1 500**

NEWSPAPER-MAGAZINE INTERNET CAFE

Many newspapers and magazines are published in Turkey. Daily newspapers are delivered to news stands, and can be bought from these news stands. You see many buffets that sell newspapers and magazines, and news agents in Istanbul. In city centers, you can also find the daily newspapers and magazines published in Europe.

There are a lot of Internet cafes in the city which provide access to internet and international call service.

CULTURE-ARTS CENTERS

There are centers that contribute to culture-arts life in Istanbul. These centers are exhibition-theatre halls, concert-conference halls, libraries, cafeterias, and have multi-functional characteristics. You can follow up the events in your fields of interest closely by following up the activities of culture centers.

The 1300-person capacity hall of **Atatürk Kültür**

Atatürk Cultural Center at Taksim Square.

Merkezi *(Atatürk Cultural Center)*, which is administrated by **the Ministry of Culture and Tourism**, is used by the *State Opera Ballet and State Symphony Orchestra*. Orchestra and various events are conducted in the other 500-person capacity concert hall. The 300-person capacity **Oda Tiyatrosu**, **Aziz Nesin Sahnesi** *(Room Theatre, Aziz Nesin Stage)*, and on the Sıraselviler Street, and the over 500-person capacity **Taksim Sahnesi** *(Taksim Stage)* administered by A.K.M. are used for staging the State Theatre plays. **Cemal Reşit Rey Konser Salonu** *(Cemal Reşit Rey Concert Hall)* has a 860-person capacity main concert hall and some exhibition halls. The symphony orchestra and opera community are within the building, where various cultural and arts events are organized and which hosts some other organizations.

Entrance to AFM Fitaş Cinemas.

CINEMA

Movies which are one of the indispensables of the cultural and entertainment world meet their audience in many cinemas of Istanbul. As movies are played in their original languages (generally English) with Turkish subtitles, you can watch the movie

CULTURAL CENTERS

Akbank Art: *İstiklal Avenue No: 8, 34435 Beyoğlu* ☎ **+90 (212) 252 35 00-01**
German Goethe Institute: *Yeniçarşı Avenue No: 32, 34433 Beyoğlu* ☎ **+90 (212) 249 20 09**
Atatürk Cultural Center: *Taksim (Square) Meydanı* ☎ **+90 (212) 251 56 00**
Barış Manço Cultural Center: *Moda Avenue Nailbey Street No: 37 Kadıköy* ☎ **+90 (216) 418 16 46**
Beşiktaş Cultural Center: *Has Fırın Avenue No: 75, 80690 Beşiktaş* ☎ **+90 (212) 327 24 27**
Cemal Reşit Rey Concert Hall: *Darülbedai Avenue No: 1, Harbiye, Şişli* ☎ **+90 (212) 231 54 97**
Profilo Cultural Center: *Cemal Sahir Avenue No: 33, Profilo Shopping Center, Mecidiyeköy* ☎ **+90 (212) 216 44 00**
Yapı Kredi Cultural Center: *İstiklal Avenue No: 161-161A, 34433, Beyoğlu* ☎ **+90 (212) 252 47 00**

CINEMAS

AFM Fitaş: *İstiklal Avenue, No: 24-26 Beyoğlu*
☎ **+90 (212) 251 20 20**
AFM İstinye Park: *İstinye Park Shopping Center, İstinye*
☎ **+90 (212) 345 62 45**
Atlantis: *Bahariye Avenue, No. 46 Kadıköy*
☎ **+90 (216) 336 06 22**
Atlas: *İstiklal Avenue, Atlas Passage No. 209*
☎ **+90 (212) 252 85 76**
Cine Majestic: *İstiklal Avenue, Ayhan Işık Street No. 10 Beyoğlu*
☎ **+90 (212) 244 97 07**
Feriye Eurimages: *Çırağan Avenue No: 124 Ortaköy*
☎ **+90 (212) 236 28 64**
Rexx: *Sakızgülü Street No: 20-22 Bahariye, Kadıköy*
☎ **+90 (216) 336 01 12**
Sinepop: *İstiklal Avenue, Yeşilçam Street No: 22*
☎ **+90 (212) 251 11 76**
Şafak Movieplex: *Yeniçeriler Av.Çemberlitaş*
☎ **+90 (212) 516 26 60**

you want to watch in any cinema. To this end, you can go to the cinemas in large shopping centers, and the cinemas in **Çemberlitaş, İstiklal Avenue-Taksim** and **Kadıköy** regions.

INTERNATIONAL EVENTS

Istanbul, which is one of the leading cities in the world with its historical value, hosts international theatre, music, jazz and film festivals up to its reputation in the fields of culture and arts. These festivals, which are the international arts circle's focus of attention, are organized by **Istanbul Kültür Sanat Vakfı** (Istanbul Foundation for Culture and Arts).

Istanbul Foundation for Culture and Arts: *İstiklal Caddesi No: 64 Beyoğlu /* www.iksv.org
+90 (212) 334 07 00

International Istanbul Music Festival: This festival which is organized in June hosts the important artists and groups of Turkey and the world. Famous guests and local and foreign orchestras make music lovers experience unforgettable moments at historical places like **Hagia Eirene.**

International Istanbul Jazz Festival: International Istanbul Jazz Festival, which is a member of the Association of International Jazz Festivals, satisfies Istanbul with jazz in the first two weeks of July. During the jazz festival, where famous guests meet music lovers, the excitement overflows to the streets through concerts given at Cemil Topuzlu Açıkhava Sahnesi (Cemil Topuzlu Open Air Stage) and various historical places.

International Istanbul Film Festival: This film festival organized in the first two weeks of April presents a nice film festival to the people of Istanbul with selections from international festivals, documentaries, films of high quality and film classics. Interviews, panels and exhibitions are held with the atten-

HOSPITALS IN ISTANBUL

German Hospital: *Sıraselviler Avenue No: 119 Taksim*
☎ **+90 (212) 293 21 50**
American Hospital: *Güzelbahçe Street No: 20, Nişantaşı*
☎ **+90 (212) 444 37 77**
European Florence Nightingale Hospital: *Abide-i Hürriyet Avenue No: 164, Şişli*
☎ **+90 (212) 224 49 50**
Bakirköy Psychiatric and Neurologic Diseases Hospital: *Zuhuratbaba Mahallesi, Demirkapı Avenue, Bakırköy*
☎ **+90 (212) 543 65 65**
Balat Or-Ahayim Jewish Hospital: *Demirhisar Avenue No. 46-48 Ayvansaray – Balat* ☎ **+90 (212) 491 00 00**
Balıklı Greek Hospital; *Belgradkapı Yolu No: 2 Zeytinburnu*
☎ **+90 (212) 547 16 00**
Baltalimanı Bone Diseases Hospital: *Rumelihisarı Avenue No: 62 Baltalimanı* ☎ **+90 (212) 323 70 75**
Bezm-i Alem Valide Sultan Vakıf Gureba Hospital: *Adnan Menderes Bulvarı, Aksaray* ☎ **+90 (212) 453 17 00**
Paşabahçe State Hospital; *Saip Molla Avenue, Kısayol Street No: 1, Beykoz* ☎ **+90 (216) 413 09 09**
Cerrahpaşa Faculty of Medicine; *Cerrahpaşa Tıp Fakültesi 34098 Cerrahpaşa* **+90 (212) 414 30 00**
Göztepe Education Hospital: *Doktor Erkin Avenue, Göztepe* ☎ **+90 (216) 566 40 00**
Haseki Education Hospital; *Millet Avenue, Aksaray*
☎ **+90 (212) 585 00 00**
Haydarpaşa Numune Hospital: *Tıbbiye Avenue No. 40, Üsküdar* ☎ **+90 (216) 414 45 02**
Istanbul Çapa Faculty of Medicine: *Millet Avenue 34093 Çapa* ☎ **+90 (212) 414 20 00**
Istanbul Memorial Hospital: *Piyale Paşa Bulvarı Perpa yanı, Okmeydanı* ☎ **+90 (212) 444 78 88**
İstinye State Hospital: *Emirgan Avenue No: 98 34465 İstinye* ☎ **+90 (212) 323 44 44**
Marmara University Hospital: *Tophanelioğlu Avenue No: 13-15, Altunizade* ☎ **+90 (216) 327 10 10**
Okmeydanı Education and Research Hospital: Darülaceze Avenue No. 25, *Okmeydanı-Şişli* ☎ **+90 (212) 314 55 55**
Pendik State Hospital: *Dr. Orhan Maltepe Avenue No: 17, Pendik* ☎ **+90 (216) 483 11 87**
Şişli Etfal Education and Research Hospital: *Etfal Street No: 10, Şişli* ☎ **+90 (212) 373 50 00**
Taksim Education and Research Hospital: *Sıraselviler Avenue No: 112, Taksim* ☎ **+90 (212) 252 43 00**

dance of worldwide famous guests. The film competition, where films are assessed by local and international jury is among the events of the festival.

Autumn Film Week / Filmekimi (Film October): In this festival which lasts a week in October, you can have the opportunity to watch award-winning films and some films to be in vision.

HOSPITALS

There are two types of hospitals; state hospitals and private hospitals. The fees of private hospitals, which offer more luxurious service and try to do everything completely, are higher than the state hospitals *(page 197)*.

AMBULANCE (☎112)

You can contact **112 Emergency Aid and Resque Center** by dialing 112 in case of an emergency. The medical staff members are informed on the phone about the address and the type of emergency. The emergency aid team contacted by wireless or phone come to the emergency site with a full-equipped ambulance. The team that includes a doctor and medical staff members do a medical examination to the ill or injured person in a short time.

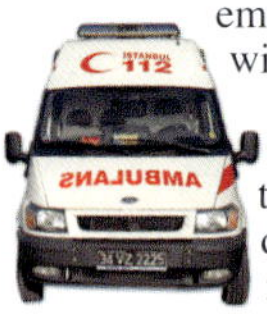

PHARMACIES/ DRUGSTORES

You can buy nonprescription or over-the-counter medications that do not require directive from a doctor from many pharmacies you can find in every region of the city, especially around the hospitals. Pharmacies on duty at night or during a holiday are announced on the windows of the other pharmacies in that region. From the pharmacies, you can buy not only medicine, but also various cosmetics, shampoo and hair care products, vitamin-minerals etc.

A police car on duty in Istanbul.

POLICE

Normally, people living in Istanbul dial **155** for calling the police for emergencies. You can seek assistance from police stations available in every district. The **Tourism Police** that is a unit offering service to tourism sector with its foreign language speaking staff provide the security of tourists visiting Istanbul. You can seek assistance from the Tourism Police located opposite of Yerebatan Sarnıcı *(Basilica Cistern)*.

Tourism Police:

Address: Yerebatan Avenue, No: 6, Sultanahmet

+90 (212) 527 45 03

Building of Tourism Police in Sultanahmet.

SOME CONSULATES IN ISTANBUL

U.S.A.: *Kaplıcalar Mevkii Street No: 2, 34460 İstinye*
☎ +90 (212) 335 90 00
Germany: *İnönü Avenue 10, 34437 Gümüşsuyu-Taksim*
☎ +90 (212) 334 61 00
Australia: *Asker Ocağı Avenue No: 15, 34367 Elmadağ-Şişli* **☎ +90 (212) 243 13 33**
Austria: *Köşbaşı Avenue No. 46, 34464 Yeniköy*
☎ +90 (212) 363 84 10
Belgium: *Sıraselviler Avenue No. 39 Taksim*
☎ +90 (212) 243 33 00-01
Bulgaria: *Ahmet Adnan Saygun Avenue No: 44 Ulus-Levent* **☎ +90 (212) 281 01 15**
Denmark: *Meygede Street No: 2, 34342 Bebek*
☎ +90 (212) 359 19 00
France: *İstiklal Avenue, No.4 34435 Taksim*
☎ +90 (212) 334 87 30
Holland: *İstiklal Avenue, No: 197, 34433 Taksim*
☎ +90 (212) 393 21 21
England: *Meşrutiyet Avenue No:34, 34435 Tepebaşı*
☎ +90 (212) 334 64 00
Spain: *Karanfil Aralığı Street, No. 16, 34330 1. Levent*
☎ +90 (212) 270 74 10
Israel: *Büyükdere Avenue Yapı Kredi Plaza, C Blok Kat: 7, 34330 Levent* **☎ +90 (212) 317 65 44**
Sweden: *İstiklal Avenue No: 247, 34433 Tunnel-Taksim*
☎ +90 (212) 334 06 00
Italy: *Tom Tom Kaptan Street, No: 5, 34433 Taksim*
☎ +90 (212) 243 10 24-25
Russia: *İstiklal Avenue No: 219, 34430 Taksim*
☎ +90 (212) 292 51 01-02
Greece: *Turnacıbaşı Street No: 22, 34433 Taksim*
☎ +90 (212) 393 82 90-91-92

SHOPPING CENTERS

Akmerkez: *Nispetiye Avenue, Etiler*
☎ +90 (212) 282 01 72
Capitol: *Mahir İz Avenue, Altunizade*
☎ +90 (216) 554 77 77
Carousel: *Halit Ziya Uşaklıgil Avenue No:1, 34710 Bakırköy*
☎ +90 (212) 570 84 34
Cevahir: *Büyükdere Avenue No: 22 Şişli*
☎ +90 (212) 368 69 00
Galleria: *Bakırköy Sahilyolu, Ataköy*
☎ +90 (212) 559 95 60
İstinye Park: *İstinye Bayırı Avenue, İstinye*
☎ +90 (212) 345 55 55
Kanyon: *Büyükdere Avenue, No: 185, 1. Levent.*
Tel: (212) 317 53 00
Metrocity: *Büyükdere Avenue, No: 171, 1. Levent*
☎ +90 (212) 344 06 60
Olivium: *Muammer Aksoy Avenue No: 1 Zeytinburnu*
☎ +90 (212) 547 74 53
Profilo: *Cemal Sahir Avenue, No: 33 Mecidiyeköy*
☎ +90 (212) 216 44 00

The areas that are not within the police's province are of the Gendarmerie's responsibility. In such places within the gendarmerie's province, you can seek assistance from the Gendarmerie by calling 156.

SHOPPING CENTERS

There are many stores including famous brands in the shopping centers where you can provide your various shopping needs easily. You can go to these shopping centers not only for shopping, but also you can eat something in the restaurants and fast food restaurants, drink something and have a rest in the cafes, and watch the movies at the cinemas in them. There are large car parks on the basement floors of these shopping centers for those who come by car.

Metro City, 1. Levent.

Kanyon, 1. Levent.

Profilo, Mecidiyeköy.

Cevahir, Şişli.

Akmerkez, Etiler.

İstinye Park, İstinye.

BANKS

There are a lot of bank branches in Istanbul; therefore it is possible to find a bank branch nearly everywhere. *They are open from 9 a.m. to 5 p.m. except Saturdays and Sundays.* Some banks have one-hour break during lunch time. If you are around Sultanahmet, you can go to many banks on Cağaloğlu – Nuruosmaniye Street or in Beyazıt. Some of the banks in Istanbul are *Akbank, Finansbank, Ing Bank, Garanti Bankası, Yapı ve Kredi Bankası, Citibank, HSBC, Türkiye İş Bankası, T.C. Ziraat Bankası, Türkiye Halk Bankası, Türkiye Vakıflar Bankası.*

Automated teller machines where you can draw money with credit card.

FOREIGN EXCHANGE

You can exchange foreign currency you have at banks, or exchange offices at more reasonable prices. While there are many single exchange offices in Sultanahmet, Beyazıt and Taksim, you may not see them so often on the other walking routes. You can see the value of your currency in Turkish Lira on the electronic boards of these exchange offices.

NECESSARY TELEPHONE NUMBERS

Ambulance **112**
Police **155**
Gendarmarie **156**
For Reporting Fire **110**
For Reporting Forest Fire **177**
Tourist Information **170**
Unknown Numbers **11811**

ISLAMIC RELIGIOUS FEASTS AND SPECIAL DAYS

Besides the religious Feasts **Ramadan** and **Kurban** (the Feast of the Sacrifice, or called Eid el-Adha in Arabic) celebrated as a custom of Islam, there are also **Newroz,** and **Hıdrellez** *(Spring Festival)* festivals which have been celebrated since the beginning of Turkish history. Besides them, the *National Holidays*, which constitute turning points of the Republic of Turkey, are also celebrated with great enthusiasm.

RELIGIOUS FEASTS

On religious feast days, people get up early, put on their clean clothes, wear nice scents, and men go to the mosque to pray. Generally, desserts are cooked, candies and chocolates are prepared to serve guests who come during the religious feast days. The elders of the family are visited and their hands are kissed. As the religious feasts are dated according to the Muslim calendar (based on 622 A.D. the year of the Hegira), these feasts start 10 days earlier according to the Gregorian calendar.

Kurban Feast (the Feast of the Sacrifice): It starts on the tenth day of Zilhicce month according to the Muslim calendar. Muslim people are expected to cut *Kurban* (an sacrificial animal; a sheep, veal, goat etc.) and to give away the meat to poor people. After the cutting ceremony which is generally carried out on the first day of the feast, meat is placed in plastic bags and given away to poor families.

Ramadan Feast (also called Candy Festival) This is the feast coming after the completion of the holy month of fasting. It starts on the first day of the month of Shevval according to the Muslim calendar. As children go to different houses one by one and collect candies, this feast is also known as **Şeker Bayramı** (Candy Holiday). Muslim people who are financially strong enough give *zekat* (ritual of **offering** alms to the poor).

NATIONAL HOLIDAYS

National holidays are celebrated with great enthusiasm. Military parades, shows of *seymen* and *zeybeks (local folk dancers)* in their local costumes, and competitions are held during these carnival-like celebrations. The official ceremonies held in Ankara, the capital city of Turkey, are broadcasted live on all television channels. You can also watch these ceremonies on TRT TURK channel, the channel of Turkish Radio Television institution broadcasted in Europe. In Istanbul there are also parades and shows on Aksaray Vatan Street during **Victory Day** (30th August Victory Day, Commemoration of the victory at the final battle in Dumlupınar ending the Turkish Independence War in 1922, dedicated to the armed forces) and **Republic Day** *(*Commemoration of the proclamation of the republic in 1923. Also the halfday in the afternoon of previous day*).*

23rd April National Sovereignty and Children's Day: The first Grand National Assembly of Turkey, which administered the War of Independence, was founded on 23rd April 1920. This day which Atatürk dedicated to children is celebrated with great enthusiasm with the attendance of children coming from many countries of the world. Turkish elementary school children and guest children coming from various countries of the world present shows.

19th May Commemoration of Atatürk, Youth and Sports Day: 19th May 1919, the day when Atatürk landed in Samsun, is accepted as the beginning of the War of Independence, and it is celebrated with great enthusiasm every year. Various marathons and events are organized on this day.

30th August Victory Day: 30th August 1922, when the Supreme Command Square War (Large-Scale Attack) ended in victory, is celebrated with ceremonies every year.

29th October Republic Day: On 29th October 1923, it was announced that the administration type of the newly founded Turkish state would be Republic. Therefore, shows are held and it is celebrated with enthusiasm on every 29th October.

Official parade in front of the audience on 30 August Victory Day.

OTHER DAYS AND PERIODS

10th November: Mustafa Kemal Atatürk passed away in *Dolmabahce Palace* at 09:05 a.m. on 10th November 1938, Thursday. On 21st November, he was buried in his temporary tomb in the *Etnography Museum* in Ankara. After the construction of Anıtkabir in Rasattepe was completed, his tomb was moved to Anıtkabir with a ceremony on 10th November 1953. Turkish people stand up for a minute at 9:05 a.m. in commemoration of their great leaders Mustafa Kemal Atatürk on 10th November every year.

Ramazan Month: Fasting, which is one of the five conditions of Islam, requires not eating, drinking anything, and not having sexual intercourse from dawn to dusk. Fasting lasts one month during *Ramazan month* of the Muslim calendar. Because of inconsistencies between the Gregorian calendar and Muslim calendar, Ramazan month starts earlier than the previous year. Fasting is a religious duty required from all healthy adult Muslims, but it is not an obligation. Those who fast don't eat or drink anything and smoke during the daytime. In the evening, Ramazan dinners are set in houses or restaurants, and those who fast break their fast following the evening ezan (Islamic call to prayer).

1 Lira

200 Liras.

50 kurush

100 Liras.

25 kurush

50 Liras.

10 kurush

20 Liras.

5 kurush

10 Liras.

TURKISH LIRA

The banknotes of Turkish Lira, which is the currency of the Republic of Turkey, are 5 liras, 10 liras, 20 liras, 50 liras and 100 liras, 200 liras. The coins are 5 kurush, 10 kurush, 25 kurush, 50 kurush and 1 lira. In other words; 1 lira is equivalent to 20 coins of 5 kurush, 10 coins of 10 kurush, 4 coins of 25 kurush, 2 coins of 50 kurush, respectively.

Direction sign.

5 Liras.

TRAFFIC

The traffic in Istanbul is generally congested during work start hours in the morning and during rush hours when people leave work in the evening. There is congested traffic on the main roads. The traffic lights, signs and boards in Turkey are in

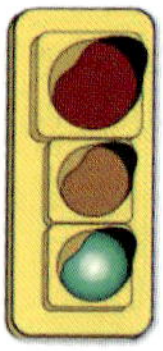

compliance with the international standards. At the crossroads, if there is a traffic police officer, his signs should be followed, or else the traffic lights and signs should be complied with. Pedestrian crossings, overpasses or underground passages are used at the places where there is no traffic police officer or traffic lights.

If there is none of those mentioned above, you should cross the street as fast as possible at right places considering the distance and speed of vehicles, and after you decide that it is safe to cross.

Traffic lights are of international standards, and **green light** means you can cross, **yellow light** means you must get ready and be careful, and **red light** means you must wait. Flashing yellow light means you must cross slowly and carefully; and flashing red light means you must stop first to see if the road is open and available. In Turkey, vehicles run on the right of the road, and distance is given in km. If you are travelling on foot, use the pavements on the routes you are walking through. On the roads where there is no pavement, you can walk one after one on the side walks called banquette. As steering wheels are on the left side of cars in our country, it may be safer to go through the left side of the road according to your direction.

PHOTOGRAPH

It very a natural right of every tourist to take photos of the places he or she visits. You can take photos of most of the places you go such as mosques, museums, palaces and cisterns. However, taking photos is forbidden in some places. If you want to take pictures at the palaces and museums you visit, you have to pay an extra amount of money for taking photos or videos. However, you need to have special permission issued for tripot shots. Some places don't allow flashlight photography. You should read the warning signs at the places you go. Taking photos may not be allowed in some sections of museums. For example, taking photos in the treasury section of *Topkapı Palace* has been forbidden; and you can see that on the warning signs. Besides, if you want to take photos of people, you should ask for permission first as you may not anticipate their reaction. It is strictly forbidden to take photos of military facilities.

LAVATORIES

Public lavatories are chargeable in Istanbul. It is easy to find lavatories around museums, mosques and large squares. Furthermore, every restaurant and mosque has a free lavatory in it. You will see some signs on the doors of these lavatories suc has "Bay", "Bayan", and "WC". **"Bay"** means 'Gentlemen', and **"Bayan"** means **'Ladies'**. At some places you can also see these signs in English.

WORK HOURS AND HOLIDAYS

In Turkey, although minor changes are possible according to the season, people at public offices generally work from 9 a.m. to 5 p.m.. Public offices and banks are closed on Saturday and Sunday. Museums are open at the weekend, but they are also closed one day in the week. Private sector offices generally offer service until noon or until the end of day on Saturday. Grand bazaars like *Grand Bazaar* and *Spice Bazaar,* and some shops are closed on Sunday, but Shopping Centers are open seven days a week. Sunday is holiday, and except restaurants in tourist regions most of the shops are closed.

FOOTBALL

The football teams in Turkey could achieve little success despite million dollars of investment they made. **Galatasaray** (1905), **Fenerbahçe** (1907) and **Beşiktaş** (1903), the three football teams which have been named 'three leaders' due to their championships, are the football teams which have large numbers of supporters in Turkey. Besides these football teams which have championships, another leader football team of the Anatolia is **Trabzonspor** (1967). The greatest success of Galatasaray is winning the **UEFA Cup** in 2000. It won the **Super Cup** by defeating Real Madrid in the same year.

Turkish National Football Team achieved great success in the **World Cup** at which it played after many years by becoming the third football team in the 2002 World Cup. The goal *Hakan Şükür* kicked in the 11th second of the World Cup match was recorded as the earliest goal of World Cups.

TIME DIFFERENCE

Turkey is two hours ahead of the Greenwich, which is accepted as the prime meridian of the world. Therefore, local time of Turkey is one hour ahead of the local times of the European countries such as

France, Germany, Spain, Italy and Switzerland, and two hours ahead of the local time of England. There is no time difference between Turkey and Balkan countries Greece, Bulgaria and Romania. Turkey's local time is 8-10 hours ahead of that of America.

ELECTRICITY

Please check the operation voltages of the electronic devices you have brought to Turkey because electric current is 220 watts in Turkey. Don't forget to use an adapter to avoid burning your devices that operate with different volts.

Circumcised child.

CIRCUMCISION

Circumcision, which means circumcising the foreskin of the penis, has both a religional and traditional aspect. Every Muslim boy is circumcised especially in his childhood through a ceremony like a wedding ceremony, where the child wears a white suit. Therefore, it turns into an enjoyable event rather than a frightening situation. After the completion of circumcision ceremony, people say '*oldu da bitti maşallah*', which literally means 'how wonderful that it has happened and finished'. At the ceremony, the child who is circumcised lies on a decorated bed, and his relatives come to his bed and give him various gifts.

MILITARY SERVICE

Military service is compulsory in Turkey. Every man who becomes 20 years old is obliged to carry out his military obligation unless he is a student. The military service period which lasts 15 months contributes to development of men under different conditions. Men who have received higher education serve 6 months as private soldier, or 12 months as commissioned officer according to the needs and the examination results.

EDUCATION

Compulsory education is 8 years in Turkey. Children start school when they are 6 or 7 years old, and receive education for 8 years. After these 8 years, they start high school. At the end of high school period, a competition starts between the graduates to enter university. While there are 100 universities including foundation universities, more than 1 million high school graduates try to enter universities, and this causes problems.

CERAMIC TILING

Ceramic tiles are colourful and glazed plates which cover walls. Ceramic tiles which developed in parallel to Turkish architecture have an important place in Turkish art of decoration. The ceramic tiles of **Iznik** and **Kütahya**, which are made using a lot of colours, are famous worldwide. In the 17th century, Kütahya and Çanakkale ceramic tiles replaced İznik ateliers respectively. Good type of clay which undergoes various processes and mixed with some ingredients is poured into a shape tablet. Later, it is dried in the sun and cooked in oven at high temperatures. Ceramic tiles that are left somewhere to dry naturally for avoiding cracking are decorated with different motifs and coloured. After

Decoration of ceramic tiles.

these motifs are drawn, ceramic tiles are glazed for protection. Plates that are covered with liquid glaze with the help of a brush are cooked in ovens again until the glaze gets hard in glass-like form. Ceramic tiles used in the structures in Istanbul very commonly nearly replaced wall pictures.

CARPET

Motifs used in Turkish carpets and the knotting technique, which started to be used for the first time in the regions of Middle Asia Turks, have a long history. Hand-made knotted carpets have developed as a handcraft since Middle Asia Turks, who used to live a nomadic life. Some carpets dating back to

Silk Carpet.

the period of Anatolian Seljuq Empire, which was another Turkish state before the Ottomans in Anatolia, have been found. 8 carpets made for Konya Alaeddin Mosque in Konya in this period (13th century) are evidences of the success of Turkish people in making carpets. Quality palace carpets were made in the carpet factory established in *Hereke*, on the coast of İzmit Bay, in the

Ceramic ewer.

Ottoman period in 1883. You can see large numbers of valuable carpets all together by visiting the **Museum of Turkish-Islamic Arts** in At Meydanı (literally Horse Square).

TURKISH CUISINE

At breakfast; besides tea, milk and fruit juice, bread, olives, cheese, eggs and jam are preferred bisedes Tea. The types of soups are *ezogelin, süzme mercimek, yayla* and also shops that sell *poğaça* (flaky), *börek* (flan) and *simit* (savory roll covered with sesame secd) serve alternatives for breakfast.

Turkey gives a special importance to tea *(çay)* that people drink right after every meal. A good steeped tea shows itself with its color that is also called blood red.

Turkish Delight

During lunch, besides soup, vegetable and dessert, the main meal can be meat or vegetables with minced meat or meat balls. Rice, boiled and pounded wheat or pasta is important to keep the stomach full. Among with these; yoghurt, cacik (yoghurt mixed with cucumber) and stewed fruit are the choices of many.

Tea.

Delicious Meat Döner Kebab.

As side dishes, "coban salad" or "green salad" are plates where summer season vegetables are used abundantly. During dinners, soup, olive oil meals and milk desserts are served on tables. In the heat of the summer, because the olive oil meals are made of vegetables, they are light and they don't trouble the stomach. Besides red meat, chicken and fish can be preferred during the day.

Among pulses, beans take the first placc. "Beans and pilav (rice)" is a most common meal. Besides meat balls, *"piyaz"* made with boiled beans and minced onions or potato chips are preferred. As for drinks, *"ayran"* is very common made from a mixture of yoghurt and water. *Yoghurt* and *ayran* are natural food that Turks presented the World.

Turkish Coffee cooked in *cezve* (Turkish coffee pot) on charcoal fire.

The traditional drink "Turkish Rakı" has the trademark of the country. Among with it, *"meze"* is presented as a snack. The main meal can be, as the order of choice, fish, *kebab* or meat. "Pickles" made of vegetables is a good snack besides meals.

Turkish Raki ready to drink.

In Turkey, which is a grape country, because it is the "homeland of wine", wine making is rapidly developing and unique types can be found very commonly.

Fırın Sütlaç (Rice pudding roasted in oven)

A variety of beers that comes from barley and hop that is planted specially is very suitable for the taste of foreigners.

In Turkish kitchen, milk desserts such as *muhallebi, keşkül, kazandibi* and dough desserts such as *baklava, kadayıf* have a rich variety with different ingredients.

Adana Kebab.

Coffee which was spread in Europe by Turks is cooked in a special pan with a long grip called *cezve*. *Turkish Coffee* that is drank in small cups and preferred with bubbles have different types of sugar in it, namely little sugar, medium sugar and with sugar.

***Sultanahmet Köftesi* (Sultanahmet meatball)**

Maps Showing Streets

The maps used in the last section will help you find the address you want to go as there is an index including the list of streets and avenues. The maps which are divided into sections comprise four different regions. The map number 1 and 2 belongs to the **Historical Peninsula**, the map number 3 belongs to **Beyoğlu** (Taksim and around), the map number 4 belongs to **Bosphorus**.

The index part has been prepared seperately for each map, and streets and avenues are in alphabetical sequence. Besides these maps, the regions mentioned are shown in detail in many maps in the book. The symbols below will help you reach at some places you need to go within the region you are.

1 2 → **Historical Peninsula**
3 → **Beyoğlu**
4 → **Bosphorus**

PTT *PTT*	Hastane *Hospital*	Tarihi Anıt *Historical Monument*	Deniz Feneri *Lighthouse*	Belediye Birimleri *Units of Municipality*
Polis *Police*	Sağlık Ocağı *Health Clinic*	Alışveriş Merkezi *Shopping Center*	İDO Feribot *İDO Ferry boat*	Banliyö hattı *Suburban railway line*
Surlar *City Walls*	Üniversite *University*	Liman *Seaport*	İDO İskele *İDO, Pier*	Jandarma *Gendarmarie*
İtfaiye *Fire Station*	Saray-Kasır *Palace-Summer Palace*	Deniz Dolmuşu *Sea Bus*	Türbe *Tomb*	Hamidiye *Hamidiye*
Tünel *Tunnel*	Cami *Mosque*	Tren İstasyonu *Train Station*	Stadyum *Stadium*	Halk Ekmek *Public Bread Buffet*
Metro Durağı *Subway Stop*	Sinagog *Synagogue*	Otogar *Bus Station*	Spor Alanı *Sports Field*	
Metro Hattı *Subway Line*	Kilise *Church*	Tramvay Durağı *Tramway Stop*	Mesire Yerleri *Popular Excursion Spots*	
Otel *Hotel*	Kültür Merkezi *Cultural Center*	Tramvay Hattı *Tramway Line*	Belediye Başkanlığı *Municipality*	

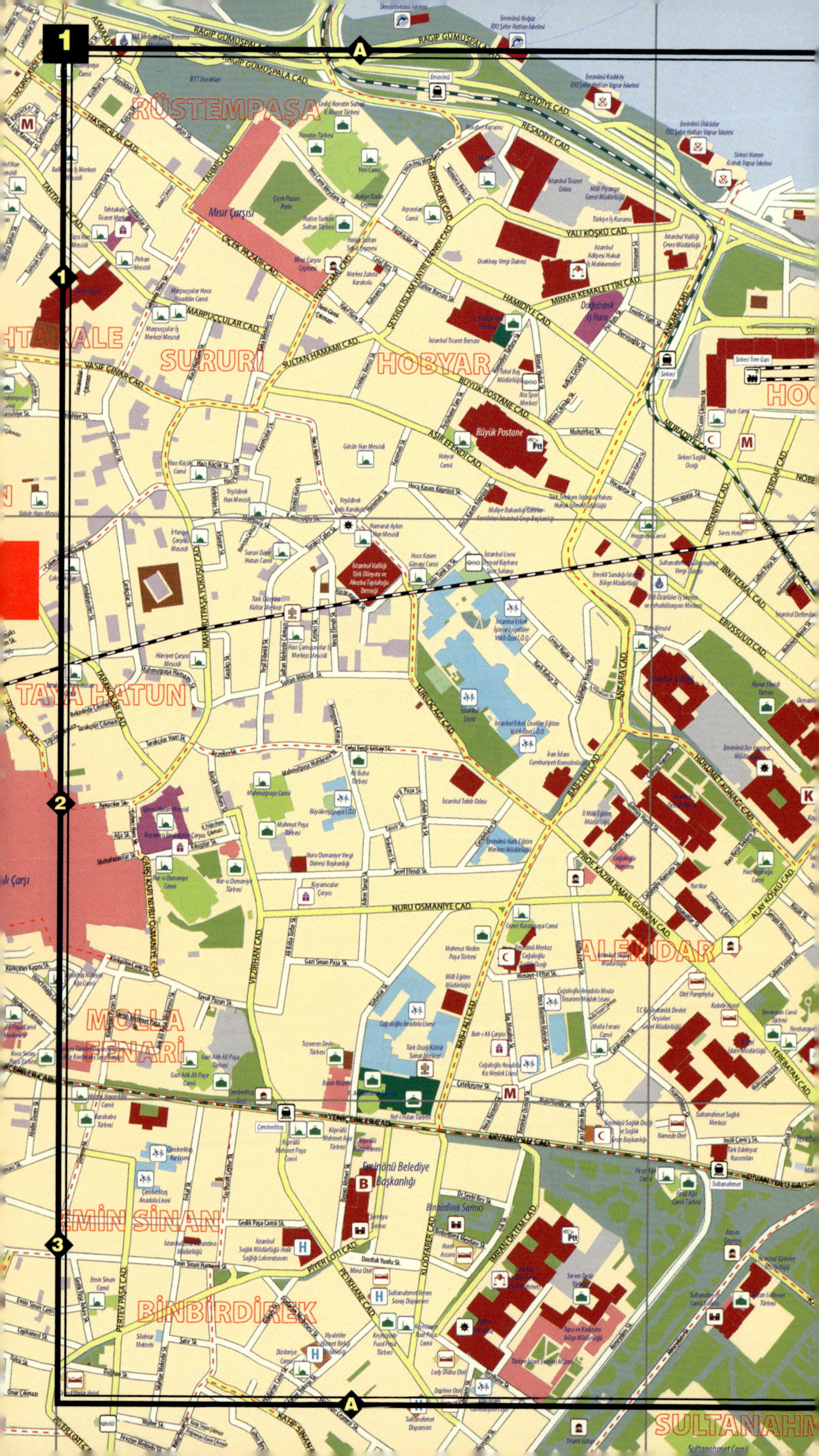
1
A
RÜSTEMPAŞA
HTAKALE
SURURİ
HOBYAR
TAYA HATUN
MOLLA FENARİ
EMİN SİNAN
BİNBİRDİREK
ALEMDAR
SULTANAHM
RAGIP GÜMÜŞPALA CAD.
REŞADİYE CAD.
HASIRCILAR CAD.
Mısır Çarşısı
ÇİÇEK PAZARI CAD.
YALI KÖŞKÜ CAD.
MİMAR KEMALETTİN CAD.
HAMİDİYE CAD.
MARPUÇÇULAR CAD.
VASIF ÇINAR CAD.
SULTAN HAMAMI CAD.
BÜYÜK POSTANE CAD.
Büyük Postane
AŞİR EFENDİ CAD.
ANKARA CAD.
Sirkeci
İBNİ KEMAL CAD.
ERUSSUUD CAD.
MAHMUTPAŞA YOKUŞU CAD.
TÜRKOCAĞI CAD.
BABIALİ CAD.
HÜKÜMET KONAĞI CAD.
PROF. KAZIM İSMAİL GÜRKAN CAD.
ALAY KÖŞKÜ CAD.
NURU OSMANİYE CAD.
VEZİRHAN CAD.
YEREBATAN CAD.
YENİÇERİLER CAD.
DİVANYOLU CAD.
Eminönü Belediye Başkanlığı
PİYERLOTİ CAD.
2
3
Sultanahmet Camii

B
C
MARMARAY YENİK
(İNŞAAT
KENNEDY CAD.
PAŞA
Saraybumu Parkı
DEMİRKAPI ORTA. AD.
GÜLHANE PARKI YOLU
Gülhane Parkı
Topkapı Sarayı
CANKURTARAN
Darphane
Aya İrini Müzesi
Arkeoloji Müzesi
KENNEDY CAD.
BAB-I HÜMAYUN CAD.
İSHAKPAŞA CAD.
KABASAKAL CAD.
ALEMDAR CAD.
Ptt
H
M
1
2
3

2
D
E
4
5
6
KİRMASTİ
SİNANAĞA
HÜSAM BEY
KIRK ÇEŞME
SOFULAR
KENDER PAŞA
KALEN
BABAHASAN ALEMİ
GURABA HÜSEYİN AĞA
KEMALP
Fatih Camii ve Külliyesi
Fatih Sultan Mehmet Türbesi
Fatih Mezarlığı
Fatih İ.Ö.O
Fatih Parkı
Fatih Kızılay Dahiliye Merkezi
Fatih Hastanesi
Medical Park Hospital
Şht. Mustafa Yelkenci Parkı
İstanbul Büyükşehir Belediye Başkanlığı
Saraçhane Parkı
Teyyare Parkı
Olimpik Spor Salonu
Yıldırım Spor Okulu
Molla Hüsrev Sofular Camii
İÜ Tıp Fakültesi Tıp Tarihi Anabilim dalı
İÜ Türkiye Araştırmaları Enstitüsü
Pertevniyal Lisesi
Valide Camii Mezarlığı
Pertevniyal Valide Sultan Camii
Oğlanlar Türbesi
Murat Paşa Camii
Yusufpaşa
Aksaray
HALİÇ CAD.
İSLAMBOL CAD.
FEVZİPAŞA CAD.
MİHCILAR CAD.
ESKİMUHTAR CAD.
ÇIRÇIR CAD.
HAYDAR CAD.
ZEYREK CAD.
İTFAİYE CAD.
YESARİZADE CAD.
HATTAT NAFIZ CAD.
NEVŞEHİRLİ İBRAHİMPAŞA CAD.
BÜYÜK KARAMAN CAD.
KIZTAŞI CAD.
HAYDARBEY CAD.
MACAR KARDEŞLER CAD.
KIZANLIK CAD.
SARIGÜZEL CAD.
SOFULAR CAD.
DOLAP CAD.
HORHOR CAD.
ATATÜRK BULVARI
ADNAN MENDERES BULVARI
ŞEHZADEBAŞI CAD.
GENÇTÜRK CAD.
HAŞİM İŞCAN GEÇİDİ
ORDU CAD.

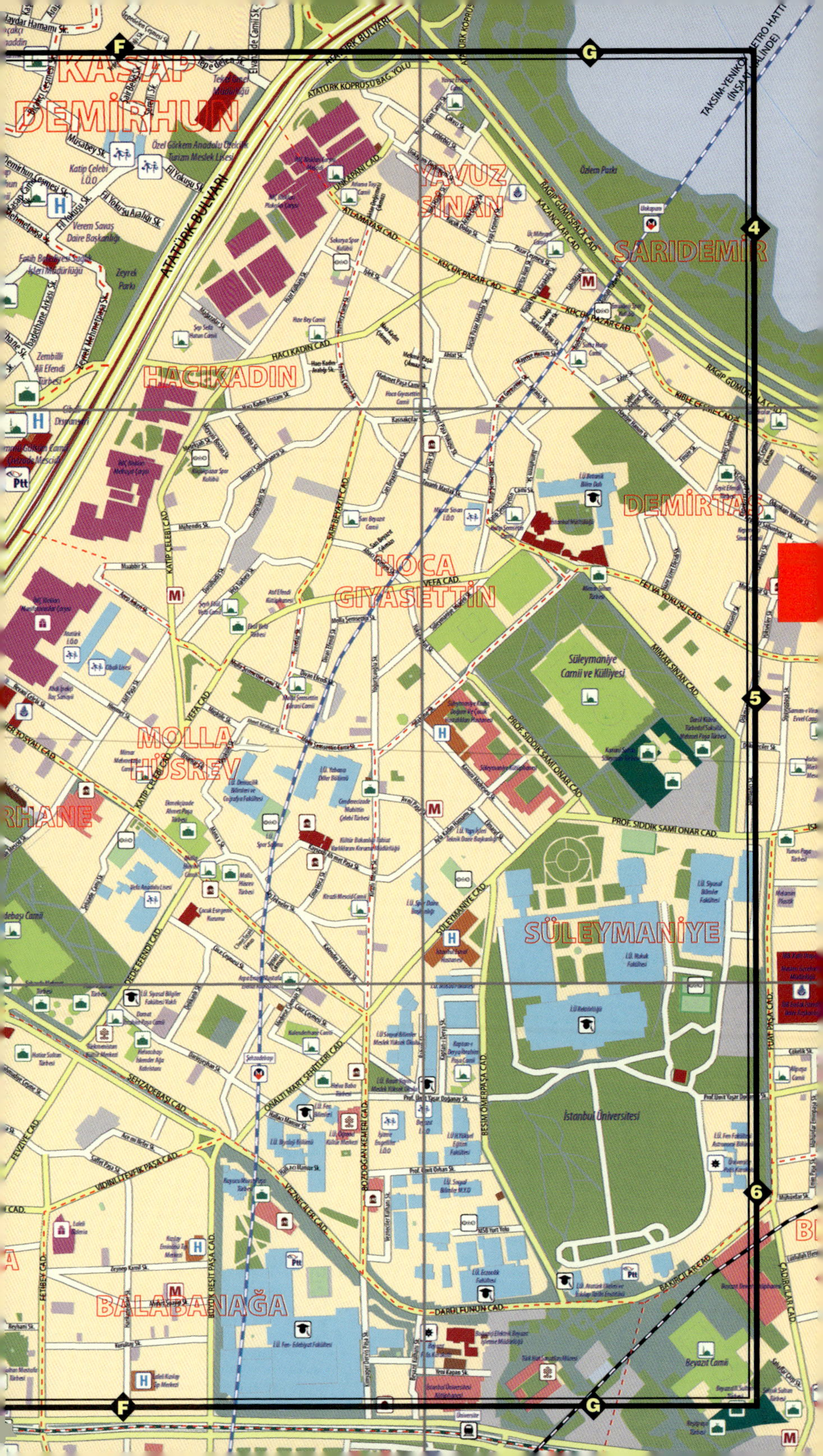
KASAP DEMİRHUN
YAVUZ SİNAN
SARIDEMİR
HACIKADIN
DEMİRTAŞ
HOCA GIYASETTİN
MOLLA HÜSREV
SÜLEYMANİYE
BALABANAĞA
ATATÜRK BULVARI
ATATÜRK KÖPRÜSÜ BAĞ. YOLU
TAKSİM-YENİKAPI METRO HATTI (İNŞAAT HALİNDE)
Özel Görkem Anadolu Otelcilik Turizm Meslek Lisesi
Katip Çelebi İ.Ö.O.
Zeyrek Parkı
Zembilli Ali Efendi Türbesi
Özlem Parkı
RAGIP GÜMÜŞPALA CAD.
KÜÇÜKPAZAR CAD.
HACI KADIN CAD.
ATALARYASI CAD.
KIBLE ÇEŞME CAD.
KATİP ÇELEBİ CAD.
VEFA CAD.
FETVA YOKUŞU CAD.
MİMAR SİNAN CAD.
PROF. SIDDIK SAMİ ONAR CAD.
Süleymaniye Camii ve Külliyesi
ŞEHZADEBAŞI CAD.
ONALTI MART ŞEHİTLERİ CAD.
BOZDOĞAN KEMERİ CAD.
BESİM ÖMERPAŞA CAD.
SÜLEYMANİYE CAD.
VİDİNLİ TEVFİK PAŞA CAD.
VEZNECİLER CAD.
BÜYÜK REŞİT PAŞA CAD.
DARÜLFÜNUN CAD.
BAKIRCILAR CAD.
ÇADIRCILAR CAD.
FEVZİYE CAD.
FETHİBEY CAD.
DEDE EFENDİ CAD.
İstanbul Üniversitesi
İ.Ü. Fen-Edebiyat Fakültesi
Beyazıt Camii
Şehzadebaşı
İ.Ü. Rektörlüğü
İ.Ü. Hukuk Fakültesi
İ.Ü. Siyasal Bilimler Fakültesi
F
G
4
5
6

3
A
1
2
3
A
KÜÇÜK PİYALE
SURURİ MEHMET EFENDİ
BOSTAN
KALYONCU KULLUĞU
ÇUKUR
KAMER HATUN
YAHYA KAHYA
ÇATMA MESCİT
ASMALI MESCİT
BEDRETTİN
EVLİYA ÇELEBİ
ŞAHKULU
TOMTOM
EMEKYEMEZ
BEREKETZADE
MÜEYYEDZADE
ARAP CAMİ
PİYALEPAŞA BULVARI
KURTULUŞ DERESİ CAD.
IRMAK CAD.
AYNALI ÇEŞME CAD.
DORT KUYU CAD.
BÜLENT DEMİR CAD.
TEPEBAŞI CAD.
MEŞRUTİYET CAD.
REFİK SAYDAM CAD.
ŞİŞHANE CAD.
EVLİYA ÇELEBİ CAD.
YOLCUZADE İSKENDER CAD.
GALİP DEDE CAD.
SERDAR-I EKREM CAD.
YÜKSEK KALDIRIM CAD.
LÜLECİ HENDEK CAD.
MUMHANE CAD.
NECATİBEY CAD.
TERSANE CAD.
TERSANE KAVŞAĞI
YELKENCİLER CAD.
FERMENECİLER CAD.
KEMANKEŞ CAD.
RIHTIM CAD.
Haliç Tersanesi
Bilgi Üniversitesi
Galatasaray Lisesi
Karaköy İDO Deniz Otobüsü İskelesi
YENİKAPI-TAKSİM METRO HATTI (İNŞAAT HALİNDE)

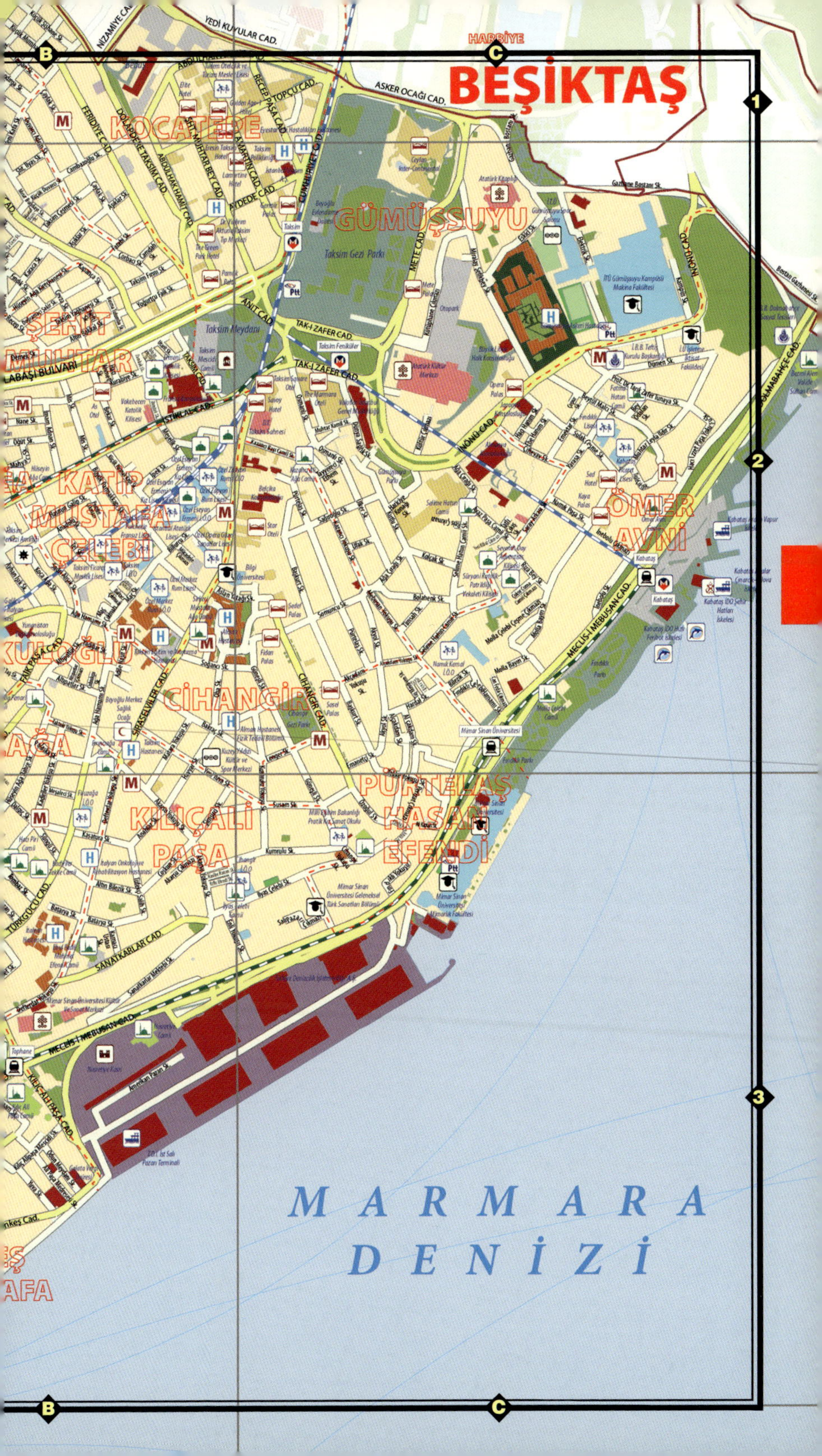

BEŞİKTAŞ
HARBİYE
KOCATEPE
GÜMÜŞSUYU
Taksim Gezi Parkı
Taksim Meydanı
ŞEHİT MUHTAR
KATİP MUSTAFA ÇELEBİ
ÖMER AVNİ
CİHANGİR
PÜRTELAŞ HASAN EFENDİ
KILIÇALİ PAŞA
TAK-I ZAFER CAD.
İNÖNÜ CAD.
MECLİS-İ MEBUSAN CAD.
İSTİKLAL CAD.
CUMHURİYET CAD.
ASKER OCAĞI CAD.
YEDİ KUYULAR CAD.
SIRASELVİLER CAD.
CİHANGİR CAD.
KILIÇALİPAŞA CAD.
DOLMABAHÇE CAD.
Kabataş
Tophane
MARMARA DENİZİ

4
Kilyos
Demirciköy
AYVAT BENDİ
KURTKEMERİ
Çiftalan
Kısırkaya
Gümüşdere
Uskumruköy
Zekeriyaköy
VALİDE SULTAN BENDİ
KÖMÜRCÜ BENT
II. MAHMUT BENDİ
FATİH ORMANI
Maden
M.AKİF ERSOY
BELGRAD ORMANLARI
TOPUZLU BENT
Merkez
Büyük Bent
BAHÇEKÖY
BÜYÜK BENT
BİNBAŞI
Kocataş
Büyükdere
Merkez
Mithatpaşa
GÖKTÜRK
GÖKTÜRK GÖLETİ
FATİH ÇEŞMESİ
KİRAZLI BENT
Kazımkarabekir
PTT Evleri
Cumhuriyet
Kemerburgaz
Çamlıtepe
Mimar Sinan Paşa
AYAZAĞA ORMANLARI
Ayazağa
Maslak
Yayla
ŞİŞLİ
Pınar
Reşitpaşa
Alibeyköy Baraj Gölü
Huzur
AZİZPAŞA
Konaklar
Cebeci
Hamidiye
Seyrantepe
Sanayi
GAZİOSMANPAŞA
Güzeltepe
Gazi
Zübeyde Hanım
Emniyet Evleri
Çeliktepe
Levent
İsmet Paşa
Uğur Mumcu
Esentepe
Yunus Emre
75. Yıl
Kazım Karabekir
KAĞITHANE
Ortabayır
Sultan Çiftliği
50. Yıl
Aksemsettin
Alibeyköy Merkez
Merkez
Karayolları
Nurtepe
Gürsel
Cumhuriyet
Karadeniz
Yeni Mahalle
EYÜP
Merkez
SENLER
Fulya
Halide Edip Adıvar
19 Mayıs
Dikilitaş
ŞİŞLİ
İNÖNÜ STADYUMU
Yıldırım
Turgut Reis
Yüzyıl
BAYRAMPAŞA
BEYOĞLU
O-3
Kocatepe
Güneştepe
Fatih
Kemalpaşa
İsmet Paşa
Altıntepsi
HALİÇ
BAĞCILAR
Fatih
Menderes
Nine Hatun
Çınar
Merkez
Gençosman
FATİH
SARAY BURNU
EMİNÖNÜ
Evren
Havuzlar
Merkez
Bağlar

KETENDERE KOYU
HAMİDİYE BURNU
Rumelifeneri
PAŞA BURNU
MARMARACIK
Garipçe
KARATAŞ BURNU
FİL BURNU
Poyraz
Anadolufeneri
Çayağızı (Riva)
ÇAYAĞIZI
Alibahadır
Paşamandıra
KEÇİLİK KOYU
İSTANBUL BOĞAZI
Anadolu Kavağı
Kaynarca
Mahmutşevketpaşa
Tokatköy
Dereseki
KAYMAKDONDURAN
Akbaba
Örnekköy
Elmalı
Zerzevatçı
Camlıbahçe
Ortaçeşme
İBRAHİM PAŞA KORUSU
SELVİ BURNU
Merkez
Yalıköy
Polonezköy
BEYKOZ KORUSU
Gümüşsuyu
POLENEZKÖY TABİAT PARKI
İncirköy
Yeniköy
Görele
Acarlar
Paşabahçe
Soğuksu
Çiğdem
Çengeldere
İstinye
BEYKOZ
İSTİNYE KOYU
Çubuklu
Emirgan
EMİRGAN KORUSU
MİHRABAD ORMANI
Rüzgarlıbahçe
MİHRİBAT
Kanlıca
Fatih
Çiftlik
Yavuz Selim
FATİH SULTAN MEHMET KÖPRÜSÜ
Kavacık
Elmalı Baraj Gölü
ÇAVUŞBAŞI
Anadolu Hisarı
Rumeli Hisarı
Göztepe
Etiler
Bebek
AYŞE SULTAN KORUSU
KANDİLLİ BURNU
Göksu
GÖZTEPE
Baklacı
Yeni Mahalle
Kandilli
KANDİLLİ KORUSU
Küçüksu
Arnavutköy
Hekimbaşı
İSTANBUL KENT ORMANI
Merkez
Vaniköy
Emek
ÇEKMEKÖY
Kuruçeşme
Bahçelievler
Kazım Karabekir
Kuleli
Mimar Sinan
Hamidiye
Havuzbaşı
Güzeltepe
Aşağı Dudullu
Mehmet Akif Ersoy
Yavuztürk
Mehmet Akif
Beylerbeyi
Hasippaşa
İnkılap
BOĞAZİÇİ KÖPRÜSÜ
O-1
O-2 E80
Ihlamurkuyu
020-07
Küplüce
Kirazlıtepe
Ferah
BÜYÜKÇAMLICA TEPESİ
Meclis
ABDULLAH AĞA ÇEMİL BEY KORUSU
Atatürk
İstiklal
ÜMRANİYE
Kuzguncuk
Burhaniye
Emniyet
Kısıklı
Namık Kemal
ÜSKÜDAR
İcadiye
Atakent
Yukarı Dudullu
Esenşehir
KÜÇÜK ÇAMLICA TEPESİ
Altunizade
Cumhuriyet
Çakmak
ÇAMLICA GİŞESİ
Bulgurlu
Barbaros
Acıbadem
O-4
Fatih
Esatpaşa
Mustafa Kemal
Yeni Çamlıca
Ferhatpaşa
Koşuyolu
Ünalan
Barbaros
Atatürk
Acıbadem
Örnek
Kayışdağı
Hasanpaşa
Küçük Bakkalköy
ŞÜKRÜ SARAÇOĞLU STADYUMU
Fikirtepe
İnönü
KAYIŞDAĞI ORMANI
Eğitim
Merdivenköy
Sahrayıcedid

HISTORICAL PENINSULA-1

A
Adem Yavuz Sk. **A2**
Adliye Sk. **B3**
Ağa Sk. **A2**
Akbıyık Cad. **B3**
Alaca Hamam Sk. **A1**
Alay Köşkü Cad. **B2**
Alemdar Cad. **B2,B3**
Ali Baba Türbe Sk. **A2**
Ankara Cad. **A1,B1,A2**
Arif Paşa Sk. **A2**
Arpacılar Cad. **A1**
Asmaaltı Cad. **A1**
Aşir Efendi Cad. **A1**
Atik Ali Paşa Medresesi Sk. **A2**
Atmeydam Sk. **A3,B3**
Aynacılar Sk. **A2**

B
Babayani Sk. **A3**
Bab-ı Ali Cad. **A2,A3**
Bab-ı Hümayun Cad. **B3**
Bankacılar Sk. **A1**
Baş Musahip Sk. **A2**
Bekirdede Çıkmazı **A2**
Bestekar Osman Sk. **A2,A3**
Biçki Yurdu Sk. **A2,A3**
Bileyciler Sk. **A2**
Binbirdirek Meydanı Sk. **A3**
Boyacı Ahmet Sk. **A3**
Büyük Postane Cad. **A1**
Büyükbaş Sk. **A1**

C
Cağaloğlu Yokuşu Sk. **A2**
Cambazhanı Sk. **A1**
Celal Bey Sk. **A1**
Celal Ferdi Gökay Sk. **A2**
Cemal Nadir Sk. **A1,A2**
Ceridehane Sk. **A2**
Cömert Türk Sk. **A1**

Ç
Çakmakçılar Yokuşu Sk. **A1,A2**
Çarıkçılar Sk. **A2**
Çarşı Kapı Nuru Osmaniye Cad. **A2**
Çatal çeşme Sk. **A2,B2**
Çeşnici Sk. **A2**
Çiçek Pazarı Cad. **A1**
Çuhacı Hanı Sk. **A2**

D
Dağhan Sk. **A3**
Darüssade Sk. **B1,B2**
Demirkapı Orta Cad. **B1,C1**
Dervişler Sk. **B1,B2**
Dervişoğlu Sk. **A1**
Direkli Hanı Sk. **A1**
Divan Yolu Cad. **A3,B3**
Dizdariye Cami Sk. **A3**
Dizdariye Çeşmesi Sk. **A3**
Dizdariye Medresesi Sk. **A3**
Dizdariye Yokuşu Sk. **A3**
Dostluk Yurdu Sk. **A3**
Dr. Eminpaşa Sk. **A2,A3**
Dr. Şevki Bey Sk. **A3**

E
Ebussuud Cad. **A1,A2,B2**
Emin Sinan Hamamı Sk. **A3**
Erdoğan Sk. **B2**
Eryılmaz Çıkmazı **B2**
Evkaf Sk. **A3**

F
Fincancılar Çıkmazı **A1**
Fincancılar Sk. **A1**
Fındıkçı Remzi Sk. **A1**
Fındıkçılar Sk. **A1**

G
Gazi Sinan Paşa Sk. **A2**
Gedik Paşa Arkası Sk. **A3**
Gedik Paşa Camii Sk.**A3**
Gülhane Parkı Yolu **B1,C1,B2**
Gümüş Haneli Sk. **A2,B2**
Güzel Sanatlar Sk. **B2**

H
Hacı Beşir Tekkesi Sk. **B2**
Hacı Küçük Sk. **A1**
Hacı Tahsin Bey Sk. **A3**
Hakkı Tarık Us Sk. **A2**
Hamam Sk. **A2**
Hamidiye Cad. **A1**
Hamidiye Türbesi Sk. **A1**
Hanımeli Sk. **A1**
Hasırcılar Cad. **A1**
Hekim Çıkmazı Sk. **A1**
Himaye-i Eftal Sk. **A2**
Hoca Hanı Sk. **A1,A2**
Hoca Kasım Köprüsü Sk. **A1**
Hoca Paşa Sk. **A1,B1**
Hoca Rüstem Mektebi Sk. **A2**
Hoca Rüstem Sk. **A3**
Hocapaşa Hamam Sk. **A1**
Hocapaşa Sk. **A1**
Hüdavendigar Cad. **B1,B2**
Hükümet Konağı Cad. **A2,B2**
Hüseyinağa Cami Sk. **A2**

I
Işık Sk. **A3**

İ
İbni Kemal Cad. **B2**
İmran Öktem Cad. **A3**
İncili Çavuş Sk. **B3**
İrfaniye Sk. **A2**
İş Mürekkebi Sk. **A2**
İshakpaşa Cad. **B3**
İstasyon Arkası Sk. **B1**

K
K.Yıldızhanı Çıkmazı **A2**
Kabasakal Cad. **B3**
Kafkas Geçidi Sk. **A1**
Kalçın Sk. **A1**
Kaputçular Sk. **A1**
Kargaşa Sk. **B2**
Kargılı Çıkmazı **B2**
Kargılı Sk. **B2**
Katırcıoğlu Sk. **A1**
Kefelihan Sk. **A1**
Kenedy Cad. **B1,C1,C2,C3**
Kılıççılar Sk. **A2**
Kızılhan Sk. **A1**
Klodfarer Cad. **A3**
Kömürcü Bekir Sk. **A1**
Kum Meydanı Sk. **B1**
Kutlugün Sk. **B3**
Küçük Sk. **B2**
Küçük Yıldızhanı Sk. **A2**
Kürkçüler Çariş Sk. **A2**
Kürkçüler Kapısı Sk. **A2**
Kürkçüler Pazarı Sk. **A2**

M
Macuncu Çıkmazı **A2**
Macuncu Sk. **A1,A2**
Mahkeme Sk. **A1**
Mahmutpaşa Yokuşu Cad. **A1,A2**
Mahmutpaşa Yokuşu Sk. **A1**
Marpuççular Cad. **A1**
Mehmet Murat Sk. **B2**
Mengene Çıkmazı **A2**
Mesih Mehmet Paşa Sk. **A2**
Mimar Kemalettin Cad. **A1,B1**
Mimar Vedat Sk. **A1**
Molla Fenari Çıkmazı **A2**
Molla Feneri Sk.**A2**
Muhafazacılar Sk. **A2**
Muhterem Efendi Çıkmazı **B2**
Muhzirbaş Sk. **A1**
Muradiye Cad. **B1**
Mustafa Dede Sk. **B2**

N
Narh Bahçe Sk. **A2**
Nasuhiye Sk. **A1**
Necip Efendi Sk. **A2**
Nöbethane Cad. **B1**
Nöbethane Çıkmazı Sk. **B1**
Nuru Osmaniye Cad. **A2**

O
Orhaniye Cad. **B1,B2**
Osman Hamdi Bey YokuşuSk.**B2**

Ö
Ödev Sk. **A3**

P
Pertev Paşa Cad. **A3**
Peykhane Cad. **A3**
Piri Reis Sk. **A1**
Piyer Loti Cad. **A3**
Postahane Yanı Sk. **A1**
Prof. Kazım İsmail Gürkan Cad. **A2,B2**

HISTORICAL PENINSULA-2

BEYOĞLU - 3

TABLE OF CONTENTS

*We thank **Uğur Ayyıldız**, the prefessional tourist guide who has carried out the review of the book, **Güngör Özsoy** the professional photographer who contributed from his archive of photographs, **İdris Atmaca** and **Cenk Kargı**, who have shared his ideas on many subjects, and **Sezen Alan**, who has prepared the index part with great care.*

Dictionary

Polis: *Police*
Hastane: *Hospital*
Eczane: *Pharmacy, Drugstore*
Ambulans: *Ambulance*
Postane: *Post Office*
Posta: *Post*
Sinema: *Cinema*
Tiyatro: *Theatre*
Telefon: *Telephone*
Telefon Kartı: *Telephone Card*
Cami: *Mosque*
Türbe: *Tomb*
Saray: *Palace*
Müze: *Museum*
Otel: *Hotel*
Hamam: *Turkish Bath*
İtfaiye: *Fire Station*
Kilise: *Church*
İnternet Kafe: *Internet Cafe*
Seyahat Acentesi: *Travel Agency*
Turizm Danışma: *Tourist Information*
Banka: *Bank*
Kitapçı: *Bookstore*
Pastane: *Patisserie*
Market: *Market*
Kuaför: *Hairdresser*
Berber: *Barber*
Tuvalet: *Toilet, WC*
Antikacı: *Antique Shop*
Fırın: *Oven*
Açık: *Open*
Kapalı: *Closed*
Giriş: *Entrance*
Çıkış: *Exit*

EXPRESSIONS
Evet: *Yes*
Hayır: *No*
Lütfen: *Please*
Tamam: *Ok*
Günaydın: *Good Morning*
Hoşçakalın: *Good Bye*
Merhaba: *Hello*
Teşekkür Ederim: *Thank you*
Pardon / Özür Dilerim: *I'm sorry*
İyi: *Good*
İyi Akşamlar: *Good Evening*
İyi Geceler: *Good Night*
İyi Günler: *Have a nice day*
Anlamıyorum: *I don't understand*
Nasılsınız?: *How are you?*
Memnun Oldum: *Nice to meet you*
Boş Odanız var mı?: *Do you have a vacant room?*
İki kişilik oda: *Room for two*
Tek kişilik oda: *Single Room*
Fiyata kahvaltı dahil mi?: *Is breakfast included in the price?*
Fiyatı Ne Kadar: *Howmuch is it?*
... kişilik masa lütfen: *Table for ...., please.*
Yemek Listesi: *Menu*
Hesap Lütfen: *Bill, please*
Yardımcı olur musunuz?: *Can you help me?*
Satın Almak İstiyorum: *I want to buy*
Kredi Kartı geçerli mi?: *Do you accept credit cards?*
.... Var mı?: *Is/Are there ....?*
.... İstiyorum: *I want ....*
İmdat / Yardım Edin: *Help me*
Ambulans çağırın: *Call an ambulance*
Polis çağırın: *Call the police*

FOOD-BEVERAGE
Ayran: *Ayran (diluted yoghurt with salt)*
Çay: *Tea*
Kahve: *Coffee*
Kola: *Coke*
Meyve Suyu: *Fruit Juice*
Maden Suyu: *Spring Water*
Su: *Water*
Süt: *Milk*
Sütlü ....: *...... with milk*
Yoğurt: *Yoghurt*
Şarap: *Wine*
Rakı : *Raki (an anise-flavored alcoholic drink)*
Viski: *Whisky*
Çorba: *Soup*
Börek: *Pastry*
Ekmek: *Bread*
Kebap: *Kebab*
Meze: *Appetizers*
Peynir: *Cheese*
Lokum: *Delight*
Yumurta: *Egg*
Pide: *Pita*
Pizza: *Pizza*
Salata: *Salad*
Tatlı: *Dessert*
Şeker: *Sugar*
Tuz: *Salt*
Lokanta/Restoran: *Restaurant*
Büfe: *Buffet*
Garson: *Waiter*
Kahvaltı: *Breakfast*
Öğle Yemeği: *Lunch*
Akşam Yemeği: *Dinner*
Bardak: *Glass*
Bıçak: *Knife*
Çatal: *Fork*
Kaşık: *Spoon*
Peçete: *Napkin, Tissue*

TRANSPORT
Otobüs: *Bus*
Otobüs Durağı: *Bus Stop*
Otogar: *Bus Station*
Metro: *Subway*
Tramvay: *Tramway*
Taksi: *Taxi*
Tren: *Train*
İstasyon: *Station*
Uçak: *Plane*
Havalimanı: *Airport*
Dolmuş: *Shared Taxi*
Minibüs: *Mini bus*
Vapur: *Ferry Boat*
İskele: *Pier*
Bilet: *Ticket*
Jeton: *Token*
Gişe: *Ticket Office, Ticket Window*
Adres: *Address*
Cadde: *Avenue*
Sokak: *Street*
Meydan: *Square*

TIME
Bugün: *Today*
Yarın: *Tomorrow*
Dün: *Yesterday*
Sonra: *Later*
Şimdi: *Now*
Sabah: *Morning*
Akşam: *Evening*
Öğle: *Afternoon*
.... Dakika sonra: *...... minutes later*
.... Saat sonra: *.....hours later*
Ne Zaman / Saat Kaçta?: *When / What time?*
Saat Kaç?: *What time is it?*
Gün: *Day*
Hafta: *Week*
Ay: *Month*
Yıl: *Year*
Pazartesi: *Monday*
Salı: *Tuesday*
Çarşamba: *Wednesday*
Perşembe: *Thursday*
Cuma: *Friday*
Cumartesi: *Saturday*
Pazar: *Sunday*

DIRECTIONS
.... Nasıl Gidebilirim?: *How can I go to .....?*
.... Nerede?: *Where is ....?*
Sağa Dön: *Turn Right*
Sola Dön: *Turn Left*
Sağda: *On the right*
Solda: *On the left*
Doğruca Gidin / Düz Devam et: *Go straight / Carry straight on*
Uzak: *Far*
Yakın: *Close*
Önce: *Before*
Sonra: *After*

MEASURE
Az: *A few, A little*
Çok: *A lot of, Many*
Daha Çok: *More*
Daha Az: *Less*
İyi: *Good*
Kötü: *Bad*
Sıcak: *Hot*
Soğuk: *Cold*
Küçük: *Small*
Büyük: *Big*
Daha Büyük: *Bigger*
Pahalı: *Expensive*
Ucuz: *Cheap*
Fiyatı Ne Kadar?: *How much is it?*

NUMBERS
Bir (1): *One*
İki (2): *Two*
Üç (3): *Three*
Dört (4): *Four*
Beş (5): *Five*
Altı (6): *Six*
Yedi (7): *Seven*
Sekiz (8): *Eight*
Dokuz (9): *Nine*
On (10): *Ten*
Yirmi (20): *Twenty*
Otuz (30): *Thirty*
Kırk (40): *Forty*
Elli (50): *Fifty*
Altmış (60): *Sixty*
Yetmiş (70): *Seventy*
Seksen (80): *Eighty*
Doksan (90): *Ninety*
Yüz (100): *A hundred*
İki yüz (200): Two hundred
Bin (1.000): *A thousand*
On bin (10.000): *Ten thousand*

AKSARAY-AIRPORT (metro-subway)
TAKSİM-DARÜŞŞAFAKA (metro-subway)
ZEYTİNBURNU-KABATAŞ (TRAMWAY)
ZEYTİNBURNU-ESENLER (TRAMWAY)
EDİRNEKAPI-SULTANÇİFTLİĞİ (TRAMWAY)
TAKSİM-KABATAŞ (FUNICULAR)
KARAKÖY-TÜNEL (TUNNEL) (FUNICULAR)
TAKSİM-TÜNEL (TRAMWAY)
SİRKECİ-HALKALI (SUBURBAN)
EYÜP-PIERRE LOTI (TELEFERIK)
İDO Ferry Boat
City Lines
Shopping Center
HABİBLER
MESCİD-İ SELAM
CEBECİ
SULTAN ÇİFTLİĞİ
YENİ MAHALLE
HACI ŞÜKRÜ
50. YIL - BAŞTABYA
CUMHURİYET
METRİS
KARADENİZ
TAŞ KÖPRÜ
ALİ FUAT BAŞGİL
BOSNA - ÇUKURÇEŞME
SAĞMALCILAR
ULUYOL
RAMİ
TOPÇULAR
KARTALTEPE KOCATEPE
MENDERES
OTOGAR
SAĞ-MALCILAR
ÇİN ÇİN DERESİ
ESENLER
BAĞCILAR
TERAZİDERE
BAYRAMPAŞA
GÜNEŞTEPE
YAVUZ SELİM
DAVUTPAŞA
TOPKAPI
SOĞANLI
AKINCILAR
CEVİZLİBAĞ
GÜNGÖREN
MERTER
P.TEKKE
MERTER
MERKEZ EFENDİ
MEHMET AKİF
SEYİT NİZAM
ZEYTİNBURNU
HALKALI
ATAKÖY ŞİRİNEVLER
AKŞEMSETTİN
KANARYA
YENİBOSNA
BAHÇELİ-EVLER
BAKIRKÖY İNCİRLİ
MİTHATPAŞA
EXPO CENTER
SOĞUKSU
BAKIRKÖY
YENİ MAHALLE
ZEYTİNBURNU
KAZLIÇEŞME
HAVA LİMANI (AIRPORT)
KÜÇÜKÇEKMECE
MENEKŞE
FLORYA
YEŞİLKÖY
YEŞİLYURT